F. S. TURN

BRITISH OPIUM POLICY

AND ITS RESULTS TO

INDIA AND CHINA

Elibron Classics
www.elibron.com

Elibron Classics series.

© 2005 Adamant Media Corporation.

ISBN 1-4021-8082-9 (paperback)
ISBN 1-4021-2914-9 (hardcover)

This Elibron Classics Replica Edition is an unabridged facsimile
of the edition published in 1876 by Sampson Low, Marston, Searle, &
Rivington, London.

BRITISH OPIUM POLICY

AND ITS RESULTS TO

INDIA AND CHINA.

BY

F. S. TURNER, B.A.

FORMERLY OF THE LONDON MISSIONARY SOCIETY;
SECRETARY OF THE ANGLO-ORIENTAL SOCIETY FOR THE SUPPRESSION
OF THE OPIUM TRADE.

London :

SAMPSON LOW, MARSTON, SEARLE, & RIVINGTON,
CROWN BUILDINGS, 188, FLEET STREET.

1876.

LONDON :
GILBERT AND RIVINGTON, PRINTERS,
ST. JOHN'S SQUARE.

PREFACE.

THESE chapters were written in the earlier months of 1874, in response to an advertisement inserted in several newspapers inviting competitive essays upon " British Opium Policy, and its Results to India and China." The author did not see the advertisement until some time after its appearance, and the brief interval allowed for the composition of the book was for him abbreviated by the necessity of simultaneously carrying on other labours. Marks of haste were inevitable ; these have been, as far as possible, removed in the process of revision for the press ; but he fears that the following pages still bear some traces of the circumstances of their production.

Several months after the book was completed a society, of which the author had the honour to be appointed secretary, was formed to diffuse information upon the subject, and to appeal to the conscience of our Government and people against the trade. This society now publishes the present work, hoping that it will do service by promoting a discussion of the real merits of the question. The particular statements and opinions herein contained, however, are put forth on the author's sole responsibility; and the society he has the honour to serve must not be held accountable for more than a general approval of the design of the book.

Nearly two years have elapsed since the book was written, during which time the opium question has been debated in Parliament and the press. The author has taken advantage of the process of revision to alter statistics to the latest dates, to add a few foot-notes and introduce some new matter into the appendix, and to excise or qualify a few hasty expressions. But the substance of the book remains the same, and the chief result of two years' farther study of the subject, and of interchange of thought with many minds upon it, has been to intensify the writer's conviction that England is verily guilty in this matter. If only the nation could be aroused to feel the absolute necessity of some change for the better, the writer's chief end will be gained; and he would not repine though the spirit of reformation should work in other modes than he has indicated. In the meantime he has seen no cause to alter his opinion that the right course would be to abandon the opium monopoly, and to relieve China from the treaty obligation to admit opium, promising her, in lieu thereof, our honest and hearty aid in every effort put forth by the Chinese authorities to prohibit the trade on their own coasts.

A word or two may be permitted here in explanation of the author's dislike to the opium monopoly. An able writer in the *Contemporary Review* (Feb., 1876) urges that the wickedness lies, not in raising money from opium by monopoly rather than by tax, but in encouraging the production of opium, and in compelling the Chinese to admit the opium thus produced. The author admits that the monopoly powers now possessed by the Indian Government might conceivably be used for exactly the contrary purpose to that for which they have been and are used, viz. to prevent, instead of to provide for export to China. It is also possible, on the other hand, that the Indian Government, if dispossessed of the monopoly, might encourage the production of opium by private individuals for the sake of revenue. Therefore, if such a change should ever be proposed by the Government, it will be needful to watch the process, for the purpose of preventing the public being deceived by a sham reform. Nor will it be wise to expect from any such change a substantial and permanent relief of the Chinese. The Chinese themselves must put down the opium trade in China. Our business is to remove the obstacles we have placed in the way of their doing so, and to encourage and assist them in contending against the vice to the best of our ability.

While so far agreeing with the *Contemporary*, the author nevertheless cannot recant his profession of political faith. To his mind, promotion of an evil and permission of an evil are not the same thing, either in the case of an individual or of that collection of individuals called a Government. There are evils which we cannot wisely interfere with, but which it would be shame for us to encourage. Besides this theoretical objection, there is a very grave practical objection to the monopoly. As the Marquis of Salisbury pointed out to the deputation the other day, by means of the monopoly the Government secures for itself the merchants' profit as well as the tax. The trade never having been in private hands from time immemorial, there is no class of persons deprived of an advantage which they miss through the prohibition of private trade. Hence it has happened that the Government of India has been able to extract millions from China without their own subjects feeling the pressure at all. The temptation has been irresistible, and the writer fears it will be irresistible unto the end. So long as that monopoly endures the Indian Government will work it, as they have hitherto worked it, to enrich their treasury, regardless of the consequences to China.

The author, therefore, cannot withdraw his protest against the Indian Government's direct participation in the opium trade. Nevertheless, as this book will show, he always regarded the iniquity of forcing the drug into China as incomparably greater than that of having a Governmental connexion with it in India. If insisting upon the removal of the lesser evil has diverted attention from the more serious one, nobody more sincerely regrets the error in policy than himself. A new session of Parliament is before us, and events have drawn the public attention to China. It is to be hoped that we shall prove we have learned wisdom by experience, and shall not fail to make good use of future opportunities.

Canada Building, King Street, Westminster,
24th February, 1876.

CONTENTS.

CHAPTER I.

THE QUESTION STATED.

CHAPTER II.

OPIUM AS A STIMULANT, MORALLY CONSIDERED.

CHAPTER III.

The East India Company's Opium Policy.

CHAPTER IV.

Opium Policy of the British Government.

CHAPTER V.

CHINESE ANTI-OPIUM POLICY.

CHAPTER VI.

ON OPIUM CULTIVATION IN CHINA.

APPENDIX A.

APPENDIX B.

APPENDIX C.

ACTION OF THE INDIAN GOVERNMENT IN INCREASING THE SUPPLY OF OPIUM FOR THE FOREIGN TRADE.

APPENDIX D.

HISTORICAL.

APPENDIX E.

APPENDIX F.

PROGRESS OF POPPY CULTIVATION IN CHINA.

APPENDIX G.

STATISTICAL.

Anglo-Oriental Society
FOR THE SUPPRESSION OF THE OPIUM TRADE.

Vice-Presidents.

THE RIGHT REV. THE LORD BISHOP OF RIPON.
THE RIGHT HON. RUSSELL GURNEY, M.P., P.C., Q.C.
MR. ALDERMAN W. McARTHUR, M.P.

General Council.

STAFFORD ALLEN, Esq.
WM. S. ALLEN, Esq., M.P.
Professor SHELDON AMOS, M.A.
EDWARD BAINES, Esq.
Rev. G. S. BARRETT.
J. GURNEY BARCLAY, Esq.
Dr. T. J. BARNARDO.
Rev. W. BRADEN.
Rev. GORDON CALTHROP, M.A.
W. T. CHARLEY, Esq., D.C.L., M.P.
Lord ALFRED CHURCHILL.
J. J. COLMAN, Esq., M.P.
Sir ARTHUR COTTON.
JAMES COWAN, Esq., M.P.
Rev. C. C. FENN, M.A.
Sir H. M. HAVELOCK, Bart., M.P.
ALFRED HOWELL, Esq.
THOMAS HUGHES, Esq., Q.C., F.S.A.
WALTER H. JAMES, Esq., M.P.
Sir J. H. KENNAWAY, Bart., M.P.
A. LANG, Esq.
PROFESSOR LEONE LEVI, F.S.A., F.S.S.
Rev. Canon LIDDON, D.D., D.C.L.

FRANCIS N. MALTBY, Esq.
HUGH MASON, Esq.
DONALD MATHESON, Esq.
A. McARTHUR, Esq., M.P.
DAVID M'LAREN, Esq.
Rev. Canon MILLER, D.D.
Rev. H. C. MILWARD.
Hon. Capt. MORETON.
Rev. J. MULLENS, D.D.
ERNEST NOEL, Esq., M.P.
J. W. PEASE, Esq., M.P.
Rev. G. T. PEEKS, M.A.
A. A. REES, Esq.
HENRY RICHARD, Esq., M.P.
HUDSON SCOTT, Esq.
THOMSON SHARPE, Esq.
Rev. C. H. SPURGEON.
Rev. R. TABRAHAM.
J. THOMSON, Esq., F.R.G.S.
E. O. TREGELLES, Esq.
E. B. UNDERHILL, Esq., LL.D.
Rev. C. J. VAUGHAN, D.D.
Rev. H. WRIGHT, M.A.

&c., &c., &c.

Executive Committee.

ARTHUR ALBRIGHT, Esq.
General R. ALEXANDER.
ROBERT BAXTER, Esq.
F. W. CHESSON, Esq.
F. C. CLAYTON, Esq.
R. N. FOWLER, Esq.
Rev. H. GRATTAN GUINNESS.
SAMUEL GURNEY, Esq., F.R.G.S., F.L.S.
THOMAS HANBURY, Esq.
JOHN HILTON, Esq.
HENRY HIPSLEY, Esq.

EDW. HUTCHINSON, Esq.
Rev. JAMES LEGGE, D.D., LL.D.
W. LOCKHART, Esq., F.R.C.S., F.R.G.S.
Mr. Alderman W. McARTHUR, M.P.
W. MORGAN, Esq.
J. C. PARRY, Esq.
EDWARD PEASE, Esq.
ROBERT SAWYER, Esq.
T. B. SMITHIES, Esq.
EDMUND STURGE, Esq.
JOSEPH STURGE, Esq.
J. F. THOMAS, Esq.

Treasurer—R. N. FOWLER, Esq.   Secretary—F. S. TURNER, B.A.

Bankers—Messrs. DIMSDALE, FOWLER, BARNARD, & DIMSDALE, 50, Cornhill.

Offices—CANADA BUILDING, King Street, Westminster, S.W.

Contributions in aid of the Society's operations will be thankfully received by the Treasurer, at Messrs. DIMSDALE, FOWLER, & Co.'s Bank, 50, Cornhill, by any member of the Executive Committee, or by the Secretary at the Office.
Post-Office Orders please make payable at Parliament Street, S.W.; Cross Cheques, DIMSDALE, FOWLER, & Co.

BRITISH OPIUM POLICY.

CHAPTER I.

THE QUESTION STATED.

OPIUM is the milky juice which exudes from the seed-pods of the *papaver somniferum*, the somniferous or white[1] poppy. The name, derived from ὀπός, vegetable juice which flows naturally from a plant, or is drawn off by incision, indicates the high repute of the drug in antiquity. Opium still maintains its pre-eminence. In Pareira's great work on medicines the virtues of this precious drug are thus described : " Opium is undoubtedly the most important and valuable remedy of the whole Materia Medica. For other medicines we have one or more substitutes, but for opium, none,—at least in the large majority of cases in which its peculiar and beneficial influence is required. Its good effects are not, as is the case with some valuable medicines,

---

[1] " The petals vary from white to red or violet, with usually a dark purplish spot at the base of each."—*Pharmacographia*, by Flückiger and Hanbury.

remote and contingent; but they are immediate,
direct, and obvious; and its operation is not attended
with pain or discomfort.   Furthermore, it is applied,
and with the greatest success, to the relief of
maladies of every day's occurrence, some of which
are attended with acute human suffering."   Indigenous in Asia, the first abode of the human species,
the poppy has long been cultivated in Egypt, Turkey,
Persia, India, and recently in China and Manchuria.
It is well known in our gardens, grows wild in
some parts of England, and is cultivated in Surrey
for the supply of poppy-heads to the London
market.   From the time of Hippocrates to the
present day it has been the physician's invalu-
able ally in his struggles against disease and
death.

But man's greatest banes are next door to his
chief blessings.   The knowledge of good and evil
have always grown on the same tree.   This bene-
ficent medical agent opium has been perverted from
its rightful use into a means of vicious, because
highly injurious, sensual pleasure.   When and where
this perversion first took place we cannot even
conjecture.   It is not until comparatively modern
times that this secondary use of opium has pushed
itself into world-wide notoriety.   One medical writer
attributes the growth of the practice to the progress
of Mohammedanism, which operated as a check to the
consumption of intoxicating liquors, and thus cleared
the way for the insidious advances of this gentler
but more enslaving stimulant.   The drug is not

equally acceptable to all races and all constitutions. In Turkey and Persia it has had numerous votaries. In India, the great source of supply, it is, in comparison with the population, but sparsely consumed. It is in China that the habit of using opium as a luxury has made the mightiest strides, and has produced those grave consequences which make "the opium question" one of the most serious questions of the day. More opium is consumed in China than in all the rest of the world, and nearly the whole of the opium imported into China is shipped from Calcutta and Bombay. The East and the West, England, India, and China, act and react upon each other through the medium of poppy-juice. Simple mention of the relations which these three great countries bear to the drug is enough to show that a very grave question is involved in the trade: England is the grower, manufacturer, and seller; India furnishes the farm and the factory; China is buyer and consumer. The question which obviously arises is this, is it morally justifiable and politically expedient for the English nation to continue the production and sale of a drug so deleterious to its consumers? Before, however, we enter upon a consideration of this question, we must explain how it has come to pass that the British nation has got into this unseemly position. Otherwise the fact that the British Government is actually implicated in such a trade may well appear incredible.

If, for instance, any minister could be shameless enough to suggest that England should embark on a vast scale into the business of distillers, and with national funds, by servants of Government, under inspection and control of Parliament, produce and export annually ten or twenty millions' worth of gin and whiskey to intoxicate the populous tribes of Central Africa, he would be greeted by a general outcry of indignation. Yet the very thing which we scout as an imagination, we consent to as a reality. We are maintaining our Indian Empire by our profits as wholesale dealers in an article which, to say the best of it, is as bad as gin! The predicament is so humiliating, that the reader will be inclined to resent having it thrust upon his attention. By whose blunder, by what strange combination of affairs has it come to pass that Great Britain has got into this miserable position? We find a certain measure of relief in casting the responsibility upon the East India Company. That Company was at first simply a trading association, and it seems not incongruous that it should have mixed up government and commerce in this undesirable fashion.

It is again a relief to learn that the Directors of the East India Company did not primarily institute the opium monopoly. The historian of British India, James Mill, tells us, and we find his statement confirmed by evidence presented to the House of Commons in 1830, that the " Mogul government uniformly sold the opium monopoly, and the East India Company followed their example." At the same time the East India Company inherited from the oriental despotism which it overthew another monopoly repugnant to our western ideas, that of salt. This, however, must be noted to their credit, that the directors refused to allow these monopolies of opium and salt to be carried to the accounts of the shareholders of their stock. From the first, the proceeds were carried to the Government account, and applied to state purposes. As we shall see when we come to treat of their policy, the Committee in Leadenhall Street were fully aware of the evil effects of opium-eating; and we may suppose them to have continued the customary monopoly as much in order to restrict the consumption as to add to their revenues. But the export to China, which had been up to 1767 only some two hundred chests a year, a supply which legitimate medical use could account for, gradually increased, until the hundreds had become thousands, and the thousands tens of thousands. The Company sedulously fostered this export trade which poured lacs of rupees in a steadily increasing stream into their treasury. As the revenue derived therefrom swelled in amount, the trade became more and more the object of their solicitude. Long before the Directors resigned their functions to the British Parliament, the millions of profits had become indispensable to the solvency, and therefore to the stability of their Government. Since India came directly under imperial rule the opium revenue, and with it the dependence of our Indian Empire upon the profits of the trade, have increased to still more formidable dimensions. In one year nearly eight millions sterling accrued from opium, about two-thirds of which consisted of direct profits from the sales of the opium produced by Government. During recent years between a sixth and a seventh of the annual income of our East Indian estate has been derived from this source. There is, therefore, no exaggeration in saying that we are maintaining our splendid sovereignty in Asia, and thus the integrity and glory of the British Empire, by the profits of our drug-selling speculations. Should the trade be suddenly closed—a catastrophe by no means beyond the range of possibility—then bankruptcy and ruin would stare our Indian Government in the face.

Whether this dependence upon opium profits is politically expedient is a question not unworthy the consideration of those who love their country. But a much more profound and solemn question is this, whether it can be morally justifiable for a nation to uphold its sway by profits derived from the encouragement of the vices of mankind? We invite the reader to a candid consideration of these grave questions. We shall state facts and arguments that make against the conclusion we have arrived at, as well as those preponderating considerations which appear to us to establish it, and shall make no attempt to locate the criminality of the trade in this quarter or that. To anathematize the wickedness of corporations and to fulminate reproaches against the dead would be waste of breath. We continue the deeds of our fathers, and must bear our own responsibility. Nor can we get rid of the burden by shifting it on to the shoulders of the British or the Indian Government. The responsibility rests upon the whole people. No minister, no Parliament could touch a matter so vital to the maintenance of our empire without the constraining influence of a mighty expression of public opinion to support them. Every British citizen therefore, who, directly or indirectly, has the smallest share in determining the course of the Government of his country, is in that measure responsible for our opium policy. If we in our hearts prefer to let a bad system alone, because it would be troublesome and expensive to interfere with it; because perchance the wrong could not be righted without our having to contribute an infinitesimal fraction of the cost out of our own pocket; then, though we may verbally condemn, we in fact endorse the system, and make the guilt our own.

But is there guilt? Many persons will shrink from admitting this. Deriving a revenue in this way has, they admit, an ugly look; but they are loth to grant that it is necessarily immoral. Do we not in England derive an immense proportion of our national revenue from the taxes on intoxicating drinks? Is the consumption of opium any worse than that of alcohol? Is it quite so bad? Whatever makes a deleterious article more costly must so far lessen its use, and limit vicious indulgence. These extenuations and defences must receive a candid consideration. De Quincey,[2]—author of the

---

[2] See Note, De Quincey, in Appendix (A).

English classic of opium, those "confessions" which
are not confessions, but an *apologia pro vitâ suâ*, an
elaborate essay to whitewash his reputation, and
varnish over the smirching blot of a self-indulgent
habit by the glitter of a fascinating literary style,—
De Quincey boldly anticipates assaults upon his
beloved narcotic, and tries to forestall adverse judgments against his lifelong bondage to it, by a
passage which might be supposed to be expressly
aimed against the present writer. "I say," he
writes in his preface, "that opium, or any agent of
equal power, is entitled to assume that it was
revealed to man for some higher object than that it
should furnish a target for moral denunciations,
ignorant where they are not hypocritical, childish
where not dishonest; that it should be set up as a
theatrical scarecrow for superstitious terrors, of
which the *result* is oftentimes to defraud human
suffering of its readiest alleviation, and of which the
purpose is ' *Ut pueris placeant et declamatio fiant.*' "
This quotation he is pleased to translate: "that
they may win the applause of school-boys and
furnish matter *for a prize essay.*" Unmoved by the
ingenious device of the brilliant opium-eater to
cast contempt upon our subject, and insinuate
suspicion of our impartiality, we shall proceed now
in the next chapter to consider the moral standing
of the use of opium as a pleasurable stimulant.
That it was revealed for some higher object than to
minister to the voluptuous reveries of a De Quincey
has already been sufficiently established by the

medical authority of Pareira. Its use by persons in health as a means of procuring sensuous gratification, no one " is entitled to assume " to be innocent and lawful. Nor on the other hand would it be fair to assume *à priori* that a practice to which some millions of our race are addicted is a vice, and a worse vice than any *we* have a leaning to. Let us try to weigh it in the scales of justice and truth, and decide according to the facts.

CHAPTER II.

THE subject of this essay can be discussed without requiring writer or reader to commit himself to an extreme opinion upon stimulants in general. The use of stimulants is well-nigh universal. It would be difficult to point out the nation or tribe, almost the individual, altogether independent of them. As tea, coffee, chicory, coca, chocolate, tobacco, betelnut, wine, beer, spirits, haschisch, opium, &c., they enter into the daily diet of nearly all mankind. Most of these stimulants are liable to serious abuse, and hardly the most innocent of them has escaped vehement condemnation. Coffee was much opposed on its first introduction. The wise and good John Wesley earnestly deprecated the practice of drinking tea. The blast which King James blew against tobacco still has its echoes. Mr. William Hoyle tells us, "All the maltsters, brewers, distillers, publicans, &c., are persons who are not only unproductively, but destructively employed. They take the good grain and produce, which a bountiful Providence has given us for food, and destroy it by manufacturing from it a maddening and poisonous drink, which is distributed broadcast over the country, to the destruction both of the health, morals, and material weal of the people." Opium has been inveighed against as " a vile poison," " an infernal drug," which has " annually slain its hundred thousand victims;" the seller of which is " a murderer," and the consumer " a suicide." Our inquiry, however, need not be cumbered by irrelevant issues. The question before us relates to opium alone. We have nothing to do here with tea, tobacco, or alcohol, except as they may be used for illustrations. We have to consider whether *opium-smoking* is an innocent enjoyment or a vicious indulgence, and we must rigidly confine ourselves to the question before us. In order to discuss it fairly, we need to guard ourselves both against the prejudice which may unconsciously result from the similarity of this question to other questions about which we may already have formed strong opinions, and also against the natural tendency of the mind to react against excited, perhaps exaggerated, language.

Now in considering this grave and difficult question, we must deal with it as a practical question, to be determined by the facts, so far as they are ascertainable. All theories about stimulants notwithstanding, the practical sense of mankind has already passed different judgments upon particular stimulants. The " cup which cheers but not inebriates " is blessed alike by rich and poor. Tobacco has its ardent advocates and its determined foes.

When we come to alcohol we are touching one of
the burning questions of the day.   Though the
Bible can be quoted in praise of the juice of the
grape, though poets of all nations have sung its
joys, though it can plead immemorial antiquity,
world-wide custom, and an unquestionable moderate
use in its favour, yet the evils of intemperance
among our own Anglo-Saxon race are so flagrant,
that no one with a heart in his breast can fail to be
staggered by the contemplation of them.   Would it
then, be the right thing to lay alcohol under a ban,
to set our breweries and distilleries in a blaze, to
pour the contents of the wine and brandy vaults
of our docks into the Thames, to prohibit absolutely
the most innocent use of the intoxicating beverages,
in order to save our country from the unquestionably
fearful consequences of their abuse?   There are true
philanthropists and Christians who shrink from
such a measure as impracticable, unwise, not the
true, Divine method of fighting against vice; but
while not prepared for such decisive action, they
will readily acknowledge that the evils produced by
drink in this Christian England of ours are of such
appalling magnitude as to give the advocates of total
suppression a good *primâ facie* case, for an opinion
which is, if an error, at least an error leaning to
virtue's side.

If such be the state of the case as regards alcohol,
a careful perusal of the evidence we are about to
present in this chapter, and of that in our Appendix
(A), will convince the impartial reader, that opium

cannot pretend to a more favourable judgment than
alcohol : the only question being whether it must
not receive a worse condemnation.   " Few," to
quote the *Quarterly Review*,[1] " few will be found to
believe the assertion of the great opium dealers
Messrs. Jardine, Matheson, and Co., that opium is
eminently beneficial to the Chinese, and that they
themselves are, mere commercial considerations
apart, philanthropic benefactors of the human race."
It is true that arguments have been adduced in support of this amazing assertion : but these arguments
will avail most where least is known of China and
the Chinese.   These curious arguments are two.
First, that the universal predilection of the Chinese
for opium is owing to the malarious character of the
country.   Secondly, that the use of opium is a
wholesome corrective to the unwholesome, even
putrid, food which the Chinese consume.   The
reply to the first is that the country over which
opium is smoked is, in area, about the size of
Europe, and includes perhaps an equal variety of
sites, soils, and climates ; great plains level as
our Fen district, and mountainous regions like the
highlands of Scotland.   " Ague is almost unknown
in many of the provinces."[2]   Yet everywhere, in all
climates, on all soils, under every variety of condition and circumstance throughout that vast empire,
the Chinese smoke opium.   But nowhere do they all
smoke.   The smokers are but a percentage, greater

[1]   Volume 130, p. 101.
[2]   *Vide* Dr. Dudgeon's Peking Hospital Report, 1873, p. 15.

or smaller, in any place. If eighty or ninety out of a hundred persons enjoy good health in a certain district without the use of opium; those who do take it cannot expect the necessity of their doing so to be taken for granted. The second argument is likely to tell among untravelled Englishmen who imagine that the celestials dine upon puppy and sup upon rat. The Chinese are on the whole clean feeders. Their universal food, rice and vegetables, fish and pork, is as far as possible from " putrid and unwholesome." They will eat some things that we will not: for instance, eggs which are decidedly rotten. But they strongly object to certain kinds of food which delight the European epicure: such as high-flavoured game, and cheese with insect life visible in it. These are matters of taste; but the assertion that the nature of the Chinese food requires opium as a corrective, is as true as the Chinese notion that Englishmen cannot digest their food and perform natural functions without the regular con-sumption of Chinese rhubarb! Neither of these arguments is known to the Chinese as an excuse for indulgence in opium: both were invented for their effect on this side of the water. Possibly there are physiological peculiarities which determine the pre-dilection of races for particular stimulants; but if so, these are at present undiscovered.

Among the testimonies collected in the Appendix we especially call attention to the statements of Dr. Lockhart, not only because they proceed from a medical man, whose long residence in China, and frequent personal intercourse with opium-smokers, and careful study of the subject give him a strong claim to most respectful hearing; but because of the evident effort to set aside prejudice, and present nothing beyond the plain facts.

Those who set aside all missionary testimony as inevitably coloured by prejudice would do well to consider that there is prejudice and prejudice. The bias of the missionary who has no object but the glory of God and the salvation of mankind is a very different thing from the bias of the merchant who every year adds to his profits by the questionable traffic. How gladly the missionary would explain away the inconsistency between the opium trade and the Christian name, if he could! Is it a pleasure to him to be compelled to confess before a Chinese crowd, that he can make no apology for his countrymen in this matter? There is no one who would be relieved of a heavier incubus if this trade could be cleared from the stigma attaching to it. Sneers at " Exeter Hall philanthropy " are cheap, and in some quarters telling. But the philosophical student of human nature will acknowledge that though nearly all men are prejudiced in respect to every matter they take deep interest in, there are some prejudices which, from their very nature, dispose a man to see the truth, and others which tend to blind his eyes to the most obvious facts. Clarkson and Wilberforce, Lloyd Garrison, Wendel Philips, and Mrs. Beecher Stowe, were undoubtedly steeped in prejudice up to the eyes against slavery, while slave-holding planters were immersed over-head in prejudice in its favour. But now that we look back upon the controversy, the judgment of mankind hesitates not to say which party was right. There is a prejudice the spirit of which is, "We can do nothing against the truth, but for the truth." We are not careful, therefore, to clear missionaries from all imputation of prejudice. Let the reader weigh their evidence as scrutinizingly as he pleases. In matters of opinion he may find it necessary to allow some deduction on this account. In matters of fact we are persuaded that their testimony will abide scrutiny.

That, on the most lenient view, the consumption of opium produces physical and moral evils, fully commensurate with those produced by intoxicating drinks, is a proposition which can be established apart from missionary testimony. Pareira, in "Materia Medica," and Dr. Anstie, author of a standard work on Stimulants, are decisive upon this point. Drs. Eatwell and Impey, opium examiners under the Bengal Government, venture no more in defence of the manufacture, than to suggest that the use of opium is not a more serious evil than the use of alcohol amongst ourselves. Mr. Cooper, the traveller —extracts from whose evidence will be found in the Appendix—uses stronger language as to the terrible results of opium smoking to China generally, than I have found in the writings of any missionary. A quotation here of a witness, whose high position and intimate connexion with the subject combine to render his testimony of prime importance, and who is free from suspicion of any leaning to the missionary side, ought to be sufficient alone to set this question at rest. Sir Rutherford Alcock, K.C.B., her Majesty's Minister in China, examined before the Committee of the House of Commons, June 6, 1871, gave his evidence thus:[3]—

"5738. 'Can the evils, physical, moral, commercial, and political, as respects individuals, families, and the nation at large, of indulgence in this vice be exaggerated?'—(Sir R. Alcock.) 'I have no doubt that, where there is a great amount of evil, there is always a certain danger of exaggeration; but looking to the universality of the belief among the Chinese, that whenever a man takes to smoking opium, it will probably be the impoverishment and ruin of his family—a popular feeling which is universal both amongst those who are addicted to it, who always consider themselves as moral criminals, and amongst those who abstain from it, and are merely endeavouring to prevent its consumption—it is difficult not to conclude that what we hear of it is essentially true, and that it is a source of impoverishment and ruin to families.' "

The evident care employed here to express as moderate an opinion as possible should give these sentences great weight. Note particularly the important statement about the "universal belief of the Chinese." To the testimony of our late repre-

---

[3] *Vide* Report, East India Finance, 1871. (363.) Page 275.

sentative at the Court of Peking we can add that of
Sir Thomas Wade, who now occupies that important
post. He says,[4]—

"I cannot endorse the opinion of Messrs. Jardine,
Matheson, and Co., that 'the use of opium is not a
curse, but a comfort and a benefit, to the hard-
working Chinese.' As in all cases of sweeping
criticism, those who condemn the opium trade may
have been guilty of exaggeration. They have been
especially mistaken in representing the British
Government and people as responsible for the introduction of opium to the knowledge of the Chinese;
the Chinese knew it long before we brought them
opium from India. But it is impossible to deny
that we bring them that quality which—in the south,
at all events—tempts them the most, and for which
they pay dearest. It is to me vain to think otherwise of the use of the drug in China than as of a
habit many times more pernicious, nationally speaking, than the gin and whiskey drinking which we
deplore at home. It takes possession more insi-
diously, and keeps its hold to the full as tenaciously.
I know no case of radical cure. It has insured, in
every case within my knowledge, the steady descent,
moral and physical, of the smoker, and it is, so far,
a greater mischief than drink, that it does not, by
external evidence of its effect, expose its victim to
the loss of repute which is the penalty of habitual
drunkenness. There is reason to fear that a higher

---

[4] China. No. 5, (1871). Correspondence respecting the Revision of the Treaty of Tientsin, page 432.

class than used to smoke in Commissioner Lin's day are now taking to the practice."

For Chinese testimony we cannot quote more satisfactory evidence than that of the Mandarin Heu Naetse, who in 1836 memorialized the Emperor Taou Kwang to legalize the importation of opium, and therefore is not to be suspected of going out of his way to magnify its evils : [5]—

"I would humbly represent that opium was originally ranked among medicines ; its qualities are stimulant ; it also checks excessive secretions, and prevents the evil effects of noxious vapours. In the 'Materia Medica' of Le Shechin of the Ming dynasty it is called *Afoo-yung*. When any one is long habituated to inhaling it, it becomes necessary to resort to it at regular intervals, and the habit of using it, being inveterate, is destructive of time, injurious to property, and yet dear to one even as life. Of those who use it to great excess the breath becomes feeble, the body wasted, the face sallow, the teeth black ; the individuals themselves clearly see the evil effects of it, yet cannot refrain from it. . . . . . . It will be found, on examination, that the smokers of opium are idle, lazy vagrants, having no useful purpose before them, and are unworthy of regard, or even contempt."

Not only a long series of official documents, of which the above is a specimen, but numerous pamphlets, ballads, pictures, and illustrated sheets, proclaim the Chinese popular conviction that opium

[5] Correspondence relating to China, 1840, page 156.

is a terrible curse to their land. An old Chinese scholar thus summarized the evils of opium :— " 1st. It destroys and shortens life; 2nd, it unfits for the discharge of *all* duties ; 3rd, it squanders substance, houses, lands, money, and sometimes, it is reported, wives and children are sold to obtain it; and 4th, it injures population. The children of confirmed opium-smokers are said to be childless in the third generation. More than half of such smokers are themselves childless, and the other half have fewer children than those of other countries, and their offspring seldom live to become old men."

As abundant evidence of Chinese antagonism to opium will be found in subsequent chapters, let us now turn to other countries, and see what reputation the drug has acquired for itself there.

In the Report of the Select Committee already adduced, we have the evidence of Sir Cecil Beadon, Lieutenant-Governor of Bengal, respecting Assam :—

" 3523. 'Now I will ask you just to turn your eye in the direction of Assam. Is it not the fact that the population of Assam is almost entirely demoralized by the quantity of opium which is produced and used there ?'—(Sir C. Beadon.) ' It was.'

" 3524. 'There has been a change lately, has there ?'—' Some ten years ago the Government prohibited the manufacture of opium in Assam; up to that time it had been free.'

" 3525. ' And during that time the population was immensely demoralized ?'—' Very much demoralized.

The reason that was assigned for it was, that it was eaten by the women and children; the children from their earliest years were accustomed to suck rags saturated with opium.'"

This evidence of Sir C. Beadon is illustrated by the following extract from Mr. Bruce's tea report, date 1839 :—

"This vile drug has kept, and does now keep, down the population; the women have fewer children compared with those of other countries, and these children seldom live to be old men, but in general die at manhood—very few old men being seen in this country in comparison with others. Few but those who have resided long in this unhappy land know the dreadful and immoral effects which the use of opium produces on the native. He will steal, sell his property, his children, the mother of his children, and finally commit murder to obtain it."

Passing from Assam to Burma, the same Parliamentary Report gives us, in the words of Dr. George Smith, a fearful account of the ravages of the opium vice in British territory :—

"5097. 'Does the Excise department promote the consumption of opium in India as zealously as that of alcohol ? '—' In the Indo-Chinese districts of British Burma, the action of the departments in promoting the sale of opium has long been a public scandal. The evil has been officially reported to the Government of India by the late Chief Commissioner, Sir Arthur Phayre; and in a published official report

by Mr. Wheeler, Secretary to the present Chief
Commissioner, the evil is again described for the
information of Government in the following language :—" Mr. Hind, Assistant Commissioner, came
on board. This gentleman appears to have a large
local experience of Aracan, dating back from 1835.
The principal object of his conversation was to
impress me with the demoralizing effects of the
Bengal akbâri laws upon the impulsive, pleasure-
loving people of Burma ; and certainly he furnished
sufficient data to prove the utter fallacy of the
general conclusion, that what is good for India is
good for Burma. Prior to the introduction of
British rule into Aracan, the punishment for using
opium was death. The people were hard-working,
sober, and simple-minded. Unfortunately, one of
the earliest measures of our administration was the
introduction of the akbâri rules by the Bengal Board
of Revenue. Mr. Hind, who had passed the greater
part of his long life amongst the people of Aracan,
described the progress of demoralization. Organized
efforts were made by Bengal agents to introduce the
use of the drug, and to create a taste for it amongst
the rising generation. The general plan was to
open a shop with a few cakes of opium, and to invite
the young men and distribute it gratuitously. Then,
when the taste was established, the opium was sold
at a low rate. Finally, as it spread throughout the
neighbourhood, the price was raised, and large
profits ensued. Sir Arthur Phayre's account of the
demoralization of Aracan by the Bengal akbâri rules

is very graphic; but Mr. Hind's statements were more striking, as he entered more into detail. He saw a fine healthy generation of strong men succeeded by a rising generation of haggard opium-smokers and eaters, who indulged to such an extent that their mental and physical powers were alike wasted. Then followed a fearful increase in gambling and dacoity." ' " [6]

As in Assam and Burmah, so in China, opium is accused of ruining the moral character of its votaries. The Rev. Griffith John writes :—

" The moral effects of opium-smoking are of the most pernicious kind. It seems to paralyze the moral nature. It bedims the moral vision, blunts the moral instincts, and extinguishes every virtue. Strong drink may upset the balance of the mind for the time, but opium seems to absorb all its virtues, and leave it a dead, emotionless thing. The Chinese say that an opium-smoker is always devising some mischief, and that not the slightest confidence can be safely reposed in him. Whilst in affluent circumstances, the danger is not so great; but the moment penury sets in, he becomes an object of suspicion and aversion to all around him. There is nothing too mean or too corrupt for him to attempt in order to allay the insufferable craving for the drug. He will ruin his parents, and even sell his wife and children to procure the necessary supply." '

After reading this combination of testimony, few

---

[6] Report, East India Finance, 1871, page 235.
' *Nonconformist*, 1870.

will dispute that opium must be reckoned as at least on a par with alcohol as to its evil influence on health, wealth, and morals. We have no data to enable us to make a statistical comparison of the effects of the two stimulants. Rhetoric might have put down the deaths from opium in China at half a million instead of one hundred thousand, and yet fall short of the death-rate ascribed to drink in this country. And the money value of all the opium consumed in China in twelve months perhaps would not exceed one-fifth of the 131,601,490*l*. which, according to Mr. Hoyle, was expended upon intoxicating liquors in the United Kingdom during the year 1872. But then it must be remembered that China is a very poor country compared with Great Britain, and also that opium-smoking is quite a *new* vice in the Middle Kingdom. It dates, in any serious dimensions, no farther back than the present century. Give it time, and it bids fair to outdo alcohol in the race of destruction, and carry off the palm as most fatal of all the stimulants to the weal of the human race.

" But these lamentable consequences result from the *abuse* of opium and alcohol, not from their moderate use." Undoubtedly. We cordially concede to the opium merchant, and the defender of the East India monopoly, that it must be the *abuse* of the good gifts of God which turns them into awful plagues. This brings us to the inquiry whether or not the use of opium as an article of luxury and enjoyment is not much *less defensible* than is the use of alcohol. Is

there any "moderate" opium-smoking or opium-
eating at all analogous to the moderate use of
wines, beer, and spirits?   This is a question difficult
to answer, important as it is in this controversy.
Assertion can be pitted against assertion.   The Rev.
Griffith John says :—" I would observe that it is a
great mistake to refer opium to the same category as
tobacco and spirits.   On this point there is a wonderful unanimity of opinion among those who are
capable of forming an opinion on the matter.
Tobacco, beer, and wine, may be taken in moderation,
and are generally believed to be harmless, if so used ;
but even the *moderate* use of opium is baneful, and,
what is worse, it is impossible to take it in moderation.   The smoker is never satisfied with less than
the intoxicating effects of the drug.   He smokes
with the view of making himself drunk, and his
cravings are never appeased until he gets drunk.   If
time and means permit, he lives in a state of ecstatic
trance or intoxication, from which he desires never
to be waked up.   Opium-smoking cannot be compared with moderate drinking, but with drunkenness itself.   The habit is more insidious in its
approach than that of drinking, and holds its victim
with a far more tenacious grasp. "   For the sake of
a speedy end to the controversy, we could wish that
we had found that " wonderful unanimity " of opinion
which Mr. John encountered.   If this point were
once plainly established, that there is, there can be,
no moderate opium-smoking, there would be an end
of all debate.   The dealers in opium, the upholders

of the monopoly, would simply be aiders and abettors of self-murder. British merchants, and the British Government itself, could not escape the charge of wholesale poisoning on a gigantic scale. The vast scale of the opium-poisoning operations, involving the death of unknown numbers of Chinese, the enrichment of merchant princes, the maintenance of one of the largest Empires of the world, and the slow ruin of another Empire still larger, would not elevate the opium trade beyond the reach of the fatal accusation that it is making gain out of the very life-blood of mankind. But it would be premature to press this charge, because all defenders of the traffic assert that opium may be used in moderation, and that, thus used, it is no more injurious than ardent spirits. Mr. Winchester, formerly H.M. Consul at Shanghae, is an instance to our hand. We quote again from the Parliamentary Report :—

"5935. 'I think you said that you were a medical man?'—(Mr. Winchester.) 'I studied medicine, but I have not been practising.'

"5936. 'Would you recommend persons who lived in close rooms, without much air, to smoke opium?'— 'I believe that I would not recommend any man to smoke opium under any circumstances.'

"5937. Mr. R. Fowler: 'You have had experience of the effects of opium on the Chinese who take it, I presume?'—'I have observed the effects; I have never smoked it myself.'

"5938. 'But it would be your opinion that it has a

very prejudicial effect on the health of the people ?'—
'On the whole, I should say yes. But there are two
conditions of opium-smoking; there is what you
might call the moderate opium-smoking, and there
is that stage which I would call *opiamismus*, as being
equivalent to what may be called *alcoholismus*. I think
you must view these two conditions as entirely
separate in considering the effect of opium upon
individuals.'

"5939. 'Sir Rutherford Alcock expressed a doubt
whether people ever remained moderate smokers.
What would be your opinion on that point?'—'My
opinion is rather more in favour of the opinion that
they do; and it is derived from my observations
upon the general activity and energy of the Chinese,
both in the neighbourhood of the ports, and in the
straits, and in California, from their being, on the
whole, a useful people, and a laborious, diligent population.'

" 5940. 'Then it is your opinion that a man may
continue to use opium as we use wine and the lower
classes use beer in this country, without ever being
inclined to use it to excess ?'—' Yes, I feel sure of it.
I have known men who told me that they had
smoked opium all their lives, and who were perfectly
competent to the duties of their position.'

" 5941. 'And who were elderly people ?'—'People
of forty or fifty.'

"5942. ' Any of seventy or eighty?'—' Men of the
usual ages in private life.' "

The last is an amusingly ambiguous answer. Nor

will the argument founded on the generality of the Chinese being laborious and diligent count for much. If opium-smoking were the rule among them, and non-smoking the exception as teetotalism in England, it would hold good : but this is far from a correct representation of the case. But Mr. Winchester's assertion, that " opium has a beneficial use and an injurious use," may be set-off against Mr. Griffith John's. Dr. Eatwell, who passed three years in China, upholds the same view as Consul Winchester: and, in general, all apologists for the traffic assert that opium may be used in moderation, and, so used, is no more injurious than alcohol ; while all assailants of the traffic support, more or less categorically, the opposite view. What shall we make of this conflicting evidence ? When, in the famous Tichborne trial, hundreds of witnesses had sworn that the Claimant was Sir R. Tichborne, and their oaths had been neutralized by those of other hundreds who swore that he was not, the Lord Chief Justice commenced his summing-up by intimating that in his opinion these opposing testimonies proved that the defendant was, if not Sir Roger, at least, in personal appearance, something like the Baronet. I think a fair summing-up of the evidence in our present controversy will necessitate a verdict that the use of opium as a stimulant is *something like* that of alcohol, if not identical with it. I think we cannot deny that some opium-smokers are " moderate " *for a time:* that, while they are moderate, their indulgence does them no visible harm, and that *in some cases* they are able to keep to this moderation even to old age. So much the evidence in favour of opium seems to require. But as the judge found the defendant to be Orton and not Tichborne, despite of the resemblances, so, in the end, it may be found that opium is not as alcohol, although there is a measure of resemblance between the two. I say "it may be found in the end," because I believe that the matter must at present be regarded as *sub judice.* We have no reliable statistics as to the number of opium-smokers in China. We have no statistics at all as to the amount smoked by each, and the average length of life of smokers. In the meantime, all one can do is to estimate with care that amount of evidence we have, and form an *interim* opinion. For my own part, before looking closely at the case, I inclined rather to the view that there is a moderate use of opium—and for this reason: it appeared to me that, if the habit of opium-smoking were certainly, or well-nigh certainly, fatal within a few years to all smokers, then the practice could not maintain itself and spread. In spite of an absurd delusion to the contrary met with in England, the Chinese value their lives quite as much as we do. Human nature is pretty much the same all the world over. Men will run a certain amount of danger in the practice of pleasant vices, but they would not long continue to indulge these vices if the punishment were in all cases certain and never long delayed. If there were no moderate drinking, there would be no drunkenness, the teetotallers say; and they are right. If sexual indulgence were sure to bring painful disease and an early grave, few would have the hardihood to gratify their propensities at such an expense. Reasoning in a similar way, it seemed to me that if *every* smoker of opium passed, by a swift and inevitable process, from pleasant dallying with the pipe to a state of chronic disease and torture, ending in a premature death, the vice of opium-smoking would soon cure itself. It would hardly require a second generation of victims to warn all society against the fatal indulgence.

This reasoning is, I think, valid, and it is corro-borated by the evidence of Consul Winchester and others. We can hardly doubt that there are *some* Chinese to whom the opium-pipe is no more harmful than the moderate use of wine and spirits is to many persons in Europe. But we must be on our guard against hasty analogies. I have already repudiated the notion that stimulants can be reasoned upon as a class. Their action is very imperfectly understood as yet, according to the acknowledgment of one of the latest medical authorities. Dr. Anstie assures us that instances of indulgence in tea and coffee to an injurious extent are by no means so rare as some persons imagine. Yet neither he nor any one else would for a moment dream of comparing the effects of tea and coffee with those of beer and gin. Every stimulant must be examined by itself, and sentence passed upon it according to its own merits. Now as regards alcohol, the moderate use of it is well known. In the case of opium, the moderate use is little better than hypothetical. In England there are, perhaps, ninety-nine moderate drinkers for every drunkard. In China there is no *class* of moderate opium-smokers which can be appealed to, who openly avow and defend their practice. Individuals there may be, like those Mr. Winchester adduces, but they are few and far between. The evidence goes to show, and the essayist's own personal knowledge confirms it, that the Chinese regard opium-smoking as a vice, and a pre-eminently seductive and dangerous vice. If all the opium imported into China and grown in the country were equally consumed by the whole population, the amount falling to each smoker would be so small as to be innocuous. But, on the other hand, if all the smokers consumed as much as one Chinese ounce per day, they would all be opium-slaves. We do not know the exact number of smokers who divide the total amount of the drug between them ; but the evidence before us certainly tends to lead to the opinion that the smokers are comparatively few in number to the whole population, and that the majority, or at least a very large proportion of them, are *immoderate* in their consumption. Without exact computation our conclusion must necessarily be conjectural. But there are certain evident considerations which ought not to be overlooked.

(1) Multitudes partake of wine, beer, and spirits, as regularly as they do of beef and mutton. These beverages are a part of daily food. The use of them is general, open, and reputable. It is not so with

opium-smoking. The opium pipe is not regarded as forming a part of regular diet. Smokers and non-smokers agree in regarding it as a vicious indulgence; as a consequence, smokers almost invariably hide their addiction to the pipe, if possible. I have caught a man smoking who had only half an hour before denied to me that he was a smoker, and condemned the habit. Opium-smoking is classed by the universal popular opinion of China with gambling and debauchery. There is no reason why this should be so, except the practical experience the Chinese have had of its fearful consequences. A special pleader might argue that opium-smoking is regarded as a vice, because the Chinese Government made it a crime. I unhesitatingly believe that the Chinese Government made it a crime because it was unmistakeably a ruinous vice. We shall hear more about this in the chapter on the Chinese history of opium, to which I refer the reader. There may be moderate smokers, but this state of things points to an immense prevalence of immoderate smoking.

(2) The mass of evidence, Chinese and foreign, points to a fascinating, enthralling power in opium, which renders it more enslaving than alcohol. It is well known that alcohol by no means necessarily imposes any constant increase upon those who use it. A man may drink his quantum at seventy years of age and be perfectly satisfied therewith, although it is exactly what he used to take at twenty years of age. But if the reader carefully weighs the

evidence about opium he will hardly avoid concluding that, very generally if not always, the use
of this stimulant *imposes the necessity of continual
increase.* If the smoker could always keep to
what sufficed him during the first year or two
it might be as innocent a stimulant as tobacco.
But he cannot. There is a fatal charm about
the drug—he must go on to more and more.
English readers are familiar with this quality of
opium from De Quincey's fascinating but horrible
narration. The experience of the Chinese tallies
with that of the brilliant English writer, except that
he by almost superhuman efforts broke off the habit,
while in China this is so rare as to be regarded as
impossible.

(3) Even between drunkenness and opium-smoking
there are perceptible distinctions. We must allow
that opium-smoking is a much more pacific and
polite vice. The opium sot does not quarrel with
his mate, nor kick his wife to death. He is quiet
and harmless enough while the spirit of the drug
possesses him. But against this one must set off
the more terrible slavery in which the opium-smoker
is held fast. Many drunkards only give way to their
propensity by fits and starts. Others are drunk
perhaps regularly once a week, when pay-day puts
them in funds. But the victim of opium *must* have
his allowance *every* day. There is no pause, no
intermission for him.

(4) This brings us to the difficulty of giving up
the two vices. It may be nearly impossible to break

D

off drinking habits.   It is quite impossible to give
up opium once a certain stage has passed.   The
drunkard may have to pass through a terrible
struggle for recovery.   The confirmed opium-smoker
gives up his pipe only to die.   There is universal
unanimity of evidence upon this point, that after the
smoker has gone on for a certain time, and got to
use daily a certain amount, it is physically impossible
for him, without the help of medicines, to pause in
his career and retrace his steps.

It avails little, therefore, to argue that there may
be, that there actually is, a moderate use of opium,
just as there is of alcohol.   Each must be studied
by itself, and verdict pronounced according to the
facts.   We do know there is a moderate use of
alcohol, so extensive that even the great prevalence
of intemperance in our land does not generally convince men that they ought to banish alcohol from
society altogether.   We do not know that there is
any such use of opium.   Some moderate smoking
no doubt there must be.   But the question is what
is its amount compared with the whole amount of
smoking.   We have no figures to go upon.   The
evidence we have is vague and indefinite.   Who then
shall decide ?   Surely none ought to know, none can
know, so well as the Chinese people themselves.
And what do they say ?   From the Emperor through
all grades of society down to the lowest classes, one
and all, without dissentient voice, they condemn the
practice as fatally insidious and destructive.   They
are well acquainted with other stimulants.   Tea,

tobacco, betel-nut, spirits, they are familiar with them all. Drunkenness is known and condemned as a vice among them as among us, though it is not so prevalent there. But for opium alone they reserve a condemnation altogether unanimous, altogether unparalleled.

In Appendix (B) such information about the probable amount of opium smoked by the Chinese as we have been able to obtain is recorded. But the absence of any accurate estimate of the amount of poppy cultivation within the eighteen provinces of China renders the best attempts at calculation unsatisfactory. Even if we possessed returns of the whole quantity of opium annually consumed in China, that alone would shed no light upon the moral aspects of the question ; for it is not the total amount, but its distribution, which would determine the matter. The same quantity which would be harmless if divided equally among sixty millions, would be ruin of body and soul if consumed by two or three millions. The estimates by such authorities as Sir R. Alcock and Dr. Lockhart indicate three or four millions of smokers. Mr. Cooper and Dr. Dudgeon vastly increase the number. The discrepancy may be perhaps explained by supposing that the larger number includes all those who at one time or another take an occasional pipe, but never use the drug regularly. In this, however, there is a general *consensus* of testimony that the habit once formed can hardly ever be renounced, and that in the majority of cases it compels its votaries to increase their dose, until it reaches a highly-injurious quantity.

Statistics fail us, but this we know, that the missionary hospitals from Peking to Canton are everywhere visited by large numbers of opium victims praying for aid to release them from bondage to the pipe ; that everywhere travellers receive numerous applications for " anti-opium pills " for the same purpose; that opium beggars are frequent spectacles in all large places ; and deaths of impoverished smokers occur, in what numbers we know not, but certainly they are anything but rare. For all this we cannot justly say that it is *proved* that opium as a stimulant is essentially worse than alcohol ; but we can most assuredly say that the assertion that the two stand morally on exactly the same footing is also not proved ; that, on the contrary, very grave doubt is cast upon it ; that the evidence points to a *peculiarly enthralling* power in opium, which marks it a more dangerous stimulant than alcohol. Opium lacks any clear, positive evidence of a generally-diffused moderate use. In fine, Sir Rutherford Alcock has very fairly represented the general opinion of foreign observers in China ; and the natives would corroborate his view in stronger terms. To quote the Report once more :—

" 5756. You say, if I rightly understand you, that you never in China met with a moderate opium-smoker, that is to say, one who you think would not have been better without even the amount that he did consume ?—As a rule, that may be so ; but for instance, all our domestic servants smoke, and they do not smoke in excess, or we should not keep them.

" 5757. What do you mean by excess ?—To such a degree that if deprived of their opium, or delayed, they would collapse like the prisoner I have mentioned.

" 5758. But they all go on steadily to that stage, as I gather from you ?—That is my impression; I am obliged to speak vaguely, however, because we have not the data or statistics on which we could dogmatize at all about it."

This then is the conclusion of one who has had very great opportunities for forming an opinion, and whose position and responsibilities could not but incline him to judge as leniently as possible of the practice. Sir R. Alcock thinks that moderate opium-smoking lasts only for a time, and that " they all go steadily on " to that stage which is self-destructive. If this be the fact, it will harmonize the conflicting evidence.

Travellers like the botanist Mr. Fortune testify that they have seen opium-smokers who seemed no whit the worse for the practice. Missionaries and others say the habit is enslaving, and ruins its victims. Mr. Fortune might possibly have come round to this latter opinion, had he again seen those very persons he describes after they had used the opium-pipe for ten years longer. Even, however, if we admit that some proportion of the smokers are able to preserve their moderation to the last, it is important to notice that *the impression of the Chinese*

Government, and of the Chinese people, is altogether opposed to that of those who class opium among harmless or only occasionally harmful stimulants.

Where we cannot procure the scientific evidence of carefully-collected statistics, the evidence of *national opinion*, not that of governments only, but popular opinion, must be received as of great weight. It is the result of a general experience much wider than that which is at the foundation of the individual opinions of this or that traveller or resident. It is, therefore, most noteworthy that China, Siam, Burma, and Japan have all distinctly declared against opium. In 1839, if not before, opium was absolutely prohibited in Siam by royal edict.[8] Our first treaty with Japan contained a clause expressly excluding opium, and the newspapers tell us that within the last few months the Japanese officials have been enforcing their laws against the Chinese smokers, on account of their great dread lest the practice should establish itself among them. The long-sustained and intense opposition of the Chinese to opium will have to be separately treated of.

In conclusion, we cannot say that it is *absolutely proved* that opium-smoking is a more pernicious habit than dram-drinking; but there is reason to think that the drug exercises a peculiar enslaving power, which renders it more universally fatal to its votaries. For the purposes of this essay, however, it is not necessary to bring absolute proof that opium is always pernicious. It is enough that the

[8] "China Repository," vol. viii. p. 125.

Chinese, who know a great deal more about it than we can know, are, one may say, unanimously agreed in regarding it as a fearful curse to their land. " British Opium Policy " has to do with a system by which we are the producers of the drug, the Chinese the users of it. It is for them to say whether they think it a harmless luxury or a national poison. Hesitation of judgment, contrariety of opinion, may characterize the testimonies of English witnesses, but nothing of the kind can be observed in China; those persons who are the actual slaves of the opium-pipe being the loudest in its condemnation. Granting, then, that we are doubtful about the exact measure of its evils, nothing can justify us for forcing it upon an unwilling people.

CHAPTER III.

THE East India Company's opium policy may be expressed in two words, repression and revenue: at home repression, revenue from abroad. The Directors of that Company, being sovereign masters of a hundred millions of their fellow-creatures, were by no means careless of the physical and moral welfare of their subjects. Unhappily their sense of responsibility found its limit here, and no qualms of conscience interfered to prevent their pandering to the vicious tastes of a distant population beyond the seas.

No decent government can welcome the replenishing of its finances by the vices of mankind. Were governments unscrupulous, the moral sense of the masses would compel them to profess to deplore the fruitfulness of such sources of revenue. Nevertheless, it so happens, as matter of fact, that governments do continually receive large revenues from the vicious excesses of their citizens. In our own country the taxes upon strong drink bring in over thirty millions a year, a large proportion of

which is contributed by drunkenness. As this fact
is pleaded in defence of our opium revenue, it may
be well to consider the principles which ought to
determine government action in such cases.

All luxuries obviously are exposed to taxation
in preference to necessaries. It is better to tax tea
than bread; better to tax spirits than tea. When
the article of luxury is frequently injurious to its
consumers, and its consumption cannot be prevented, it is thereby plainly marked out for taxation,
because taxation checks consumption by making
the article more expensive. On this ground opium
presents itself as a positive claimant for taxation, and
every argument for taxes upon alcohol supports the
justice of deriving revenue from the poppy.   If
absolute prohibition of the use of opium be assumed
to be impossible, or beyond the proper functions of
Government, then the institution of a tax upon it
becomes positively commendable.   But here we
must lay down another principle which inheres
in all wise policy in respect to such taxation.
The Government only accepts revenue from this
source under the compulsion of circumstances,
admitting it in order to diminish evils which Government cannot altogether prevent.   Statesmen of all
parties would abhor the suggestion that they should
encourage drunkenness in order to swell a surplus.
Even that consumption of intoxicating drinks which
can only be characterized as improvident is not
atoned for because it contributes largely to the
revenue.   This terrible waste of national resources

" kills the goose which lays the golden eggs," cripples the power of the people to support the demands which Government must make upon them. We may lay it down as a guiding principle that taxation of articles liable to abuse, such as alcohol and opium, can only be justified because of its effect in restricting their consumption. The acquisition of revenue must not be the primary object.

The East India Company's Directors proved both by professions and acts that, so far as their own subjects were concerned, they were animated by wise and benevolent views. From an early date they distinctly deprecated the consumption of opium by Hindoos, and aimed at its repression. Mr. C. W. Bell, of the Revenue Department of Bombay, said to the Committee of the House of Commons:[1] " I find it frequently stated in the Government records, that they endeavour not so much to look for an increase of revenue as for a diminution of the consumption of spirits and the prevention of drunkenness." In respect to opium, this honourable policy is attested by Mr. H. St. George Tucker, the eminent finance minister, who wrote in 1829: "It is scarcely necessary for me to speak of the policy which had been pursued by the East India Company, systematically for a long course of years, with relation to the monopoly of opium in Bengal. The leading feature of that policy was, to limit the manufacture to a moderate quantity, seldom exceeding 4500 chests —to confine the cultivation of the poppy to those

[1] Report, East India Finance, 1871, p. 206.

districts in which the drug could be produced of the
best quality and at the lowest cost—and to prevent
as far as possible the sale and use of it in our territory, except for medicinal purposes. In prosecuting
this policy we went so far as to prohibit the cultivation of the poppy in the districts of Bangulpore
and Rungpore, where it had long been grown extensively, and where the produce had been heretofore appropriated to the purposes of the monopoly ;
and at a period not very remote, on information
being obtained that the cultivation in Rungpore had
been clandestinely renewed, the Government did not
hesitate to order the plant to be eradicated, in the
most peremptory and arbitrary manner. In short
the very essence of all our arrangements had been to
draw the largest revenue from the smallest quantity
of the article." [2]   To this unexceptionable testimony
we can add the explicit avowal of the Court of
Directors. In their despatch to the Governor in
Council in Bengal, under date 24th October, 1817,
they say : [3] "The sentiments expressed in our despatch
of 18th September, 1816, will have prepared you to
expect our approbation of the measures adopted by
you for the purpose of supplying from the Government
stores a quantity of opium for the internal consumption of the country. We wish it at the same time
to be clearly understood, that our sanction is given
to these measures, *not with a view to the revenue*

---

[2] Kaye's "Memorials of Indian Government," p. 149.

[3] Appendix to Report on the Affairs of the East India Company, 1831, p. 11. In British Museum, vol. vi. of 1831, p. 359.

*which they may yield, but in the hope that they will
tend to restrain the use of this pernicious drug,* and
that the regulations for the internal sale of it will be
so framed as *to prevent its introduction into districts
where it is not used,* and to limit its consumption in
other places as nearly as possible to what may be
absolutely necessary. WERE IT POSSIBLE TO PREVENT
THE USE OF THE DRUG ALTOGETHER, EXCEPT FOR THE
PURPOSES OF MEDICINE, WE WOULD GLADLY DO IT IN
COMPASSION TO MANKIND." Noble sentiments these,
which would have covered the Directors with im-
mortal honour had they been consistently carried
out.

In accordance with their deliberate policy of
" employing taxation less as an instrument of raising
a revenue than as a preservative of the health and
morals of the community," the Directors absolutely prohibited cultivation of the poppy in certain
districts,[4] restricted it within limits in others, kept

---

[4] Government Letter, No. 1359, to the Revenue Commissioners, dated 18th June, 1835. " In reply, I am instructed to
observe, that as this Government has been directed by the Supreme
Government (and in their directions the Court of Directors have
concurred) *to afford no encouragement whatever to the growth of opium
in the territories under this presidency* (Bombay), and to prevent, as
far as possible, the extension of the cultivation ; and as the growth
of the drug is new to the Poona district, the Right Honourable
the Governor in Council considers it incumbent on this Government, *however disinterested it may be to the interests of individuals,
to discourage it by all means in its power.*"

Government Resolution, No. 479, of 21st January, 1854.—
" The Government will neither purchase the opium produced nor
forego the duty thereon ; and that in the event of the duty not
being paid, the collector will be required to enforce the pro-

vigilant control of the sale of opium, and made their charge for it as high as possible without making the temptation to illicit dealings too powerful.   The result of this policy appears satisfactory.[5]   Through-out their wide dominions, and during a long course of years, it is not surprising if sometimes good intentions were imperfectly executed.   Critics aver that the excise system tended to introduce, and pro-mote a taste for, the excisable articles.   But if these criticisms can be substantiated, they amount to no more than convictions of errors in judgment.   Whether owing to the Company's regulations, or to the tem-perance of the people, the consumption of opium in British India has been very moderate.   The value of the opium sold from Government stores in 1868-9 was only 300,000*l.*, and of this sum 200,000*l.* was clear Government profit.   The cost of production being about 30*l.* per chest, this sum represents about 3400 chests of Government opium consumed in India.   Comparing this quantity with the 50,000 chests sent to China, it is clear at a glance that the Company's own territories are insignificant con-tributors to the opium revenue; and we have no difficulty in giving the Directors and their agents full

visions of the existing law, *it being the earnest desire of Govern-ment to discourage the production of the drug in their own terri-tories.*"   Papers relating to the Opium Question, 1870, p. 7.

[5] When this was written the author had not seen the Official Reports about the progress of the opium vice in British Burma.   The reader can refer to the extracts in the Appendix and judge for himself whether or not the British Government is directly responsible for the introduction and propagation of the vice in that portion of our territory.

credit for sincerity in carrying out their repressive policy to the best of their ability. This small consumption in Bengal is the more striking in contrast to the immense amount consumed in the native states of Central and Western India, the internal government of which is in the hands of native princes. Mr. W. Neville Sturt, in his Report to Parliament,[6] estimates the consumption in Rajpootana and Central India at 20,000 chests. The Rajpoots and the Sikhs are almost universally addicted to opium-eating.

A few words in explanation of the East India Government's connection with opium may be useful. Popular language constantly speaks of " our Indian Empire " as if it were a homogeneous unity; and probably multitudes of Englishmen have the impression that all the vast peninsula, from the Himalayas to the eastern and western oceans, belongs directly to the British crown. This is not the case. Speaking roughly, about two-thirds belongs to Britain, and one-third is still under the rule of Indian sovereigns, Maharajahs, Rajahs, Nawabs, Begums, and other Hindoo designations of thrones, principalities, and powers. The independence of these native states is fettered by the presence of British residents at their courts, who hold varying degrees of influence, but as far as opium is concerned they are now practically independent. This important difference between British territory and

---

[6] East India (Progress and Condition) during the year 1870-71, p. 78.

native territory divided the opium concerns of the Company into two quite dissimilar sections. Patna and Malwa conveniently designate these sections. Patna opium is produced on British territory; Malwa opium is grown in the native states.

Patna opium alone is the subject of the "monopoly." It is important to remember that when we speak of " the opium monopoly " this does not cover the whole of the opium which is produced in India, and sent to China. The monopoly only exists for the British territory, and as in British territory the poppy is only allowed to be cultivated in two districts, Behar and Benares,[7] of which Benares is the larger, the monopoly opium is commonly called Benares opium, or from the chief station in Benares, Patna opium. This Patna opium is in amount considerably more than the Malwa, and contributes say two-thirds—rather over two-thirds—of the revenue. For this, and for this only, the monopoly is responsible; the Company's connexion with Malwa, which was less direct, must be set forth separately. This monopoly system was very simple. The Company reserved to itself the sole right of cultivating the poppy and of selling the opium. Any infringement of this jealously-guarded right was promptly and inexorably punished by confiscation, fine, imprison-

[7] And in the Panjab, where it is grown for local consumption. Hitherto, however, there has been some uncertainty about the law in the Panjab and the Madras and Bombay Presidencies. To remove this, and place the whole of British India under the provisions of the Bengal Opium Act, Sir William Muir introduced a Bill into the Council of the Governor-General last year.

ment. All Government officials, police, native watchmen, and even the native landowners were obliged to assist in protecting the monopoly. The Company did not, however, engage directly in the cultivation. This was left to the ryots, or farmers. The Company's portion of the actual business consisted in inspecting the land offered for poppy cultivation, making advances of money to the ryot, to whom a licence for cultivating so much land was granted; receiving and examining, packing and storing, the opium brought in; retailing it to the licensed vendors in Bengal, selling it wholesale for exportation at Calcutta. Not an acre of land could be sowed with poppy seed, without licence from the Company's agent. Not a pound of opium in all Bengal but must be delivered to the Company's depôt before it could become an article of merchandise. The Company, therefore, were gigantic capitalists, doing business wholesale and retail on an immense scale, without any rivals, and engrossing the whole of the production and sale. The price for home consumption was about three times the cost of production. The opium for export, the great bulk of the trade, was sold by auction in Calcutta, realizing generally about four times the cost of production. We describe the monopoly here in the past tense, because we are treating of the extinct East India Company's affairs, but as the monopoly was in the Company's days so it is to-day. The transference of power from Leadenhall Street to St. Stephen's produced no change whatever in the system.

The monopoly has been attacked on side issues, which we shall simply allude to here. One is that this system of advances may be and has been abused. When we find the Company advancing two-thirds or nearly the whole value of the opium before it is brought to their factory, one-third before a hoe has touched the field, it is plain that it is not a policy of restriction which is at work here. And when too we hear of the amount of cultivation suddenly expanding in obedience to the declard wish of the great capitalist, who is at the same time sovereign of the poor peasants who work for him, it is difficult to believe that the action of the Government is always so clean as defenders of the system assert.[8]

[8] That this natural suspicion is justified by facts appears from the testimony of Sir William Muir, in his Minute of 22nd February, 1868.—"A few years ago, when the Government of Bengal was straining every nerve to extend the cultivation of the poppy, I was witness to the discontent of the agricultural population in certain districts west of the Jumna, from which the crop was for the first time being raised. Where the system of advances has long been in vogue, and the mode of preparing the drug well understood, no doubt the poppy is a popular crop; though even there the system of Government monopoly gives to Government officers a power of interference over those who have once taken their advances which must be liable to abuse. But the case to which I allude was that of new districts, where the poppy had not hitherto been grown, and into which the Bengal Board were endeavouring to extend the cultivation by the bait of large advances among an unwilling peasantry, and at the risk of inoculating them with a taste for a deleterious drug, and all this with the sole view of securing a wider area of poppy cultivation, and thus a firmer grasp of the China market. Witnessing this when on circuit in 1864, the impropriety of the position was to my mind so painful that, as the Governor-General may perhaps recollect, I ventured at the time to address his Excellency directly on the subject."

E

Of course there ought to be no compulsion, of course
no ryot need receive the advances unless he pleases,
of course it would appear more to the advantage of
the Company to secure willing service by liberal
payment than to make discontented serfs of its subjects. Whether or not the charges brought against
the Company by adverse critics, and stoutly denied by
its own officials, be true or not, or only true ex-
ceptionally, we cannot well ascertain, nor need we
particularly care to inquire. If the monopoly can
be defended on its general merits, this is a mere
matter of detail which may be subsequently and
separately dealt with, and we may safely leave it to
public opinion and the public press in India.

A second charge is that the cultivation of the
poppy has withdrawn a large proportion of the best
land from the production of food. This charge will
be considered in a subsequent chapter. On the
whole, so far as its operation upon India is concerned,
the monopoly is but a peculiar method of taxation.
It is foreign to the thoughts and customs of England;
it is open to the serious objection of presenting the
supreme Government before the minds of its subjects
in the humiliating guise of a dealer in noxious drugs;
it is a cumbrous device for accomplishing what
might be much more simply effected by a direct tax,
and it will always be liable to the suspicion of abuse
through unfair dealing by some of the numberless
petty officials who must be employed to carry it out.
But there is this powerful argument in its favour
which, in the minds of many Indian statesmen,

counterbalances a host of objections; it is an old, established custom. "The people of India will bear a great deal so long as they are used to it. They are very intolerant to change. They do not understand it. They are timid and suspicious. Benevolence and wisdom may go hand in hand in our measures, but the people are not easily persuaded that what we are doing is for their good."[9] Probably if our Government were now to begin, we should not establish any monopoly. But the East India Company inherited the monopolies of opium and of salt from their predecessors in sovereignty. The British Government has taken them over from the East India Company. Open as they both are to practical and moral objections, if nothing worse can be alleged against them than has appeared from our investigation into the working of the opium monopoly in India, we might be content to leave them both to be dealt with by experts in Indian affairs. On Indian soil the monopoly takes the place of a tax; it is a maximum charge upon the consumption: and, total abolition of poppy growth excepted, probably no change of name or method would do more to accomplish that repression of the use of the drug which was the avowed object of the Company's legislation.

One thing, however, must be written against the monopoly as affecting India, and this is properly not a result of legislation for the inhabitants of India, but belongs to that cultivation for revenue of which we are now to speak. The habit of opium-

[9] Kaye's "Administration of the East India Company."

eating is naturally formed and spreads round the
villages where it is grown. If the Government
restricted the cultivation within such limits as would
supply the Indian demand, it would also restrict the
area throughout which the cultivation itself would
breed the habit of use. Inasmuch as the Company
extended the cultivation vastly beyond the supply
needed for their own dominions, so they greatly
extended the influence of the cultivation in spreading a taste for the drug through the villages. It is
impossible to say how large a proportion of this
Indian consumption of 3400 chests must be attributed to this origin. But certainly the Company
did not manufacture an immense supply for foreign
use, without inoculating numbers of their own people
with a liking for the indulgence. This was the
inevitable penalty of their indifference to the moral
welfare of strangers. The publican may sternly
coerce his children to sign the pledge, or earnestly
point out to them the evils of intemperance, but if
he sedulously builds up a fortune by the sale of
intoxicating drinks, it will be strange indeed if his
children should altogether escape the influence of
the traffic. This unhappy result of the monopoly is
directly dependent upon the cultivation for the sake
of revenue, which we discern to have been the East
India Company's policy from the first. Repression
at home : revenue from outside.

We have quoted above the distinct avowal of the
intention of the Directors to repress the use of opium

in India; a parallel frank avowal of their purpose to
encourage the use abroad, we do not find in their
records.   But we do find that from so far back as
last century the Company admitted the proceeds of
sale for exportation into their books, without inquiry
and without hesitation : and that from that day to
this the monopoly has been conducted so as to derive
as great a revenue from this source as possible, and
without the slightest regard to the destination of the
opium and its effects upon the welfare of humanity.
At first the export trade was small, and may easily
have escaped the attention of the Directors.   A
Parliamentary report of 1810 tells us that the opium
sales produced 250,000*l.* in 1793, and in 1808-9 had
mounted up to 594,978*l.*   These returns appear to
include both the home sale and the export: and
whether they are gross or net receipts we do not
know.   But from these small beginnings the profits
of the manufacture gradually rose, until in 1830 the
revenue nearly reached a million sterling; in 1843 it
was about two millions ; in 1853 it was three millions
and a half, and in 1873 six millions and a half.   Such
an expansion as this did not grow in the dark.   There
is abundant evidence, and it is explicitly acknowledged by the highest representatives of the Indian
Government, that the Company managed the monopoly with the express purpose of supplying the
China trade.   Their opium factories were worked to
prepare an article saleable in the Chinese market.
Inquiries were instituted and experiments made to
discover how the drug could be prepared to suit the

Chinese palate. The profits of the China trade were the one object of the monopoly. The inconsiderable quantity consumed in their own territories was of no account for the great end of the monopoly, the acquisition of revenue. Every ball of opium filled in the Government factories was intended to transfer a certain amount of solid silver from the pockets of citizens of China into the Indian treasury. The very form of preparation marked out its destination. Opium intended for home use was not done up in balls, so that when the drug left the factories the shape it had assumed proclaimed the use it was meant for. Moreover Indian finance ministers watched with anxiety the fluctuations of the Chinese market, kept the merchants' keen glance steadily directed to quarters from which any interference or competition with the trade was apprehended. This lively concern to preserve intact the proceeds of so lucrative a trade is notably manifested in the action of the Company with regard to Malwa opium, which we must now proceed to explain.

From Bombay to Canton is only a slightly longer voyage than from Calcutta to that port. It may appear at first sight rather strange that a monopoly of the opium trade from the eastern port could be of immense value, when there were opium-producing districts in states not under the Company's rule, which could send out unlimited quantities of the article from the western port. If these native states had been really independent, and had possessed ready access to the sea, the monopoly would soon have

been despoiled of its bloom. But immediately
competition threatened, the all-powerful Company
stepped in and protected its precious traffic by
energetic measures. Mr. James Mill states that " so
long as the country between Malwa and the coast
was in the hands of the Mahrattas, and the transport
of valuable commodities was insecure, only a small
quantity reached the coast. When the country came
into our possession, and carriage was safe, it was
seen that a large supply might go to the China
market, and lower the price. To obviate this evil
we entered into treaties with the chieftains in whose
territories the opium is grown, and obtained their
consent to limit the quantity grown in their territories, and to sell the whole of it to us." In plain
terms the Company compelled these nominally
independent states to give to it the same monopoly
which it enjoyed in Bengal. Pecuniary grants were
made to the native princes, Holkar, Scindia, and
others : but the dissatisfaction of all parties was so
great, that the Company's agents repeatedly and
emphatically urged the abandonment of the treaties,
even at the cost of giving up all the gains of the
Bengal monopoly. This Malwa monopoly endured
from 1818 to 1831, an agent of the Company residing
at Indore to purchase the opium, which was then
sold by auction in Bombay. The blue-books give
us glimpses of discontented princes, oppressed
cultivators, desperate smuggling affrays, dissatisfied
merchants; but it would be waste of labour to
reproduce the picture, because the Malwa monopoly

is a thing of the past. It is only worth while to
refer to it now, as a proof of the determined zeal
with which the Directors protected their old Eastern
monopoly at all hazards. In 1831 the Company
annulled the treaties, and gave up the Malwa monopoly. How was it that they could afford to do this?
They had now obtained command of the whole coast
from which the opium could be shipped, except the
port of Damaun, to which the route from the opium
districts is long and exceedingly difficult. They
took advantage of their geographical position to
impose a duty on each chest, varying at different
times from 125 to 700 rupees [1] by which means they
raised a considerable revenue from the Malwa trade,
and prevented it from underselling their Patna opium
in the China market. This duty, fixed for several
years past at 600 rupees per chest, is payable in the
native states before the journey to the coast begins.
The Malwa monopoly while it existed, and the subsequent exaction of transit duty upon Malwa opium,

[1] The following is from the Minute of Sir William Muir:—
"It will be useful to note the various rates which have ruled
from time to time the export duty from Western India. They
are as follows:—

Period.	Pass Duty per Chest.	No. of Chests exported.
Prior to 1835 . . .	Rs. 175	
1835 to 1842 . . .	125	From 8000 to 16,000 annually.
1843 to 1845 . . .	200	
1845 to 1847 . . .	300	
1848 to 1858 . . .	400	Gradually increased to about 34,000 annually.
1859	500	
1860	600	Annual average about 35,000 chests, including Ahmedabad.
1861	700	
1862 and subsequently	600	

differed from the Bengal monopoly in this, that in the native states the Company made no pretences of morality, interfered in no way with the drug except for the sake of revenue, restricted the cultivation solely to obtain increased profits.   On the one hand they escaped in Malwa the opprobrium of being the actual producers of the drug; and on the other they did nothing to check the fearful prevalence of opium-eating in Malwa and Rajpootana.   Their action on that side was animated by pure and undissembled desire for revenue.

Such was the opium policy of the East India Company—to discourage opium-eating among its own subjects, and at the same time to acquire the maximum of revenue by the exportation of opium, whether of the Company's own manufacture, or produced in the territories of the native chiefs.   The next point to consider is who were the customers patronizing the Company's opium shop.   Was India the source of supply for all the world, and did ships of every flag resort to her ports to purchase this valuable medicine?   Had it been so, the morality of the traffic might have been the same, but its character would not have been so apparent.   India might have plausibly pleaded ignorance.   "How can I know where all this opium goes to, and what use is made of it?   All nations apply to me for a drug which is advantageously produced on my estate, and which the general consent of humanity proves it to be advantageous for other nations to buy of me. Let those nations answer for themselves as to the

use they make of their purchase. Free trade and
no questions asked is my motto." But the Company could not conceal the character of their commerce in opium by profession of ignorance of its
destination, India had but one customer, one well-
known customer, for whose special use every chest
of her opium was packed ; that customer, a neigh-
bour, with whom she had had friendly dealings for a
hundred years, the Chinese empire. The fact was
notorious, because record was kept in Government
offices of the destination of every cargo which was
exported. It is not literally exact to say that China
was the *only* customer : but if for China we substitute China and Chinese emigrants in the Malay
archipelago, we attain to an almost exact expression
for the consumers of Indian exported opium. It
appears from the returns that a small fraction, about
one-eleventh, of the whole export, was taken up by
Penang, Singapore, Java, and other places, where it
is well known that the resident Chinese are the chief
consumers. This fraction, however, is so small that
for all practical purposes we may reason upon the exportation to China itself. If that can be defended,
all can be defended ; if that must be condemned, the
whole trade is condemned. In the Appendix will
be found tables transcribed from official returns, which
show the numbers of chests exported to China and
to other ports. According to these tables in seven
years, from 1849-50 to 1855-56, there were sent
from Calcutta to China 234,986 chests; from Bombay to China 166,446 chests, making a total in seven

years of 401,402 chests. During this same seven
years 38,647 chests were sent to Singapore, Penang,
&c. Possibly some Malwa opium was sent to the
straits, though no mention is made of it in these
returns. But allowing a margin for this omission,
the returns show that nine-tenths of the export from
India went to the dominions of the Emperor of
China, and therefore nine-tenths of the Company's
revenue was paid by the people of an alien realm.

The Christian religion teaches us that we should
love our neighbours as ourselves, and refuses to
recognize distinctions between Jew, Greek, and
Scythian. Even the heathen sage Confucius is reported to have said, "All in the world are brethren."
It is painful to observe that such a man as James
Mill seems to have regarded it as the recommendation
of the monopoly, that it poured into the Indian
treasury a large income derived from foreigners.
But surely Mr. Mill would not have thought it
desirable, if it were possible, to extract ten millions
a year out of French pockets to pay for the army,
the police, the poor-rate of England. Such a suggestion would have suited the age of ancient Greece
and Rome, when the state was everything, and
humanity was not yet discovered; but it is an
anachronism in this nineteenth Christian century.
One can understand the argument of those who
maintain that the monopoly is simply equivalent to
the imposition of a heavy tax upon the " pernicious
drug," and that the Company were thereby actually
doing what they could to restrain the consumption

abroad as well as at home, although that argument
by no means tallies with the facts of the case; but
that people should find a positive ground of satisfaction in the vast consumption of a deleterious article
in China, because it enriches India, and only injures
Chinese, is so abhorrent to our feelings of justice
and humanity that it is difficult to meet such views
with a calm and courteous reply.　Why, then, should
Englishmen, who, by a wonderful series of events,
find themselves lords of two hundred millions of
Asiatics in India, be bound by every tie of human
and Christian obligation to be careful of the physical
and moral weal of these Hindoos, and yet be released
from all obligation toward four hundred millions of
Asiatics who dwell farther east ?　By what principle
of political morality were these rulers of India permitted to be utterly indifferent to the corruption and
ruin of China ?　Must we first wage war upon a
people, deprive it of its independence, usurp the
throne of its native princes, subjugate it to an alien
and unwelcome sway, before we come under an
obligation not to undermine its prosperity, de-
moralize its population, and ruin myriads of its
citizens ?

Mr. Smith and Mr. Jones were extensive sheep-
farmers in Australia, their estates being divided only
by a river.　Both gentlemen had large families and
employed many hands.　Mr. Smith was himself a
strong advocate of temperance, and used his influence to induce his sons and servants to be water-
drinkers, but if any of them declined to adopt his

advice, he took care that they should have no opportunity of giving way to excess, by strictly limiting
the supply of intoxicating drinks upon his estate.
Across the water Mr. Jones might or might not
share his sentiments, but for himself he was resolved
he would have no drunkenness upon his farm.   It
happened one night that a canoe came over from the
opposite side, and a stranger asked to purchase a
bottle of brandy.   There was no town near, no
other source from which the man could supply himself, and Mr. Smith, who saw his opportunity, asked
and received three or four hundred per cent. profit
upon the brandy.   The traffic thus begun, gradually
increased.   Mr. Smith found that brandy was always
saleable over the way, and soon disposed of all his
stock, but as soon replenished it from the nearest
town.   Something perhaps whispered that this conduct was inconsistent, but then the profits were so
great, and sheep-farming was not altogether so successful as he could have wished.   It was Mr. Jones's
business to look after his own dependents.   Did not
he, Mr. Smith, stringently repress any inclination
to excessive indulgence among his own people ?   Let
Mr. Jones maintain discipline among his sons and
shepherds ; that was his affair.   By and by rumours
reach him that Mr. Jones is much distressed at this
increase of drunkenness on his estate, that he takes
it as very unneighbourly that Mr. Smith should provide the means which sustain it, and indeed that Mr.
Jones has positively prohibited any person on his
estate from purchasing liquor from the opposite

shore.   Mr. Smith's position now became awkward.
He had always regarded himself as an honourable
and conscientious man ; and disliked the business in
which he was engaged; but then the profits were
really of consequence to him.   His expenses were so
great that he could not afford to lose them.   However, something must be done to preserve his reputation.   So he summoned his boys and his servants
together, and strictly enjoined them not to carry a
bottle across the river.   Meantime he has a hundred
dozen of Hennessy's and Martell's brands in his
store-room.   Must all that prove a dead loss ?   He
was saved from his dilemma by the offer of a third
party to relieve him of his stock.   The purchaser to
his knowledge conveyed it across the water.   From
this time Mr. Smith never failed to keep up a good
supply of spirits.   Sounds of drunken riot came
across the river : it was reported that one man had
died of *delirium tremens*, and another had robbed his
master's desk, and another had been discharged, and
wandered about begging.   Mr. Jones was old and
infirm ; and his overseer connived at the introduction
of liquor against his master's orders.   Mr. Smith
defended himself by saying that owners of large
estates ought not to be old and infirm, and ought
not to employ dishonest overseers.   He did not *send*
the brandy across : he put a stop to that at once,
directly he heard that Mr. Jones objected to it; it
was too much to expect him to keep watch over Mr.
Jones's servants as well as his own.   So Mr. Smith
kept up the brandy supply, and found the money

very useful on his farm. He read the Liturgy regularly every Sunday to his family and dependents, watched carefully over their morals, and would have been angry if any one had challenged his right to be esteemed an honourable, Christian gentleman.

Our little apologue will explain itself, but to depict the Company's policy in its real character, the imaginary sketch is all too feeble. There is but one justification attempted for this opium-trade, and that a poor one, but such as it is, it is this : that it was not the Company's affair to inquire for what use China demanded such a vast quantity of opium; for all that the Directors could tell, there might be something in the Chinese climate or constitution which made opium beneficial there ; but it was for the Chinese themselves to judge of that. The Chinese did judge of that. Before this century began, when the Company's shipments had increased the import into China from a hundred or two, to thousands of chests, the attention of the Chinese Emperor and mandarins was drawn to the increasing consumption of the drug; and they judged it decisively, once for all, and from that day to this they have never faltered in their decision. And what was their judgment ? One may put it in the Company's own words. They judged that opium was a pernicious drug, that it demoralized the people, and that they must out of compassion to their subjects prevent its use altogether. They did not say, as the Company did, " were it possible :" they believed it possible, and determined to do it. They absolutely forbade the introduction and use of the drug. They enacted severe and yet severer laws against it. The Company were well aware of all this. They, and they only, had the right of trading with China, and the superintendents of their factories kept them constantly informed of all these proceedings of the Chinese Government. What course did these Directors pursue, who would so gladly " out of compassion to mankind," have " prevented the use of the pernicious drug altogether "? They straitly charged their own servants not to introduce the drug into their ships or factories, and *continued regularly to manufacture every year a large quantity of opium expressly for the China market, knowing, one may say meaning, it to be smuggled into China.* This they did without intermission or hesitation, concealment, or apology, for more than fifty years. It is difficult to speak of the morality, or rather the degree of immorality, of such a proceeding as this.

The particular nature of this smuggling trade we shall have to notice in portraying the Chinese policy. At present it is enough to remark that the East India Company's policy was to provide the materials of a well-known smuggling trade. They, the Governors of a mighty nation, systematically encouraged the infraction of the laws of another great nation for the sake of gain to their own treasury. Though that phase of the opium-trade is a thing of the past, it is impossible to think of it even now without a deep sense of shame.

CHAPTER IV.

In 1858 the magnificent dominion of the East India Company was placed under the direct rule of the British crown. From that year our national responsibility for the opium trade became clear and immediate.

But it would be an error to suppose that the British Parliament and people can plead irresponsibility previous to 1858. At no time was the East India Company an independent authority. It was always part and parcel of the English nation, and under the control of the national Government. Its authority was not self-created, but an emanation from the supreme authority of the nation. Its charters were repeatedly revised and renewed, and at length extinguished by that authority. Again and again parliamentary committees sat for months and years, submitting all the concerns of the Company to minute inspection. In these detailed examinations of the Company's transactions, their opium policy did not escape criticism. Once and again the monopoly appeared to tremble in the balance. It main-

F

tained its ground, and that it did so, sufficiently
proves the concurrence of the British Government.
In 1810 and 1812 the opium concerns of the Company, and its commercial relations with China, were
the subjects of investigation. In 1832 we find a
distinct ratification of the Bengal monopoly, which is
especially to be noted because in the Report of the
Committee of Parliament which investigated Indian
affairs in 1831, the opposition of the Chinese Government to the introduction of opium was emphatically
brought to the notice of the committee, by letters
laid before it from the select committee of the East
India Company at Canton, expressly drawing the
attention of the Directors to the severe measures
threatened by the Chinese against this illegal traffic
in opium, and intimating their fear that the local
Government was determined to suppress the illicit
commerce.[1] It was with these letters before them, and
with the full knowledge that the trade was a smuggling trade, and that the Company had recognized
its true character by forbidding their own ships and
servants to be engaged in it, that the Committee of
the House of Commons deliberately approved and
adopted the opium policy of the East India Directors
as their own. The Report says :—

"The monopoly of opium in Bengal supplies the
Government with a revenue amounting in sterling
money to 981,293*l*., per annum ; and the duty which
is thus imposed amounts to 301¾ per cent. on the

[1] Appendix II. to Report on Affairs of East India Company,
1831, pp. 134—136.

cost of the article. *In the present state of the revenue
of India, it does not appear advisable to abandon so
important a source of revenue,* a duty upon opium
being a tax which falls principally upon the foreign
consumer, and which appears upon the whole less
liable to objection than any other which could be
substituted." [2]

From this time forth the British Parliament became distinctly the upholder of the East India Company's action in the matter.   The Report goes on to
speak of the precariousness of this revenue, and the
probability that at no distant time it may be desirable to substitute for monopoly an export duty; but
all reference to the morality of the traffic is discreetly
avoided.   The key-note of the British opium policy
was struck, and henceforth was never changed. That
key-note was, and is, *the revenue is too great to be
abandoned.*   Parliament in effect said, " We cannot
afford to examine into the righteousness of the
thing.   Are we to throw away a million sterling on
account of fine-drawn scruples ?   Smuggling trade,
is it ?   We know that : but we cannot give up so
flourishing a revenue.   The Chinese Emperor objects ?
Then let him stop the trade, if he can.   He does not
complain to us, and while we can ignore his objections, we will."   In this spirit our rulers clutched at
the profits of a scandalous commerce ; and to this
day there has been no national repentance.

In 1833 the East India Company's exclusive

---

[2] Reports from Committees, 1831-2.   East India Company's
Affairs, III. Revenue, p. 10.

privileges of trade with China were withdrawn, and the trade thrown open. From this time our Government was drawn into closer relations with the Chinese authorities. Previously the factory at Canton had been in charge of a superintendent appointed by the Company, to which he made his reports, so that the English Government had no direct communication with that of China. In the new circumstances it was considered necessary to appoint some responsible officer to represent Great Britain in China; accordingly Lord Napier was sent out in 1834 as Chief Superintendent of Trade, with vague powers, which failed to give him sufficient authority to exercise practical control over his countrymen; the power which the East India Company's officers had possessed, of excluding a refractory merchant from the trade, being withheld. His brief tenure of office is memorable only for the determined resistance which the Chinese provincial Government offered to his attempts to enter into direct communications with them. During the Company's time the mandarins had sent and received communications through the medium of a native guild of thirteen firms, styled in our books the Hong merchants or Co-hong, who were made responsible by their Government for the good behaviour of the foreigners. The Chinese officials haughtily refused to dispense with this means of intercourse. They would recognize the foreigners as private traders only, for whom sureties must be found amongst the Chinese before privilege of trade could be granted; and were resolved to ignore the existence of the foreign Governments.   When Lord Napier arrived, and pressed upon them his credentials as representative of the British crown, they rudely flung them back in his face.   The issue of the struggle was that Lord Napier was compelled to retreat to Macao, where, worn out by vexations and insults, he succumbed to the fatal effects of the climate, and died just three months after his landing in China.

This essay is strictly devoted to a consideration of the opium question, and it therefore becomes the writer's painful duty to expose the faults of his own country.   But it would be altogether a mistake to suppose that he is blind to the faults of China.   In his opinion it would not be too much to say that the Chinese Government brought upon itself all the evils of the opium trade, and the consequent wars, by its arrogant refusal to enter into intercourse with foreigners.   In review of the insulting language and behaviour of the high officials of Canton, one might fairly have addressed their successors thus:—" In your haughty conceit you believed or pretended to believe that western barbarians did not possess the same human nature as your own.   You spurned their approaches with contempt, though they came with every appearance of respect and friendship.   You determined to regard them as savage beasts; what right have you now to complain if they are wearied out by your refusal to reason with them, and employ brute force to attain their end?" This fatal defect in the Chinese character was not local nor temporary, but has been displayed throughout all their intercourse with foreigners.

Earl Macartney's embassy in 1792, and Lord Amherst's in 1816, were conceived in a most conciliatory spirit, and had the Chinese Government received them with frank cordiality, all the mischief and disgrace of the succeeding complications might have been avoided. The opium trade might have been made the subject of earnest expostulations, which the English Government neither could nor would have evaded. But in their absurd pretension to universal supremacy, the Chinese despised the golden opportunity. Lord Macartney was treated civilly, but only as bearer of tribute from a distant region bowing to the world-sovereignty of the Son of Heaven. Lord Amherst was required to perform the nine prostrations before the Emperor, and, upon his declining, was unceremoniously dismissed without an audience. China, by her overweening pride, invited, almost necessitated, the long string of calamities which succeeded. Yet faults on the other side do not atone for our own. The fatuous pride of a pagan nation, for which one may see much excuse in its venerable antiquity, its ancient supremacy over the neighbouring countries, its long isolation from, and therefore inevitable ignorance of, the rest of the world, cannot palliate the unrighteous policy of an enlightened Christian nation.

That our own Government was not, in theory, at

least, insensible to its duties, appears from the
instructions given to Lord Napier under the Royal
sign manual, upon his entering on his difficult and
delicate commission :[3]—

" And we do require you constantly to bear in
mind, and to impress as occasion may offer, upon
our subjects resident in, or resorting to China, the
duty of conforming to the laws and usages of the
Chinese Empire, so long as such laws shall be
administered towards you and them with justice and
good faith."

These were the words with which his sovereign
started Lord Napier on his way to China. Yet the
smuggling trade was at that time being carried on
in open violation of the laws and usages of the
Chinese Empire. But then " it does not appear
advisable to abandon so important a source of
revenue." Nearly a million sterling annually, and
and all from Chinese pockets! Therefore while the
principle was distinctly announced that our Government *would not protect* British subjects in any difficulties or disasters that might come upon them in
consequence of their violation of Chinese law, not a
word was said of *restraining* them from violating the
law. On the contrary, the propositions of the
superintendents, or their hints in that direction,
were met with a significant silence. The policy was
mean, but the revenue was large—1,000,000*l.* per
annum—and Parliament had decided that it must
not be abandoned. To touch the smugglers was to

[3] Correspondence relating to China, 1840, p. 3.

extinguish the revenue. Their illicit agency was an indispensable link in the collection of that revenue. The smugglers did their work quite gratuitously and independently; and could be disavowed whenever their illegalities should threaten to compromise the Government. So it seemed; but this policy was too base to work well. At the first pressure of real interference by the Chinese, our Government found that it could *not* separate itself from those who had done its work so long and so profitably. It was obliged to wage war on behalf of these opium smugglers, and the British tax-payer must pay the cost. Against the millions per annum of revenue we must set off millions that our Chinese wars have cost us, and millions more that our British manufacturers have lost through the check upon their legitimate commerce by this opium trade; and taking all into account, we easily come to the conclusion, that for nations as well as for individuals, "honesty is the best policy" after all.

Lord Napier's successor, Mr., afterwards Sir John F. Davis, within the first three months of his occupation of the vacated post, forwarded to Lord Palmerston a copy of a very stringent Imperial edict against the opium trade, which required of the Canton Government that the opium store-ships should be expelled, that cruisers should be appointed to guard against ingress of the contraband article, and that officials accepting bribes should be severely punished.[4] As usual, the Hong merchants were

[4] China Correspondence, 1840, p. 76.

employed to notify the Imperial will and pleasure to
the unmanageable foreigners, and the injunction
urging these Hong merchants to greater zeal, contains an Imperial estimate of the character of these
foreign visitors, anything but complimentary, but
alas! too exactly verified by the facts.   His Chinese
Majesty observes :—" By nature the barbarians have
no other object but gain, and their clandestine trade
having existed so long, they certainly will not con-
tentedly relinquish it."   Shrewd Chinese Majesty;
you have not studied human and barbarian nature
in vain!   Mr. Davis read this edict, but issued no
injunction to his countrymen to abstain from their
illegal and now perilous practices.   He interpreted
his instructions under the Royal sign manual, with
due recollection that the revenue of India must be
taken care of.   So he contented himself with for-
warding it to Viscount Palmerston.   He attempted
no denial of the malpractices of the English
merchants, he had not a word in defence of his
countrymen's honour and honesty.   But he has just
one word of consolation for his official chief, lest his
lordship should be seriously troubled by anxiety for
the threatened revenue.   "It is almost needless to
observe," he says, in his covering despatch to Lord
Palmerston, "that previous documents of this
nature have proved entirely nugatory, and that the
opium trade has continued in spite of them."   We
do not know what was Lord Palmerston's reply;
but we know that he sent out no orders to restrain
the opium trade.   The thunder-cloud which was

gathering on the horizon did not burst that year
nor next, and no doubt Lord Palmerston hoped,
and tried to expect, that it would never burst
at all. Why should not this add one more to
the long list of " entirely nugatory " edicts, and
the opium-trade " continue in spite of them " to
swell the East Indian revenue as before ?

Mr. Davis was soon succeeded by Sir George B.
Robinson. The new chief-superintendent, instead
of discountenancing the opium trade, took up his
abode at Lintin, and actually applied to his Government to purchase a vessel for his permanent residence
there.[5] What was there significant in Lintin ? Up
to 1821 the ships used to bring opium to Whampoa,
(the port of Canton), and to Macao. In that year
there was a flagrant exposure of the corruption of
the Chinese officials, who were bribed to admit
opium, in consequence of which the opium ships
were driven from Whampoa, and the Portuguese
dared not admit them to Macao. So these " entirely
nugatory " decrees were not without some practical
effect. Expelled from the ports, the opium merchants
established a depôt of receiving or store-ships at
Lintin, an island off one of the mouths of the Canton
river, where was their regular harbourage until 1839.
Whampoa, the port of Canton, was the only place at
which trade was permitted by the Chinese Government ; Lintin was the opium-smuggling station,
where the illegal traffic was carried on in defiance of
the Chinese Government. Yet Lintin was the place

* China Correspondence, 1841, p. 115.

this British representative selected for his permanent abode, in the very midst of the opium ships. From this place he dated his despatch of Feb. 5th, 1836 [6] to Lord Palmerston, in which he palliates the iniquity, and speculates as to the risks of the traffic. It appears from this letter that a struggle between smugglers and coast-guards was going on all along the coast, and that serious conflicts sometimes took place. But the superintendent congratulates himself that no European was personally engaged in any affray. And then, as if compelled by the terrible irony of the situation, he continues; "whenever his Majesty's Government directs us to prevent British vessels engaging in the traffic, we can enforce any order to that effect, but a more certain method would be to prohibit the growth of the poppy, and the manufacture of opium in British India; and if British ships are in the habit of committing irregularities and crimes, it seems doubly necessary to exercise a salutary control over them by the presence of an authority at Lintin." This despatch shows that Sir George Robinson was well aware of the "irregularities and crimes" of the smuggling trade; and he took care that Lord Palmerston should know also. The baronet waits only for a word, and he will at once put a stop, or a least a partial check, to these excesses. If he could not hinder the trade altogether, he could prevent British ships from taking part in it. Let Lord Palmerston only write three lines of direction, and it shall be done. But his

[6] *Vide* Appendix.

lordship speaks no word, writes no line. It was impossible to interdict smuggling into China without injuring the revenue of India, therefore his lordship preferred, to use an expressive Americanism, to "let things slide."

And sliding they were, going down hill at a rapid rate. Up to this time the opium-merchants did not need to do more than bring the drug to China, and take the silver in exchange for it. But as the opposition of the Chinese Government grew more determined, a change came over the scene. Chinese smugglers could not now be found to elude the vigilance of the custom-houses; the customs-officers no longer dared to take their bribes and let the drug through as before. The thunder-cloud was no longer on the horizon, it now frowned portentously right over head, and now and again ominous flashes leaped forth, harbingers of the coming tempest. On land opium-smokers were seized, beaten, imprisoned, beheaded. On the water, boats were destroyed, smugglers arrested and tortured. The natives were thoroughly cowed, and withdrew altogether from their old practice of fetching the drug, and running it inland. Now at last, the opium-merchants, those honourable merchant princes, the Jardines and Dents, whose wealth has won for them historical fame in the history of British relations with China, now at last they will surely for very shame pause in their career. Now at length, though too tardily, the British representative will send such missives home, as will wring the word of command from his

reluctant chief. Now, in spite of the interests of
the Indian revenue, that chief must surely speak the
word which will save his country's flag from infamy.
But no. The Chinese emperor had taken the measure
of British merchants correctly. Honourable exceptions there were, a few upright men, who never had
and never would enrich themselves by crime. But
the opium-dealers were determined to carry on their
lucrative traffic at all risks. And Lord Palmerston?
The crisis was a grave one. Perhaps his lordship
took the question to a cabinet council. If so
the result was that her Majesty's Government did
not see their way clear to act. No. Things must
slide. And they did slide. When the natives
declined to carry the drug in, the foreign merchants
carried it in themselves in their own armed schooners
manned by lascars. Fighting ships were fitted out
in Calcutta, armed to the teeth, and commanded
by buccaneering captains, who openly boasted
they would sink anything and everything which
attempted to interfere with their sale of the drug
on the Chinese coast. The East India Company
continued the steady production of the opium, sold
it to the China opium-clippers, and entered it in
their books as exported to China, noticing the
character of the trade only as it made them feel
some anxiety about the precariousness of the
revenue.

Captain Elliot was superintendent of trade from
1837 to the war. His despatches to Lord Palmerston,
from which we have given extracts in the Appendix,

present a graphic picture of those eventful years. It would occupy too much space here to attempt a detailed account of that exciting time; especially as we must go over the same ground from the Chinese point of view, in another chapter. It will be seen, then, that the magnitude of the evil daunted some Chinese statesmen into hopelessness of remedy, and led them to turn their minds toward the legalization of the traffic, as a lesser evil. The Imperial Court appeared to hesitate for a brief space, but soon recovered its spirit and urged on repressive measures more vehemently than ever before. Captain Elliot's letters reflect varied shades of hope and fear. The prospect of legalization was eagerly welcomed by him. He requested frequent visits of H.M. ships of war, as "calculated either to carry the provincial Government back to the system which has hitherto prevailed, or to hasten on the legalization measure from the Court." He thought that "the legalization of the trade in opium would afford his Majesty's Government great satisfaction," and added, "it cannot be good that the conduct of a great trade should be so dependent upon the steady continuance of a vast prohibited traffic in an article of vicious luxury, high in price, and liable to frequent and prodigious fluctuation." But soon the clouds gathered thickly again, and the glimmer of hope was extinguished. He sends despatch after despatch, enclosing edicts of the Chinese authorities denouncing and forbidding the opium-trade in the sternest terms, and requiring of him, as responsible for the foreign merchants, to send away the opium-ships stationed at Lintin.   To the Chinese authorities he makes the lame excuse " that he sees only the papers of the British ships which arrive within the port, and he is therefore without any public means of knowing which of the ships resorting to those anchorages are British, what is the nature of their pursuit, whence they come, or whither they go."   But to Lord Palmerston he writes a faithful account of the urgent position of affairs, describes in vivid terms the high-handed way in which the opium dealers were forcing the drug into the river in their own armed boats, and advises that a special commissioner should be sent with ships of war—for what?   That the representative of the British crown might not appear clothed with only the mock show of authority, made responsible in the eyes of the Chinese for disorders he was powerless to prevent?   That he might clear the river of the desperadoes who were fast precipitating England into war?   Alas! no. But " to explain that it was impossible for her Majesty to prevent the exportation of opium, and to urge the legalization of the trade."   Captain Elliot seems to have been an honourable and a brave man, and to have acted with considerable caution and firmness in a very difficult situation.   But the Indian revenue hung round his neck like a mill-stone.   He could not be thoroughly honest in speech or action, because he knew that an honest policy was not expected of him by his superiors.   He was there to keep things quiet, if possible, but not to interfere with that illegal trade which ministered to the Indian revenue. As matters drew near to a crisis, he was driven to act, with or without authority, in any case without power. His predecessor, as we have seen, considered himself competent to stop the whole smuggling trade so far as British ships were concerned in it; Captain Elliot now proved the emptiness of the boast. The smuggling depôt at Lintin he did not venture to assail, but made an attempt to stop the smuggling by armed European boats within the Bogue, only to find himself powerless. The opium dealers defied his injunction, and England's representative, superintendent of trade under Royal sign manual, officer of a power which was soon to devastate the Chinese empire with fire and sword from Canton to Nanking, was compelled to acknowledge to the governor of Canton his impotence to restrain the wretched riff-raff into whose hands the actual carrying of the smuggling trade in Canton waters had fallen. Was not this British policy too? In after-times, the consul in each treaty port was armed with full power to deal with law-breakers in summary fashion, and the British fleet was there to support him. Similar power might and ought to have been given to the superintendents of trade, when the East India Company's control ceased; and it is noteworthy that by the China Trade Act of 1833 very large powers were conferred on her Majesty in Council to enable her to give the requisite authority to her representatives in China.[7]

[7] "Hansard," third series, vol liii., p. 675.

But at this period it would never have done to invest a superintendent of trade with any actual physical power. Possibly an honest man might use it, and then what would become of the opium revenue? Obviously it was not possible for the British Government formally to sanction and exempt from interference an illegal traffic. It was equally clear that occasions might arise when the superintendents might deem it indispensable to check the opium trade, for the honour of their country, and the safety of the lawful commerce; as no doubt Captain Elliot would have checked it at this time if he could. This appointment of superintendent with full power to give good advice and no power to enforce it, wears too much the appearance of design to be taken as altogether an oversight.

In 1839 the crash came. The Chinese Imperial Commissioner, Lin, compelled the surrender to his Government of 20,291 chests of opium, worth over two millions sterling, all India-grown opium. This opium was entirely destroyed. Captain Elliot directed the surrender, "constrained by paramount motives affecting the safety of the lives and liberty of all the foreigners here present in Canton." Not a hair on the head of any European was injured; not a finger was laid upon any individual. Lin simply drew a cordon round the foreign factories, withdrew the Chinese servants, stopped the supplies of food and water, and said, "I want that opium, and must have it." He might have tried wiser measures to get it; it would have been much wiser

not to get it at all, for its destruction was the
kindest thing he could do for the East India Company and the trade. The Company had already
received their revenue. The trade, already all but
extinguished for four months, received an immense
impulse after the incubus of this vast stock was
removed. It was a blundering method of procedure,
worthy of the arrogant agent of an Oriental despot.
And yet, regarding it as an honestly meant effort to
extinguish a terrible vice at any cost and risk, was
not the destruction of that opium, after all, the
grandest act in the whole history of British and
Chinese intercourse; an act worthy of record in
the same page with Britain's payment of twenty
millions for the extinction of slavery? There can
be no question that Commissioner Lin was morally
within his right in seizing that opium, though his
method of doing so is open to objection. Every
ounce of that opium was contraband, and was forfeit
to the Emperor of China the moment it entered
Chinese waters. Lin might have taken it by the
strong hand, indeed, did take it by the strong
hand, in a way which no doubt recommended it to
himself for its effectual simplicity. There was no
fighting, no bloodshed; it does not appear that even
one Englishman went without his dinner for a single
day. To the Oriental mind, the fact that some
innocent persons suffered a little temporary inconvenience along with the guilty would appear too
trivial a matter to be noticed in the accomplishment
of a grand act of justice. When we take into con-

sideration that the British Superintendent had confessed himself impotent to secure the execution of
his own mandates, that the violation of Chinese law
had endured for a long course of years, and during
the recent years in defiance of repeated expostulations, that ample warning had been given of the
determination of China to bear the opium trade no
longer, we cannot for very shame lay much stress
upon the informality and arbitrariness of the Chinese
method of procedure.

The very ship that took Captain Elliot's despatch
to England, announcing these events, returned with
the news that the British Government had resolved
to appeal to arms.

The war which ensued is known in history as
" the opium war."   It was a war of such a character,
that it is equally difficult either to express or repress
our feelings of indignation and sorrow.   In place of
any expression of our own, take the sentence pronounced upon this war by Mr. Gladstone in his
place in Parliament in 1840 :—" They gave you
notice to abandon your contraband trade.   When
they found that you would not, they had a right to
drive you from their coasts, on account of your
obstinacy in persisting in this infamous and atrocious traffic.   You allowed your agent to aid and
abet those who were concerned in carrying on that
trade ; and I do not know how it can be urged as a
crime against the Chinese that they refused provisions to those who refused obedience to their laws
whilst residing within their territories.   A war more

unjust in its origin, a war more calculated to cover this country with permanent disgrace, I do not know, and I have not read of. The right hon. gentleman opposite spoke of the British flag waving in glory at Canton. That flag is hoisted to protect an infamous contraband traffic; and if it never were hoisted, except as it is now hoisted on the coast of China, we should recoil from its sight with horror. Although the Chinese were undoubtedly guilty of much absurd phraseology, of no little ostentatious pride, and of some excess, justice, in my opinion, is with them; and whilst they, the Pagans, the semi-civilized barbarians, have it on their side, we, the enlightened and civilized Christians, are pursuing objects at variance both with justice and with religion."[8]

Some persons protest against the phrase " the opium war." They allege that there were other causes of war, and that war must have occurred sooner or later had there been no opium trade. This may be granted. But after a review of the events narrated above, it is clear that *the* war which actually occurred took its rise and received its moral character from the opium trade. In the words of Lord John Russell, the war was set afoot " to obtain reparation for insults and injuries offered to her Majesty's Superintendent and subjects; to obtain indemnification for the losses the merchants had sustained under threats of violence; and, lastly, to get security that persons and property trading with

[8] *Vide* " Hansard," third series, vol. liii., p. 818.

China should in future be protected from insult or injury."[9] What were the "insults and injuries" complained of ? Those that occurred in Lin's high-handed seizure of the opium. For what was the indemnity demanded ? Principally for the opium destroyed. Nothing more is wanted than Lord John Russell's own description to brand the war as one caused by, and on behalf of opium; though the use of the word is carefully avoided. The British statesman would naturally have preferred to regard the drug as some unknown article of commerce, an algebraic x, and to fix the cause of dispute upon Lin's summary proceedings. The historian cannot ignore facts in this way. Whatever we had to complain of in Commissioner Lin's behaviour, opium was the root of the whole matter.

It will be instructive to quote here Williams'[1] *résumé* of the debate in Parliament upon the question of peace or war,—"It turned almost wholly upon the opium trade, and whether the hostilities had not proceeded from the want of foresight and precaution on the part of her Majesty's ministers. The speakers all showed ignorance of both principles and facts. Sir James Graham asserted that the Governors of Canton had sanctioned the trade; and Sir G. Staunton that it would not be safe for British power in India, if these insults were not checked, and that the Chinese had far exceeded, in

[9] *Ibid.*, vol. lii., p. 1223.
[1] "The Middle Kingdom," by S. Wells Williams. Vol. ii., p. 526.

their recent efforts, the previous acknowledged laws
of the land! Dr. Lushington maintained that the
connivance of the local rulers acquitted the smugglers; while Sir John Hobhouse truly stated the
reason why the Government had done nothing to
stop the opium trade was that it was profitable;
and Lord Melbourne, with still more fairness said,
'We possess immense territories peculiarly fitted for
raising opium, and though he would wish that the
Government were not so directly concerned in the
traffic, he was not prepared to pledge himself to
relinquish it.' The Duke of Wellington thought
the Chinese Government was insincere in its efforts,
and deserved little sympathy; and Lord Ellen-
borough spoke of the million and a half sterling
revenue 'derived from foreigners,' which, if the
opium monopoly was given up, and its cultivation
abandoned, they must seek elsewhere. No one
advocated the war on the ground that the opium
had been seized, but the majority were in favour of
letting it go on because it was begun. The debate
was, in fact, a remarkable instance of the way in
which a moral question is blinked, even by the most
conscientious persons, when politics or interest comes
athwart its course."

A detailed account of the military and naval
operations would be out of place here, and we are
glad to be spared the distressing narrative. Horrible as war is in any circumstances, there is nevertheless a terrible fascination in the account of a
great struggle between two mighty peoples, like

France and Germany, in which the hostile armies
are not far from equally matched in discipline and
arms.   But it gives one a sickening sensation to
read of the slaughter of mobs of Asiatics, armed
with gingalls, and carrying bows and arrows, by the
disciplined forces of Great Britain.   During fourteen
tedious months the contest moved slowly over
fifteen hundred miles of sea-coast and inland river.
Forts were bombarded, ships destroyed, cities cap-
tured, and looted or held to ransom, thousands of
Chinese soldiers were slain, and necessarily a vast
amount of suffering was inflicted upon non-com-
batants.   And, regarding the war as a fact by itself,
apart from its causes, the most painful thought
is, that this immense display of destructive energy
was mostly wasted, as we have learnt since, and
might have learnt long before.   The same amount
of force steadily directed against the capital would
have attained the desired end, with the minimum of
bloodshed.   As it was, an incalculable amount of
suffering was inflicted upon innocent people, who
had no more responsibility for the grievances complained of, no more power to atone for them, than
had the buffaloes which drew their ploughs; and a
second war had to be waged within twenty years to
repair the mistakes of the first.

In the subsequent treaty, the treaty "which
opened China," no mention of opium was made,
except the exaction of six millions of dollars indemnity for the 20,000 chests destroyed by Lin.
The English Ambassador endeavoured to induce the

Chinese officials to legalize the opium traffic;[2] but no —their Emperor would not hear of it—his ministers did not dare to name the subject. Sir H. Pottinger was therefore compelled to abandon the proposal. After all the expenditure of blood and treasure, it was provoking to be obliged to leave the opium trade an acknowledged illicit traffic. But at once to do this, and in the same breath to compel the Chinese Government to pay for the destruction of confiscated contraband property, seems almost to surpass the reach of British inconsistency. We pride ourselves upon being a practical people, upon not being governed by ideas; and certainly an amazing amount both of self-complacency and indifference to logic are needed to sustain a shock like this. Either we were in the right or in the wrong about opium. If in the right, we ought to have insisted upon the legalization. If in the wrong, how had we the face to make the Chinese pay for those 20,000 chests? But people's notions of morality seem to have got bewildered by the drug. After the treaty was signed, the opium merchants actually proposed to send opium ships into the open ports, and to *demand* that the drug should be admitted on a five per cent. duty. It seems incredible, and yet no doubt it must have also been almost beyond the powers of comprehension of the opium merchants, that her Majesty's Government had fought for them, exacted indemnity for them, and then left them

---

[2] Papers relating to the Opium Trade in China, 1842-56, pp. 1—3. Middle Kingdom, vol. ii., p. 569.

smugglers as before. And so Sir Henry Pottinger had to issue the following proclamation :[1]—

"It having been brought to my notice, that such a step has been contemplated as sending vessels with opium on board, into the ports of China to be opened by treaty to foreign trade, and demanding that the said opium shall be admitted to importation, in virtue of the concluding clause of the new tariff, which provides for all articles not actually enumerated in that tariff passing at an *ad valorem* duty of five per cent., I think it expedient, by this proclamation, to point out to all whom it may concern, that opium being an article, the traffic in which is well known to be declared illegal and contraband by the laws and Imperial edicts of China, any person who may take such a step will do so at his own risk, and will, if a British subject, meet with no support or protection from her Majesty's Consuls, or other officers.

"This proclamation will be translated and published in Chinese, so that no one may plead ignorance of it.

"God save the Queen!

"Dated at the Government House, at Victoria, this 1st day of August, 1843.

(Signed) "HENRY POTTINGER."

Still the old policy. You, British merchants, performing for our Government the useful office of collecting the East Indian revenue from Chinese pockets, remember we cannot protect nor support

[1] China Repository for August, 1843, vol. xii., p. 446.

you : for what you do is distinctly illegal. But we know that you will do it, and do not intend to prevent you. That is the business of the Chinese Emperor.

Another illustration of this policy is seen in the publication of an Order in Council, dated 24th February, 1843,[4] forbidding British ships to violate the treaty by going to trade outside the treaty ports; but when Captain Hope, of her Majesty's ship " Thalia," stopped two or three opium-ships proceeding above Shanghai, he was recalled from his station, and ordered to India, where he could not " interfere in such a manner with the undertakings of British subjects."[5] The Chinese Government desisted from the struggle against opium, when the war had convinced them that England was resolved to force it at all costs. That this was their conviction (and after what had occurred, how could it be otherwise ?) we know from their letter to Sir Henry Pottinger, making overtures for peace : " Our nations have been united by a friendly commercial intercourse for 200 years. How, then, at this time, are our old relations so suddenly changed, so as to be the cause of national quarrel ? It arises most assuredly from the spreading opium poison. Opium is neither pulse nor grain, and yet multitudes of our Chinese subjects consume it, wasting their property, and destroying their lives, and the calamities arising therefrom are unutterable ! How is it possible for us to refrain from forbidding our people to use it ?" This touch-

---

[4] China Repository, vol. xii., p. 446.

[5] Williams' Middle Kingdom, vol. ii., p. 582.

ing appeal must be regarded as the last free utterance of China as to opium. England ought then to have replied, disavowing in distinct terms any wish to force opium into China, ought to have engaged to do her part to prevent her subjects from any further illegal practices, ought to have renounced the revenue derived from these practices. England did none of these things, and China, down-trodden and bleeding, with the foot of the conqueror on her neck, could only think that, bad as the opium trade was, it was an evil which England was resolved to thrust upon her, and therefore to be tolerated as a lesser evil than an unequal war.

One step had yet to be taken to make our British opium policy complete, viz. to secure the legalization of the traffic. This was achieved by Lord Elgin in the negotiations for a treaty of peace after the second Chinese war, commonly known as the "Lorcha" or "Arrow War," of 1857. That this legalization was not the spontaneous act of the Chinese is plain from the Blue-book; though, as we have only the views of our own side depicted there, it is impossible to discover from that source the degree of repugnance the Chinese statesmen felt, and the measure of opposition they offered. The Earl of Elgin sailed from England, bearing with him instructions from the Earl of Clarendon "to ascertion whether the Government of China would revoke its prohibition of the opium trade."[6] The treaty, which was signed on the 26th June of the next year,

<hr/>

[6] Correspondence relating to the Earl of Elgin's Special Mission to China and Japan, 1857—1859, p. 5.

contained no reference to opium, apparently because
the Earl was ashamed to propose the subject.[7] Two
months later Lord Elgin concluded the first treaty
between England and Japan, in which he put his
signature to a clause expressly prohibiting the importation of opium.[8]

In the month of September the plenipotentiary of
the United States, Mr. W. B. Reed, addressed a
long letter to Lord Elgin, arguing that the existing
condition of things was the worst possible, that the
local authorities of Shanghai had virtually legalized
the trade by exacting a duty from it, and that the
British Government ought either to abandon the
trade or to procure its recognition by China. We
can judge from the following paragraph which Mr.
Reed believed to be the right course :—

" But two courses are open for us to suggest and
sustain—that of urging upon the Chinese authorities
the active and thorough suppression of the trade by
seizure and confiscation, with assurances that no
assistance, direct or indirect, shall be given to
parties, English or American, seeking to evade or
resist the process ; adding to this what, if your
Excellency agrees with me as to the expediency of

[7] " I have more than once understood your Excellency to say
that you had a strong, if not invincible, repugnance, involved as
Great Britain already was in hostilities at Canton, and having
been compelled in the north to resort to the influence of threatened
coercion, to introduce the subject of opium to the Chinese
authorities."—Letter of the U. S. Minister, Mr. Reed, to Lord
Elgin. *Ibid.*, p. 396.

[8] *Ibid.*, p. 379.

measures of repression, I am sure will be consonant with your personal conviction of what is right—the assurance of the disposition of your Government to put a stop to the growth and export of opium from India. I may be permitted to suggest that perhaps no more propitious moment for so decisive and philanthropic a measure could be found than now, when the privileges of the East India Company, and what may be termed its active responsibilities, including the receipt and administration of the opium revenue, are about to be transferred to the Crown. I am confident my Government would do ready justice to the high motives which would lead to such a course, and rejoice at the result." [9]

Being unable to take notice of this suggestion, Lord Elgin was shut up to the second of the two courses put before him by Mr. Reed, viz. to urge the Chinese to admit the drug into the tariff. This duty was discharged by Lord Elgin's delegates, Messrs. Oliphant and Wade, and their report [1] of the discussion with the Chinese delegates appointed to meet them makes it sufficiently clear that to the Chinese no real option was left. The proposition to legalize opium came from the English side, and the nearest approach to the appearance of voluntary consent on the part of the two Chinese delegates, which Messrs. Oliphant and Wade could put upon record, was, that Treasurer Wang admitted the necessity of a change; i. e. some change. The Chinese feeling appears plainly enough in the fol-

<hr />

[9] *Ibid.*, p. 396.   [1] *Ibid.*, p. 400.

lowing passage of the report which records their view, a report given us, we must remember, by the opposite party :—" China still retains her objection to the use of the drug on moral grounds, but the present generation of smokers, at all events, must and will have opium.   To deter the uninitiated from becoming smokers, China would propose a very high duty; but as opposition was naturally to be expected from us in that case, it should be made as moderate as possible "(!)   Accordingly they proposed a duty of sixty taels a chest; but the English delegates would agree to no higher than thirty; at which figure, therefore, opium was inserted in the tariff.   In 1869, during the negotiations for revision of the treaty, Sir Rutherford Alcock and the Chinese statesmen agreed that the duty should be raised from thirty to fifty taels; but her Majesty's Government refused to ratify the revised treaty, and the original treaty of Tientsin is still in force.

At last, then, the long-coveted right was won. Henceforth the opium-merchant could openly introduce " the pernicious drug " through the Chinese custom-houses, which about this time were re-organized and placed under the control of an Englishman !   The scandal of the illicit traffic is a thing of the past, and now surely the British and the Indian Governments may be allowed to share in the blessings of the blood-bought peace, and give thanks to heaven that they could extract their annual millions of revenue from the Chinese with a quiet conscience !   But conscience is a troublesome thing; before it can be satisfied we have to confront the allegation that *we forced China to legalize the trade.* The strong man knocks down the weak one, sets his foot upon his chest, and demands, " *Will you* give me the liberty to knock at your front door and supply your children with poison *ad libitum?*" The weak man gasps out from under the crushing pressure, "I will; I will; anything you please." And the strong man goes home rejoicing that he is no longer under the unpleasant necessity of carrying on a surreptitious back-door trade. That the Chinese Government yielded only to physical force it will be our business to prove in the next chapter. Indeed, this has been sufficiently proved already, if to the preceding history we add the fact that as soon as the Chinese Government began to regain a little strength it renewed its protest against the opium. But this is anticipating.

The history of British opium policy up to the present day is written. In 1832 a committee of the House of Commons deliberately stamped its character by resolving that " In the present state of the Indian revenue it does not appear advisable to abandon so important a source of revenue; a duty upon opium being a tax which falls principally upon the foreign consumer." From the principle then laid down the British Government has never swerved. In 1832 the income from opium was less than a million sterling out of a gross revenue of eighteen millions; in 1872 the net revenue from opium was more than seven millions and a half out of a gross

revenue of fifty millions. If the opium profits could
not be dispensed with when they amounted to less
than one-eighteenth of the total income, still less
can they be spared when they are more than a
seventh of the whole. A Government which deter-
mines to perpetuate a lucrative iniquity until it is
perfectly *convenient* to put an end to it, resolves in
effect to uphold the iniquity until the day of judgment.

A brief record of the attempts made in Parliament
to overthrow this iniquity will fitly close this chapter.
In 1843 Lord Ashley (the present Earl of Shaftesbury) raised a vigorous protest in the House of
Commons by moving the resolution :—

"That it is the opinion of this House that the
continuance of the trade in opium, and the monopoly
of its growth in the territories of British India, is
destructive of all relations of amity between England
and China, injurious to the manufacturing interests
of the country by the very serious diminution of
legitimate commerce, and utterly inconsistent with
the honour and duties of a Christian kingdom, and
that steps be taken as soon as possible, with due
regard to the rights of Government and individuals,
to abolish the evil." [2]

This resolution his lordship supported by an
eloquence and an array of evidence which one would
have thought irresistible. Among his supporters
was Sir George Staunton, whose long official resi-

---

[2] "Hansard," third series, vol. lxviii., 4th April, 1843.

dence in Canton, and acquaintance, then almost unique, with the Chinese language and literature, gave him an authority which was not diminished by the fact that Sir George was not generally opposed to our Government in favour of China.   He said on this occasion, "I never denied the fact that if there had been no opium-smuggling there would have been no war.   Even if the opium traffic had been permitted to run its natural course, if it had not received an extraordinary impulse from the measures taken by the East India Company to promote its growth, which almost suddenly quadrupled the supply, I believe it never would have created that extraordinary alarm in the Chinese authorities, which betrayed them into the adoption of a sort of *coup-d'état* for its suppression."   And in reply to Mr. Baring, who contended that legalization was the only remedy, and announced the expectation of Government that the very next mail would bring news that the Emperor of China had consented to it, Sir George said: "In point of fact it is well known that the Chinese authorities could and did stop the traffic effectually for four months previous to the seizure of the opium; that there was not a single chest sold for the whole of that period . . . I believe the fact to be that this traffic neither has been nor ever will be legalized in China."   Sir Robert Peel, however, had more faith in Sir Henry Pottinger's bringing negotiations for legalization to a successful issue.   We know the result; but at the time no doubt these confident expectations had great weight with the

House. Sir Robert Peel deprecated hasty action,
promised that her Majesty's ministers would take
the subject into their cautious consideration, and
asked the House to entrust the subject to them.
Lord Ashley thereupon withdrew his motion.

Fourteen years after this debate, and a few weeks
previous to Lord Elgin's departure for the East,
with special instructions to get the trade legalized,
the Earl of Shaftesbury renewed the attack in the
House of Lords, by moving that two important
questions be submitted for the opinion of her
Majesty's Judges. These were (1), whether it be
lawful for the East India Company to derive a
revenue from the cultivation of opium? and (2),
whether it be lawful for the Company to prepare
opium for the purpose of being smuggled into
China? The motion was withdrawn, but the Government itself undertook the task. The questions
were submitted by the President of the Board of
Control to four high legal authorities—the Queen's
Advocate, the Attorney and Solicitor General, and
the Company's standing counsel. And what were
the answers? In brief, yes, to the first question;
no, to the second: i. e. there was nothing in contravention of English law in the bare fact that the
Company sold opium, but, to quote the *ipsissima
verba* of this important opinion, "We think now
that opium is made contraband by the law of China,
and that its importation into China is made by
Chinese law a capital crime, the continuance of the
Company's practice of manufacturing and selling

this opium in a form specially adapted to the Chinese contraband trade, though not an actual and direct infringement of the treaty, is yet at variance with its spirit and intention, and with the conduct due to the Chinese Government by that of Great Britain as a friendly power, bound by a treaty which implies that all smuggling into China will be discountenanced by Great Britain."[3] These four eminent legal authorities, including the Company's own standing counsel among them, found that the East India Company were accomplices of smugglers; and as such, were guilty of conduct tending to provoke breach of the peace between England and China. Indeed the facts were confessed, and the equity of the case is plain. The law condemns the receiver of stolen goods as well as the thief, the manufacturer of spurious coin as well as the utterer, and it must condemn the accomplice of smugglers as well as the smugglers themselves. If China had possessed the physical force of the United States, and could have got her grievances submitted to a Grand Court of Arbitration at Geneva or elsewhere in any year between 1842 and 1858, she might have recovered damages, compared with which the Alabama compensation would have looked small. But China was weak and ignorant, and the Earl of Shaftesbury's motion for legal inquiry ended in the condemnation of England and India by their own self-chosen judges, without the slightest step being taken to restrain them in their course of injustice.

[3] Parliamentary Return, 24th August, 1857, *vide* Appendix.

This arraignment of the Company before a legal tribunal came rather late, for next year their sceptre departed from them, and the legal offence ceased by Lord Elgin's introduction of opium into the tariff. Nothing remained but to assail the trade on a direct moral issue. This course was adopted by Sir Wilfred Lawson, who moved in the House of Commons in 1870, the resolution—

" That this House condemns the system by which a large portion of the Indian revenue is raised by opium."

Again there was a gallant debate, with a formidable array of arguments and evidence in support of the resolution. On the opposite side, though the ability of Mr. Grant Duff and the high authority and splendid powers of Mr. Gladstone were displayed in defence of the revenue, we find nothing essentially new. Opium was classed with alcohol, and our taxation of the latter was urged in defence of the direct production of the former. But, as before, the importance of the revenue was the backbone of the resistance to Sir Wilfred Lawson. The House divided : forty-seven members followed Sir Wilfred Lawson, while one hundred and fifty-one voted with the Government.[*]

[*] To complete the history up to the date of publication, we may record here the latest debate in Parliament, raised last year (1875) by Mr. Mark J. Stewart's motion :—" That this House is of opinion that the Imperial policy regulating the opium traffic between India and China should be carefully considered by her Majesty's Government, with a view to the gradual withdrawal of the Government of India from the cultivation and manufacture of opium : "—in which the Government manifested the same determination not to yield a jot of the old traditional policy. The votes were—for the Government ninety-four, for the resolution fifty-seven.

CHAPTER V.

CHINESE ANTI-OPIUM POLICY.

FROM the commencement of the century to the present day the Chinese Imperial Government has persisted in prohibiting the practice of opium-smoking. Among ourselves, it is commonly held that the Government should restrict its functions as much as possible to the protection of life and property, and interfere as little as possible with the moral and religious concerns of the people. China, on the contrary, from time immemorial, has been accustomed to the idea of paternal government. Government has been looked upon as the most sacred and all-embracing of all human duties. The sovereign, and under him, his ministers are personally responsible for the temporal and moral welfare of all under their sway. The most ancient of the Chinese books attest this conviction, as when the Conqueror T'ang, founder of the Shang dynasty (B.C. 1766), declared in a proclamation "when guilt is found anywhere in you who occupy the myriad regions it must rest on me." [1]

[1] "Legge's Chinese Classics," vol. iii., p. 189.

It is a result of this idea of the duties of Government that Chinese imperial and provincial decrees are composed in a homiletic style. They are sermons as well as laws, and indeed are expected to operate by the power of moral suasion, before the material penalties denounced are put in force. To an English reader unaccustomed to this hortatory style in the utterances of secular authority, these wordy exhortations will scarcely escape seeming ludicrous. But the Chinese expect this good advice from the ruling powers. Both governors and governed hold that the people must be instructed in their duties before legal penalties are inflicted. It is involved in this Chinese idea of a paternal rule, that the Government must always denounce and repress vice of all kinds with ceaseless rebukes and uncompromising penalties. The Duke of Chow's manifesto against drunkenness (B.C. 1115) is the most ancient extant of an innumerable succession of edicts against prostitution, gambling, opium-smoking, and immoralities of every description. We smile at their pedagogical tone, and despise the executive inefficiency which made so many of these fulminations nothing better than firing blank cartridges; nevertheless they effectually dispose of the accusation of hypocrisy frequently brought against the Chinese Government by defenders of the opium-trade, who have represented Chinese antagonism to opium-smoking as if it were an isolated and unprecedented fact in their history.

The first imperial edict against opium-smoking, of

which we find record, was issued by the Emperor
Kia K'ing in the first year of this century. Opium-
smoking is a modern vice, and its rise and progress
synchronize with the increase of the trade under
the patronage of the East India Company. Chinese
medical works, of 300 years back, mention the drug
as a remedy in cases of diarrhœa, dysentery, and
other diseases. Where and when and by whom
smoking as a luxury was commenced is hidden in
obscurity. "Before the year 1767 the import of
the Indian drug into China rarely exceeded 200
chests; that year it amounted to 1000, at which
rate it continued for many years."[2] It would not
be an unreasonable conjecture that it was about
that date that the practice of smoking originated.
"In 1773 the British East India Company made a
small adventure of opium from Bengal to China."[3]
In 1798-9 the import exceeded 4000 chests. The
Report of the Governor of the two Kwang provinces
in 1836 states : "Now in regard to opium, it is an
article brought into the Central Empire from the
lands of the far-distant barbarians, and has been imported during a long course of years. In the reigns
of Yung Ching and K'ien Lung (A.D. 1723—1795) it
was included in the tariff of maritime duties, under
the head of medicinal drugs, and there was then no
regulation against purchasing it or inhaling it." In
1779 the then Governor of Kwang Tung presented
a memorial to Kia K'ing, the fifth ancestor of the

---

[2] Phipps, "China and Eastern Trade," p. 208.
[3] Chinese Repository, vol. v., p. 553.

reigning Emperor, which produced the imperial decree referred to above. In 1800 the importation of opium was prohibited, and smokers were threatened with punishment. Successive decrees increased this punishment to transportation and strangling. Now since the importation did not reach so high as 5000 chests in any year before 1820, it is plain that up to that time the Chinese Government could only have been actuated by a sincere concern for the moral welfare of its subjects. The drain of silver which caused alarm to the financialists when the import was near 50,000 chests could hardly have been subject of anxiety when it did not reach to a tenth of that amount.

The moral weight of the Chinese Government's antagonism to opium-smoking was undoubtedly weakened by the ease and regularity with which the import was effected during a long course of years by means of an established and well-understood system of bribery. It was not until 1837 that really vigorous efforts were put forth to extinguish the practice, and not until 1838 that the foreign importers of the opium were directly attacked. The immunity of nearly forty years bred a sense of security in the minds of the opium-smugglers. Nay, so quiet and regular was the trade for long periods (though not without some serious interruptions), and so uniform the scale of fees for bribing the officials, that they chose to ignore altogether the fact that they were smugglers, and felt themselves seriously aggrieved when at last the long-slumbering authorities awoke to action. Looking at the subject with English eyes, it is impossible to refrain from grave censure of the Chinese official imbecility and corruption. But the student who looks at the matter not with the eyes of a European but as surveyed from the interior, with Chinese eyes as it were, will not argue from this remissness of the executive that the Government was insincere in its opposition. A "paternal" Government, which takes the morals of 300,000,000 subjects under its care, must wink at a good many irregularities. In such a numerous family, it is not to be expected that all the children will be good boys and girls. The edicts against vice are often held in abeyance, kept suspended *in terrorem* over the heads of transgressors, but not at all times put into execution with equal vigour. The difficulty of securing honest administrators of the laws is well known, and this defect of their political system compels the central authority to shut its eyes to many evasions of the law. But this does not do away with the law, nor argue any want of sincerity in its promulgation. The memorial of Choo Tsun,[4] represents the feelings of the Chinese very fairly when it says: "It has been represented, that advantage is taken of the laws against opium by extortionate underlings and worthless vagrants, to benefit themselves. Is it not known then, that

[4] Choo Tsun was Cabinet Minister in the reign of Taou-Kwang. The memorial is translated in the Chinese Correspondence of 1840, p. 168.

where the Government enacts a law, there is
necessarily an infraction of that law? And though
the law should sometimes be relaxed, and become
ineffectual, yet surely it should not on that account
be abolished; any more than we would cease eating
because of disease of the throat. When have not
prostitution, gambling, treason, robbery, and such-
like infractions of the laws, afforded occasions for
extortionate underlings and worthless vagrants
to benefit themselves, and by falsehood and bribery
to amass wealth? Of these there have been
frequent instances; and as any instance is discovered, punishment is inflicted. But none surely
would contend that the law, because in such
instances rendered ineffectual, should therefore be
abrogated! The laws that forbid the people to do
wrong may be likened to the dykes which prevent
the overflowing of water. If any one, then, urging
that the dykes are very old, and therefore useless,
we should have them thrown down, what words
could express the consequences of the impetuous
ruin and all-destroying overflow!"

Choo Tsun was right; to the Chinaman, the law
as a protest of the Government is, to a certain
extent, a practical barrier against vice. When
temporarily inoperative it does not grow obsolete,
but retains its vitality as a witness against evil.

The habit of opium-smoking was held in check
from 1800 to 1837, by statutes which seemed
inoperative to foreign eyes. Nor is it true that
this period did pass by without enforcement of the

law against native offenders, some instances of
which produced temporary consternation among
the foreign dealers.[5] We have seen already that
as regards the foreigners they were compelled
to remove their stocks of opium outside the
limits within which the recognized trade was
carried on. Still we cannot deny that the
facility and security of the illicit trade during
a long course of years was calculated to deceive
foreigners as to the real sentiments of the Chinese
Government. Whatever spasmodic attempts were
made to deter the native from buying and using
opium, the foreign merchants were not molested.
Their great wealth, and the power the lucrative-
ness of the trade gave them of bribing to any
extent required, will of itself account for this.
Besides, it is plain enough that, for all their
grandiloquent boasting and affected contempt for
this handful of barbarians, the mandarins stood in
awe of the unknown but formidable resources of the
nations of Europe. They postponed laying a finger
upon them to the last possible moment. When at
last imperative orders from Peking compelled them
to attack the source of the smuggling trade, our
virtuous and honourable British merchants took
the interference in extreme dudgeon, affected to
believe that non-molestation for over thirty years

[5] Phipps recounts several instances between 1831 and 1834,
one, " a very extensive seizure of ninety-six chests of Patna and
Benares opium in sight of the shipping at Lintin." See " China
and Eastern Trade," pp, 212—215.

actually gave them a right to break the law ; and complained of its enforcement as an intolerable grievance !

It was not true, however, that the determined attack on the trade, which led to the opium war of 1840, burst upon the merchants without warning. So far previously as the beginning of 1832 an edict was issued to the Hong merchants, giving a graphic and faithful description of the illicit trade, and exhorting the foreigners to discontinue their evil practices. It cannot be pretended that the merchants did not receive this communication, for a translation of it was published that same year, in an English newspaper, printed in Canton. It is a fair specimen of the Chinese style of thought and expression in such documents :—

" Opium is a spreading poison, inexhaustible ; its injurious effects are extreme. Often has it been severely interdicted, as appears on record. But of late, the various ships of barbarians which bring opium all anchor about at Lintin in the outer ocean, and, exclusive of cargo ships, there are appointed barbarian ships, in which opium is deposited and accumulated, and there it is sold by stealth. That place is in the midst of the great ocean, and it is accessible from every quarter. Not only do traitorous banditti of this province go thither, and in boats make clandestine purchases, but from many places in various provinces vessels come by sea, under pretence of trading to Lintin ; and in the dark buy opium dirt, which they set sail with, and carry off; as for example, from Amoy, Ningpo, Tientsin, &c.

"At present some one in the capital has represented the affair to the Emperor, and strict orders have been respectfully received from his Majesty to investigate, consult, and exterminate by cutting off the sources of the evil. I, the Cabinet Minister and Governor, have met and consulted with the Lieutenant-Governor, &c. . . . . . .

"An order is hereby issued to the Hong merchants, that they may forthwith obey accordingly. They are commanded to expostulate with earnestness, and persuade the barbarians of the several nations, telling them that hereafter, when coming to Canton to trade, they must not on any account bring opium concealed in the ships' holds, nor appoint vessels to be opium depôts at Lintin in the outside ocean, hoping to sell it by stealth. If they dare intentionally to disobey, the moment it is discovered, positively shall the said barbarian ships have their hatches sealed, their selling and buying put a stop to, and an expulsion inflicted, driving them away to their own country; and for ever after they shall be disallowed to come to trade, that thereby punishment may be manifested. On this affair a strict interdict has been respectfully received from Imperial authority, and the Hong merchants must honestly exert their utmost efforts to persuade to a total cutting off of the clandestine introduction of opium dirt. Let there not be the least trifling or carelessness, for if opium be again allowed to enter the interior it will

involve them in serious criminality.   Oppose not !
These are commands."

Of course it seemed absurd to the Jardines and
Dents of that day that the Chinese mandarins should
expect them to abandon a trade by which they were
making princely fortunes simply in response to
moral suasion.   Of course they affected to regard it
as a proclamation put out to hoodwink the Imperial
authority, but not meant to have any practical
result.   All the more astonished were they when at
a later time a Chinese mandarin dealt with the
opium question *au grand sérieux*, and they had to
give up their opium to save their lives.   But even
in this year, 1832, seven years before the catastrophe, they could not deny they were fairly warned,
that the illegal and dishonourable character of their
proceedings was pointed out in plain terms.

To avoid the semblance of an undue leaning to
the Chinese side, it may be necessary again to
remind the reader that a defence of the Imperial
anti-opium policy by no means implies an admiration of the whole of the Chinese treatment of
foreigners and foreign trade.   A student of Chinese
history and literature will make many excuses for
their unreasonable and provoking manner of dealing
with the strangers from the far west visiting their
shores.   It would be unreasonable on our part to
demand that the prejudices of 4000 years should be
laid aside in a day upon the first appearance of a
new piece of bunting on the verge of the horizon.
The Chinese literati, the governing class, were

pedantic, conceited, arrogant, and vexatious. In some matters they were palpably unjust. But they were only what we might have expected to find them; and they did not invite us, we forced ourselves upon them. This essay, however, has nothing to do with the general intercourse of Chinese and Europeans, nor is it concerned to deny that throughout the century preceding the opium struggle there were good grounds for serious complaints against the Chinese officials. Our business is with opium, and in this matter, although the Chinese Government committed some diplomatic blunders, we cannot but acknowledge and admire the spirit of wise and philanthropic antagonism to a ruinous vice which animated the sovereign and his advisers ; a spirit of altogether a higher order than the selfish worldly wisdom of their mighty but unscrupulous opponents.

The splendid though unsuccessful effort of the Chinese Government to extinguish the opium traffic must now be briefly recounted from the Chinese side. In 1836 Heu Naetse, who had held official positions in Canton, addressed a lengthy memorial to the Emperor,[6] describing the opium-smuggling trade after the style of the edict above quoted, and dwelling upon the impossibility of coping with it. He therefore recommended that the trade should be legalized, opium being admitted as a medicinal drug under duty, as in K'ien Lung's time. Not that he thought the smoking a harmless practice, for he

[6] China Correspondence, 1840, p. 156.

recommended that all officials, scholars, and soldiers
should be prohibited from indulging in the habit;
but simply because the smuggling trade was carried
on entirely by exchange of silver for the drug, in
consequence of which China was being drained of
its bullion. This memorial was sent down by the
Council of State to the officials at Canton for
them to consider and report upon. The provincial
mandarins reported in favour of legislation. But
meantime Choo Tsun[7] and a censor, Hü Kiu,[8]
strongly opposed the temporizing policy. The
memorial of the latter mentioned the names of
several merchants, English, Parsee, and American,
who were well known as engaged in the unlawful
traffic. These memorials occupied the attention of
the Government for more than a year. Though
China has no representative government, no public
debates, no newspapers, it would be a grand error
to imagine that public opinion has no weight there.
Probably no country in the world has recognized
more distinctly that the satisfaction of the people is
the only complete justification of a policy, the
only sure support of a government. China is a
despotism, but not a military despotism. It is a
despotism by sufferance of the people. The reigning
dynasty stands, while it governs sufficiently well to
be tolerable to the country. It falls, and expects to
fall, when it ceases to possess the moral support of
the masses. *Vox populi, vox Dei*, has its Chinese

[7] *Ibid.*, p. 168.   [8] *Ibid.*, p. 173.

equivalent in the classic saying, " Heaven sees as
the people see, hears as the people hear." To
suppose that the Emperor Taou Kwang's opposition
to opium was the benevolent craze of a well-meaning
but ill-informed autocrat, legislating against, or
without taking account of, the popular wish, would
be a tremendous blunder. Taou Kwang and his
ministers took, in Chinese fashion, the sense of the
Empire on the opium question. The chief authorities of the provinces had the proposition to legalize
opium laid before them, and were commanded to
send reports on it to Peking. In the capital those
remarkable functionaries, the Censors, privileged to
criticize and exhort the Son of Heaven himself,
and bound to give impartial statements on all
important subjects, contributed their evidence as to
the state of public opinion. The official class in
China takes its tone of political thought and feeling
from the educated gentry. The opinion of the
educated gentry is the public opinion of the country,
for the masses are not independent enough to do
other than reflect the opinion of their superiors.
Hence the issue of these inquiries instituted by the
Court fairly represented the national mind. If China
were polled to-day there is no doubt that the great
mass of the people would be found to approve the
anti-opium policy; and among the votaries of the
pipe, who best know its fascinations and its curse, a
large number would join in the wish that the drug
had been effectually excluded. We question whether
the history of the world has ever seen an Imperial

policy more truly a national policy than this Chinese interdiction of opium.

Before the Imperial Council came to a final decision the Canton Government was directed in the meantime to enforce the existing edicts. Consequently the opium ships were again ordered to depart from the coast. Nine foreigners, English, Parsees, and Americans, residing at Canton, notoriously engaged in the opium traffic, who were mentioned by name in three edicts, were peremptorily ordered to leave the country. These nine persons treated the order with contempt. This is not surprising. The Chinese Government did not yet use force; and when did smugglers bow to any other argument? But it *is* surprising that Captain Elliot could write to Lord Palmerston that if the Chinese attempted to enforce this decree of expulsion, his interference on behalf of the British merchants would become indispensable on account of the great injury they and their constituents would suffer! It shows how long habit, uninterrupted success, and great wealth had blinded the eyes of the British community in Canton to the criminal character of their pursuit. We have seen that one superintendent wrote home that it was absurd to call the opium trade smuggling, because the Chinese authorities connived at it. Now another superintendent writes that he must employ his influence as representative of Great Britain to protect the smugglers, because the Chinese authorities no longer connive at their doings! We find a clue to this confused sense of right and wrong in the evidence which Mr. Jardine afterwards gave before a Committee of the House of Commons. Being asked whether he was ever troubled with doubts about the morality of the trade, he replied that " when the East India Company were growing and selling it, and there was a declaration of the Houses of Lords and Commons, with all the bench of bishops at their back, that it was inexpedient to do it away, I think our moral scruples need not have been so very great."[9] The British Government threw the responsibility upon the Government of India; the Indian Government cast it upon the opium merchants; the opium merchants shoved it back upon both the preceding. All parties quieted their consciences by pointing to the connivance of the Chinese officials; the marvel is that when this connivance ceased and active opposition took its place, Captain Elliot and the merchants should have clung so persistently to their old notions, and have resolved to set China at defiance!

After full inquiry according to the accustomed methods, the Imperial Council resolved to reject Heu Naetse's advice, and to extinguish the opium trade altogether. Foreigners raised a cry that the Chinese Government was hypocritical in pretending to care for the weal of the people, and that its only real objection was to the exportation of bullion in exchange for the drug. From that day to this defenders of the trade have never been weary of exclaiming against

[9] Report, Select Committee on China Trade, 1840, p. 100.

the *insincerity* of the Chinese.   But the charge on the
face of it is absurd.   If the loss of silver had been
the only or chief objection to the trade, the Chinese
would have adopted Heu's plan, proposed to meet
that very difficulty.   There is no reason for denying
that the Chinese statesmen were alarmed to see the
precious metals flowing out of the country; but this
consideration was almost lost sight of by them in the
overwhelming moral objections to the traffic.

The edicts requiring the opium ships, and the
chief opium dealers to depart the country, being
utterly disregarded by the foreigners; and they
persisting in the smuggling trade, now no longer
carried on in native but in foreign craft, what could
the Chinese do?   They had made the Hong
merchants securities for the foreign traders, but
these Chinese merchants were palpably unable to
control their foreign friends.   In 1838, seizures of
opium from foreign boats were made once and again,
in one case right under the foreign factories.   The
Hong merchants waited upon the foreigners and
entreated them to stop the trade, but, of course, in
vain.   At last, in December, twelve boxes of opium
were seized in broad daylight while being landed in
front of the factories.   The Governor now urged
the Hong merchants to the utmost verge.   He
required the immediate expulsion of the ship from
which this opium came, though it seems he was
wrongly informed as to its name.   He demanded
the expulsion of the man, a British merchant named
Innes, a man who, on another occasion, actually

proposed to levy private war upon the Chinese Government to avenge some real or fancied injustice, and had to be reminded by Lord Palmerston that if he did, he would be liable to be dealt with as a pirate. The ship was the wrong ship. The man was the right man. It made no difference, however. Neither man nor ship would move. The Hong merchants used all their influence with the foreign merchants; but the Canton Chamber of Commerce replied they had no power to expel individuals nor to check the smuggling trade. The Hong merchants, in despair, threatened to close the trade, no longer to rent their houses to foreigners, and to pull Mr. Innes' house about his ears, if he did not go. The Chamber of Commerce replied in effect that an Englishman's house is his castle, and that the Hong merchants must on no account dare to infringe the sacred principle. One of the Hong merchants was publicly exposed wearing the cangue, or as we should say, in the pillory. The Governor might have proceeded to severer punishments, but the inability of these unfortunate men to control the stubborn foreigners was too evident.

Next the Governor resolved to give the foreigners an ocular proof of the consequences of their trade. The penalty of dealing in opium was death. One Ho Laoukin lay under sentence. The Governor ordered that he should be executed in front of the foreign factories. An officer, followed by a few lictors, brought the criminal to the appointed spot, and began to erect the wooden stage against which he was to be strangled. The foreigners hurried out upon hearing what was intended, and drove him off the ground. The officer submitted, and performed the execution elsewhere. But the mob poured in, took possession of the square, and for a few hours there seemed likelihood of a horrible massacre. The mob had begun pulling down a house, when the district magistrate arrived upon the scene, attended by a handful of soldiers, and quelled the riot. Captain Elliot wrote to Lord Palmerston in indignant terms about this shameful attempt to make the foreign factories an execution-ground; but his lordship failed to see what right the merchants had to interfere with the Chinese Government in the execution of its own laws, on its own soil. Had the Chinese Government persisted in this plan, it would have been a novel way of fighting the opium traffic. How long could the wholesale dealers in the smuggled drug have endured to see their Chinese brethren of the retail trade strangled before their eyes daily! Such horrid spectacles frequently repeated under their windows might have taken away their appetite for their meals, and so have starved them into submission, as effectually as Lin did. Subsequently the Chinese carried out another execution on the very spot. But this satisfied the Government for the time.

In the spring of 1839 the Imperial Special Commissioner, Lin, formerly Governor of Hu Kwang, came to Canton armed with dictatorial power to put a final end to the iniquitous traffic. A few days after his arrival he issued a peremptory demand for the surrender of all the opium at Lintin and the other anchorages. The merchants offered a thousand chests, as a sop to pacify him. But he must have the whole. Troops were collected, the river was blockaded. Everything showed a spirit of determination such as the illicit dealers never expected to see in the despised Chinese authorities. Captain Elliot and the merchants professed to fear for their lives, though the worst they actually suffered was the inconvenience of losing their servants. The 20,000 chests were delivered up and destroyed. No doubt the seizure would not have held good in courts where John Doe and Richard Roe appear upon the pleadings; but the scene was China, not England. Lin was acting by what we may call martial law. Those opium dealers had no legal rights in China, they had for a long course of years inflicted illegal wrongs. Lin made a great mistake in his method of proceeding, because of his entire ignorance of foreign nations; but he acted according to the best of his judgment. He dealt what was meant to be, and what ought to have been, an annihilating blow to the traffic. When that immense amount of valuable property was poured into the sea, China delivered her loudest protest against the guilty trade, and did the utmost that lay in her power to extinguish it for ever.

The great effort was a failure. One cannot but regret that the Chinese ignorance of diplomacy prevented the statesmen who had given such signal

proofs of their hostility to opium from continuing
the struggle in ways more likely to have been
successful.   Lin published among his own people
two long letters to the Queen of England, which, if
duly forwarded through the proper official channel,
could not have failed to produce a practical result.[1]
This indeed was the fatal fault of the Chinese policy.
Their Government obstinately declined all official
communication with the nations of the West, until
forced upon them at the sword's point.   We have
seen how the British Government resolutely ignored
the opium smuggling for thirty years.   The British
Government will not protect illicit traffic, was the
consistent utterance of all that period.   We have
seen how the high legal advisers of the Crown and
the East India Company, condemned their preparation of opium for the smuggling-trade as illegal.
One can hardly doubt that if China had tried peaceful and direct negotiation with the British Government, instead of persisting in shutting her eyes to all
the outside world, and scolding the Hong merchants,
the issue would have been greatly different.

But at least the Chinese have been consistent.
Humbled and vanquished, the Emperor Tao Kwang
is reported to have made this reply to the proposition for legalizing the traffic, made by Sir H.
Pottinger.   "It is true, I cannot prevent the introduction of the flowing poison; gainseeking and
corrupt men will for profit and sensuality defeat my
wishes; but nothing will induce me to derive a

[1]   *Vide* Appendix.

revenue from the vice and misery of my people."
Thus, though victors in the physical contest, we
were morally defeated. The noble inflexibility of
the heathen Monarch made it palpably evident, that
in the whole preceding struggle England was in the
wrong.

Has the Chinese anti-opium policy undergone a
change? This is a most important question. We
have heard the indignant condemnation which Mr.
Gladstone pronounced upon the opium war; and
yet, in 1870, Mr. Gladstone condescended to
apologize for the existing opium trade. Doubtless
he did so under the impression that the character
of the trade had changed. In this, however, he
was entirely mistaken. Its *form* has changed, for
it is a legalized, instead of a contraband traffic. Its
moral character is unchanged, because the Chinese
objection to the traffic is unchanged, and the legality
given to the trade was granted under influence of
fear. We must now produce evidence for this.

The first proof that legalization of the traffic does
not indicate any change in the policy of the Government consists in the fact that the old edicts against
the use of the drug are not repealed, though allowed
to sleep for awhile. But this sleep is not so profound, but that even recently there have been active
attempts to resist the vice. Dr. Dudgeon, in his
report of the Peking Hospital for 1869, says,—

" In the capital, stringent regulations are now
and again put in force against opium-smoking; as
for example, when some great crime or calamity,

an atrocious murder, or a great conflagration takes place, or on the accession of new officials to office. The sale of the drug in the Tartar city, at the end of last year, after the death of the lieutenant-governor and installation of his successor, has been strictly prohibited. Many sellers, and a few smokers, had their goods distrained, and they themselves cast into prison for two months. To the reigning family it seems of paramount importance to keep the Manchus from this vice; but notwithstanding all their exertions and vigilance, the vice is growing and extending among these lazy pensioners and soldiers.

But it is in the despatches and evidence of Sir R. Alcock, recently her Majesty's representative at Peking, that we have the most striking testimony to China's unchanged hostility to the opium trade. Under date, Peking, May 20, 1869,[2] the ambassador addressed the Earl of Clarendon, giving a lengthy report of an interview between himself and three ministers of the Foreign Board of Peking. In the course of the discussion, Sir Rutherford had accused the Chinese literati of being actuated by a hostile animus towards foreigners. The Chinese ministers at first disputed the fact, but,—"In the end, Wen-Seang shifted his ground; and asked how could it be otherwise? They had often seen foreigners making war on the country; *and then, again, how irreparable and continuous was the injury*

---

[2] Correspondence respecting the revision of the Treaty of Tientsin, p. 396.

which they saw inflicted upon the whole Empire by the foreign importation of opium! If England would consent to interdict this—cease either to grow it in India, or to allow their ships to bring it to China— there might be some hope of more friendly feelings. No doubt there was a very strong feeling entertained by all the literati and gentry, as to the frightful evils attending the smoking of opium, its thoroughly demoralizing effects, and the utter ruin brought upon all who once gave way to the vice. They believed the extension of this pernicious habit was mainly due to the alacrity with which foreigners supplied the poison for their own profit, perfectly regardless of the irreparable injury inflicted, and naturally they felt hostile to all concerned in such a traffic . . . . If England ceased to protect the trade, it could then be effectually prohibited by the Emperor; and it would eventually cease to trouble them, while a great cause of hostility and distrust in the minds of the people would be removed.''

The interview here reported was succeeded by a formal note from the Chinese Government which amounts to a distinct application to the British Government to give up the legalized importation and permit China to return to the former system. This document is of such immense importance to the present condition of the question, that we must print it entire.[3]

" From Tsungli Yamen to Sir R. Alcock, July,

[3] Report, East India Finance, 1871, p. 268.

1869.   The writers have on several occasions, when
conversing with his Excellency, the British Minister,
referred to the opium trade as being prejudicial to
the general interests of commerce.

" The object of the treaties between our respective
countries was to secure perpetual peace; but, if
effective steps cannot be taken to remove an
accumulating sense of injury from the minds of
men, it is to be feared that no policy can obviate
sources of future trouble. Day and night the
writers are considering the question, with a view to
its solution, and the more they reflect upon it, the
greater does their anxiety become, and hereon
they cannot avoid addressing his Excellency very
earnestly on the subject.

" That opium is like a deadly poison, that it is
most injurious to mankind, and a most serious pro-
vocative of ill-feeling is, the writers think, perfectly
well known to his Excellency, and it is, therefore,
needless for them to enlarge farther upon these
points.   The Prince and his colleagues are quite
aware that the opium trade has long been condemned by England as a nation, and that the
right-minded merchant scorns to have to do with
it.   But the officials and people of this Empire,
who cannot be so completely informed on this
subject, all say that England trades in opium
because she desires to work China's ruin, for (say
they) if the friendly feelings of England are genuine,
since it is open to her to produce and trade in
everything else, would she still insist on spreading

the poison of this hurtful thing through the Empire?

" There are those who say, stop the trade by enforcing a vigorous prohibition against the use of the drug. China has the right to do so, doubtless, and might be able to effect it; but a strict enforcement of the prohibition would necessitate the taking of many lives. Now, although the criminals' punishment would be of their own seeking, bystanders would not fail to say that it was the foreign merchant seduced them to their ruin by bringing the drug, and it would be hard to prevent general and deep-seated indignation; such a course indeed, would tend to arouse popular anger against the foreigner.

" There are others again who suggest the removal of the prohibitions against the growth of the poppy. They argue that as there is no means of stopping the foreign (opium) trade, there can be no harm, as a temporary measure, in withdrawing the prohibition on its growth. We should thus not only deprive the foreign merchant of a main source of his profits, but should increase our revenue to boot. The sovereign rights of China are indeed competent to this; such a course would be practicable, and indeed the writers cannot say that, as a last resource, it will not come to this; but they are most unwilling that such prohibition should be removed, holding, as they do, that a right system of government should appreciate the beneficence of Heaven, and (seek to) remove any grievance which afflicts its people, while to allow them to go on to destruction, although an increase of revenue may result, will provoke the judgment of Heaven, and the condemnation of men.

" Neither of the above plans are indeed satisfactory. If it be desired to remove the very root, and to stop the evil at its source, nothing will be effective but a prohibition, to be enforced alike by both parties.

" Again, the Chinese merchant supplies your country with his goodly tea and silk, conferring thereby a benefit upon her; but the English merchant empoisons China with pestilent opium. Such conduct is unrighteous. Who can justify it ? *What wonder if officials and people say that England is wilfully working out China's ruin, and has no real friendly feeling for her ?*

" The wealth and generosity of England are spoken of by all; she is anxious to prevent and anticipate all injury to her commercial interest ; how is it, then, that she can hesitate to remove an acknowledged evil? *Indeed it cannot be that England still holds to this evil business, earning the hatred of the officials and people of China, and making herself a reproach among the nations because she would lose a little revenue, were she to forfeit the cultivation of the poppy.*

" The writers hope that H. E. will memorialize his Government to give orders in India and elsewhere to substitute the cultivation of cereals or cotton. Were both nations to rigorously prohibit the growth of the poppy, both the traffic in and the consumption of opium might alike be put an end to. To do away with so great an evil would be a great virtue on England's part; she would strengthen friendly relations, and make herself illustrious. How delightful to have so great an act transmitted to after-ages!

"This matter is injurious to commercial interests, in no ordinary degree. If H. E., the British Minister, cannot, before it is too late, arrange a plan for a joint prohibition (of the traffic), then no matter with what devotedness the writers may plead, they may be unable to cause the people to put aside ill-feeling, and so strengthen friendly relations as to place them for ever beyond fear of disturbance. Day and night therefore, the writers give to this matter most earnest thought, and overpowering is the distress and anxiety it occasions them.

"Having thus presumed to unbosom themselves, they would be honoured by his Excellency's reply."

We do not envy the mental condition of that Englishman who can read through the above letter without shame and sorrow, to think that we should have put it into the power of Chinese statesmen to address us thus. That document alone ought to settle the opium question. Can a Christian Government, a Christian nation, refuse to respond to such an appeal as this? Would that that document were placarded at every railway-station, published in every newspaper in Great Britain, until the aroused conscience of the people demanded to be relieved from the reproach now justly resting upon us! Would that the Chinese Government would repeat its protests every year and every month; concluding every communication to our ambassador with the expression of their desire to have the opium-trade abolished!

That the Chinese Foreign Office is thoroughly sincere in this appeal to England's justice and charity, may be regarded as set at rest by our late ambassador's emphatic assurance before the Select Committee of the House of Commons.[4]

"I have estimated the absolute interest of the Chinese Government in the Indian trade (in opium), at about a million and a half sterling; and in reference to this I may mention that not only in the conference that took place with the minister of the Tsungli Yamen, but also at different times, officially or privately, they have shown the greatest readiness to give up the whole revenue if they could only induce the British Government to co-operate with them in any way to put it down. My own conviction is firm, that whatever degree of honesty may be attributed to the officials and the Central Government, there is that in their words that they would not hesitate one moment, to-morrow if they could, to enter into any arrangement with the British Government, and say, "Let our revenue go, we care nothing about it. What we want is to stop the consumption of opium, which we conceive is impoverishing the country, and demoralizing and brutalizing our people.""

In confirmation of Sir Rutherford Alcock's testi-

[4] Report, East India Finance, 1871, p. 273.

mony, we have that of Mr. (now Sir Thomas) Wade, at present our ambassador at Peking, who wrote in 1868 :[5]—

" We are generally prone to forget that the footing we have in China has been obtained by force, and by force alone, and that, unwarlike and unenergetic as we hold the Chinese to be, it is in reality to the fear of force alone, that we are indebted for the safety we enjoy at certain points accessible to our force. . . . Yet nothing that has been gained, it must be remembered, was received from the free-will of the Chinese; more, the concessions made to us from time to time have been, from first to last, extorted against the conscience of the nation; in defiance, that is to say, of the moral convictions of its educated men ; not merely of the office-holders, whom we call mandarins, and who are numerically but a small proportion of the educated class, but of of the millions who are saturated with a knowledge of the history and philosophy of their country. To these, as a rule, the very extension of our trade must appear politically, or what is in China the same thing, morally wrong; and the story of foreign intercourse during the last thirty years can have had no effect but to confirm them in their opinion."

The assertion we made above, that the Chinese policy of absolute interdiction of opium has never changed, is established beyond controversy by this unimpeachable evidence. For a time, China outwardly con-

[5] Correspondence respecting revision of the Treaty of Tientsin, p. 432.

K

formed to our demand for legalization; but it was
through compulsion, and only by compulsion is the
legalization maintained.   The moral character of the
trade, therefore, is no better than it was in the old
smuggling days.   The scandal is simply shifted from
the shoulders of a few private individuals to that of
the nation as a whole.

CHAPTER VI.

ON OPIUM CULTIVATION IN CHINA.

The origin of the practice of smoking opium in China is wrapt in obscurity. By some Great Britain has been made responsible for the introduction and sole maintenance of the habit. Others again have tried to relieve our country from odium by asserting that the practice was known and widely spread in China before the first chest of Indian drug was landed in the country. A brief review of the scanty allusions to opium in China before the present century will enable us to judge of the merits of these conflicting opinions.

Mr. T. T. Cooper says that the habit of smoking opium has existed on the western borders of China for "a great many years, probably a couple of centuries;"[1] but adduces no evidence in support of this assertion. Mr. Hobson, Commissioner of Customs at Hankow, made particular inquiries upon this point, and informs us that[2] "The popular story in Szechuen is that 100 years ago opium was intro-

---

[1] Report, East India Finance, 1871, p. 258.
[2] *Ibid.*, p. 282.

duced into Szechuen, Shensi, Yunnan, and Kwei-
chau, from India and Thibet. At the time of its
introduction it was esteemed for its medicinal properties only; but during Kienlung's reign (1736-96)
it was discovered to be smokable, and the Szechuen
people were among the earliest indulgers." He also
states that in the " General History of Yunnan,"
revised and republished in the first year of Kienlung's reign, opium is noted as a common product
of Yung Changfoo. Dr. J. Wilson, celebrated for
his attainments in Hindoo literature, thinks that
opium was not generally known in India until about
a century ago,[3] because he has not found it mentioned in native books. It was introduced, he says,
from Turkey and Arabia into India by the Moham-
medan conquerors, and was familiar to the rulers long
before the people got acquainted with it. If this be
correct, since the progress of opium cultivation
probably moved eastwards, beginning perhaps in
Egypt, and passing by way of Turkey, Persia, India,
Assam, Burma, into Yunnan, the south-western
province of China, it seems extremely unlikely that
while the poppy was rare in India a hundred years
back, it can have been well-known, as Mr. Cooper
supposes, in western China a century earlier. The
Calcutta Blue book on opium contains a memorandum from the Delegates of the Shanghai Chamber
of Commerce appointed to investigate the origin and
extent of the cultivation of the poppy in China, in
which they report that " the opium pipe is believed

[3] Report, East India Finance, 1871, p. 346.

by the Szechuen people to have been *a Canton invention*, dating from the tenth year of Taoukwang (1830)."[4] This belief is evidently erroneous as to the date, but as an example of the unreliability of native accounts, it may be taken as a set-off against those upon which Mr. Cooper's opinion was based. It may have some weight as indicating the locality of the origin of opium smoking, but cannot be implicitly trusted in this respect.

In 1830 a censor, Shaou Chinghwuh, of Chekiang, a sea-board province, speaks, in a memorial, of the cultivation having spread within the previous ten years over a large part of the province, and says it is reported to be grown in Fohkien, Kwang Tung, and Yunnan.[5] Major Burney wrote from Ava, under date March 9, 1831, "Opium is imported by the caravans from China to Ava. The Chinese said that the poppy plant had been cultivated for the last eight or ten years at a place called Medoo, two days' journey from Tali, but that the cultivation is limited and carried on secretly, for, if the Government at Peking became aware of it the cultivators would lose their lives. The quantity imported by these caravans is insignificant."[6] Choo Tsun's memorial (1836) states that in Yunnan the poppy is cultivated "all over the hills and the open champaign," and the annual

[4] Papers relating to the Opium Question. Calcutta, 1870. p. 260.

[5] Chinese Repository, vol. v. p. 472.

[6] Phipps, China and Eastern Trade, p. 231.

produce "cannot be less than several thousand chests."[7] The Chinese are reckless in these vague numerical estimates; but nevertheless the production at that date must have been considerable, and would indicate a long acquaintance with the plant. The Roman Catholic missionaries who entertained Mr. Cooper in Szechuen informed him that the poppy was not introduced into that province when they entered it thirty years previously.[8]

These are the data upon which we have to form our opinion as to the origin of opium smoking and the date of the commencement of poppy cultivation in China. No definite conclusion can be drawn. As to the origin of the habit of smoking the drug, it is quite possible that, in a country of such vast area, consisting of provinces but loosely bound together, the vice has radiated from two centres. Mr. Cooper's statement that China may be roughly divided into halves, the line passing from north to south through Hankow, of which the eastern half consumes Indian, and the western native opium, may give some support to this hypothesis.[9] If this seems unlikely then the balance of evidence rather inclines to the conclusion that opium smoking began in Canton. It is worthy of remark, that the first memorial against opium, at least the first of which we have information, proceeded from Keihking, Governor of Canton Province in 1799, and that this

---

[7] Correspondence relating to China, 1840, p. 170.
[8] Pioneer of Commerce, p. 130.
[9] Report. East India Finance, 1871, p. 253.

stigmatizes the drug as "the vile dirt of foreign countries."

Whether the native cultivation preceded or succeeded the importation by sea we cannot positively determine. "Before the year 1767 the import of this drug into China rarely exceeded 200 chests, in that year it amounted to 1000." Now the Portuguese, who carried opium to China before 1767, had possessed commercial settlements in China since 1537. Defoe, in "Robinson Crusoe," published in 1719, makes his famous hero take opium from the Straits to China, but does not allude to the practice of opium smoking.[1] On the Chinese side we have the Yunnan history, written before 1736, which mentions the growth in that province. These dates approximate, and we may fairly infer that the drug, so valuable as a medicine, was introduced into China from the east, by sea, and the west by land, at no very distant dates, and that in the west the plant followed the drug at no long interval. However this may be, the first distinct reference on record to smoking as a common practice is in that memorial of 1799 already referred to ; and we may reasonably conclude that the vice did not attain to serious dimensions long before that time, though its early beginnings may go back a good way into the century. It is a plausible conjecture that the sudden increase

---

[1] A famous Chinese novel of the last century, the *Hung Lau Mung*, is said to refer to opium-smoking as a strange newly invented indulgence : but I have not been able to verify the reference.

of the import noted in 1767, from 200 to 1000 chests, may denote the recent discovery of the sensual indulgence.

A negative but conclusive argument remains. The silence of Chinese literature is decisive against the opinion that opium smoking prevailed long ago. China does not only possess a few old books, but has an immense and constantly increasing literature, including archæological, historical, geographical, and medical works; besides dramas, poems, and novels innumerable, which give minute descriptions of the habits of the people from a distant antiquity to the present time. It is impossible that such a practice as that of smoking opium could have established itself among such a people for long, without imprinting its mark on their literature. The very street ballads of modern days refer continually to opium smoking, and if the vice dated far back, we should surely find it alluded to in the songs and romances of the people, just as we find that wine-bibbing is. Medical works of 300 years ago describe the drug and its uses in medicine; and the absence of allusion to opium smoking sufficiently demonstrates its non-existence until a recent date. Though it is clear, from the above review, that the whole accountability does not fall upon our shoulders, it is also clear that the facts will not permit us to represent ourselves as merely having supplied the materials for the gratification of a vicious habit, already confirmed and widespread before the introduction of Indian opium into the Chinese market. The habit has grown and spread along with the increase of our supply; we have fed the eastern half of the empire with the drug almost exclusively; and there is much reason to fear that the introduction and propagation of the native cultivation in certain districts, was directly stimulated by the foreign supply.

The native growth of the poppy must now be considered as a present fact, having a most important bearing on the future prospects of the monopoly. Prince Kung and his colleagues in that biting note to Sir R. Alcock, showed themselves well informed at last as to the motive of the British Government in upholding the trade, and openly threatened to strike at the roots of our revenue, by permitting the free cultivation in their own territory. The threat is new, but the fear on our side is an old fear. Even in the Company's days, it was known that the poppy was spreading in China, and since then, almost every year, the finance ministers responsible for the Indian budget, have pointed out the risk of our losing our revenue from this cause. It is a sword of Damocles, always hanging over our heads, and rendering a secure enjoyment of the monopoly revenue impossible; but will it ever fall? As usual, in dealing with Chinese affairs, it is impossible from lack of definite statistical data, to do more than conjecture. Such conjectures are almost always influenced by our wishes or our fears. One says that the consumption in China increases at so rapid a rate, that its use will absorb all our supply, and all the native production too. Another, that the quality of the native drug is so inferior, that those who can afford the imported will always use it. Against this it is alleged that the home manufacture has improved and is improving, and that the natives are beginning to prefer their own opium, because milder in its influence, and therefore not exercising so fatal a tyranny over its votaries. Instead of adding one more to these various prognostications of the future, we will collect here what information we have been able to gather about the present state of the case; referring to the Appendix for the expressions of opinion gathered from different quarters.

The Trades Reports put forth by the Chinese Imperial Maritime Customs, which are all under foreign superintendence, give much information upon this topic. The Reports we quote from are for 1869.

Hankow.—" The importation of (foreign) opium is considerably short for the last two seasons, but this is not to be wondered at now that each opium shopkeeper in this and the surrounding districts, advertizes native drug for sale.

" The general estimate of the opium merchants is : —

Province of Szechuen, Annual Yield   6000 peculs.
   ,,   ,, Kweichow   ,,   ,, 15,000 ,,
   ,,   ,, Yunnan   ,,   ,, 20,000 ,,
               Total yield   41,000 peculs."

Thus these three provinces alone were calculated

to yield annually about 40,000 chests, and this at a time when the cultivation was prohibited. It is necessary to state for those who do not know China, that the Government prohibition is not, as many persons assert, absolutely inefficacious. No doubt when one hears of half a province being white with poppy flowers, at the very time when proclamations against its cultivation are hanging at the yamen doors, English readers naturally conclude that the prohibitory edicts are equivalent to obsolete laws of the reign of the Stuarts in our statute-book, which are known only to antiquarians, and dragged to light occasionally by magazine-writers for public amusement or instruction. This, however, is not the case. Prohibition in China has two results ; irregular taxation, and a degree of risk, and therefore operates to *diminish*, while it does not prevent the cultivation. These edicts may be dead letters one year, and be instinct with life and activity the next. The Chinese know this, and of course this knowledge has a deterrent effect of a certain amount. That these edicts are not regarded as absolutely valueless by Chinese themselves is apparent from a paragraph of this very report :—

" At the time of my visit, proclamations were already posted at Chung-King, Leang-shan, Yen-Keang, and the adjacent towns, prohibiting the cultivation of the poppy, and exhorting that more attention be paid to cereal crops. The only apparent result was, that opium smokers feeling unable to break themselves of the pernicious habit, were actually buying up and storing opium, for fear supplies should be cut short."

Though the reporter prefaces this sentence by the remark, " there is little hope that the production of opium will ever be successfully put a stop to," it is plain there was much fear in the minds of those keenly interested in the matter.

Chinkiang.—The report here is, " though the importation of Szechuen opium during the year has been peculs 25·86 over the preceding year ; the quantity is too small to affect the market to any extent ; and as it is reported that stringent measures are being adopted to prevent the cultivation of the poppy, it is likely that the trade in native drug will remain stationary or gradually decrease."

The Baron de Méritens reports from *Foochow* that " the opium produced in three districts of that province is so inferior, possesses so disagreeable a smell that the Chinese cannot smoke it except as a mixture in the proportions of ⅝ths of Malwa to ⅜ths of native opium ; but one must remember that it is probable that the Chinese will soon learn that a very simple chemical preparation will remove that unpleasant smell."

From *Tientsin* we hear that " the import of opium reached its maximum in 1866. There were two causes to account for the large import at that time, since which the quantity has decreased till the past year. It would appear from Mr. Dick's report for 1866 " that in the first place the then recently issued edict as to the cultivation of the poppy in China, though not carried out to the extent of completely stopping its production, had nevertheless tended to bring much of the land then so employed under different cultivation." The other cause was a temporary rise in price.

Kiukiang. The Customs Agent here states that "the Kiang-si grown opium is produced in three prefectures, in small patches off the main line of travel, and brought to the towns and sold. The poppy is not yet boldly raised in extensive fields as in Szechuen and Shensi, but no decided efforts are made by the authorities to check the cultivation, and native opium is purchaseable in small quantities for personal consumption in most of the large towns along the banks of the river Kan."

Mr. Dick says "the high price Indian opium has commanded, has been the result of two causes—the superiority of the article, and the prejudice of the Chinese against raising it themselves. Although the latter cause has never *prevented* home production, it has certainly made the extension of it slow. But the decay of the prejudice and the increase of the production in China are making India amenable to the laws of political economy in respect to this branch of trade." Careful consideration of the above reports will show that there is at present a considerable practical check upon the production of native opium, and that China possesses the potentiality of increasing her native supply to an indefinite extent, as well as of improving its manufacture.

From the Commercial Reports of her Majesty's

consuls in China for 1872 we glean the following : [2]—

Chefoo. " Malwa is the only kind that finds a
ready market. Patna and Benares are imported,
but only in very small quantities, but Persian finds
no market at all. Native opium appears to be
gradually making its way in the market. The
poppy is cultivated to no small extent in this
province (Shantung) though not in the immediate
neighbourhood of the port."

In *Fohkien* province [3] " the quantity produced was
small, perhaps not exceeding 100 pounds. In the
adjoining province of Chekiang there was also a
falling off in the total yield. The unusually cold
weather at Chinese New year is thought to be the
cause." [4]

Consul Hughes of *Hankow* makes a statement of
much importance. " Opium. A glance at this
Table shows a remarkable decrease in the amount
of opium imported. This is attributed to the *growing
tendency of the Chinese to use the native article*, their
preference for which is *not exclusively due to its cheapness.* It is said that the mildness of the native
is the principal cause of the growing preference
for its use. The Chinese say that it is much
easier to give up temporarily, or abandon altogether,
the habit of smoking native than that of smoking
foreign opium. The habit of smoking foreign opium
affects the system to such a degree that the sudden

[2] China, No. 3 (1873), Commercial Reports, p. 31.
[3] *Ibid.,* p. 43.   [4] *Ibid.,* p. 54.

abandonment of the use of so powerful a drug would to a certainty impair the health, whereas the smoker of native opium is by no means so seriously affected by the want of his favourite narcotic.

"As far as could be ascertained the net value of all the opium grown in the province of Szechuen would reach about 35,000,000 of taels sycee [at the price given, 360 taels a chest, 97,000 chests !], but this cipher is anything but certain. A late imperial decree is said to have abolished the *likin* (war-tax) on native opium, the growth of which was to be strictly prohibited, but this decree may perhaps only concern the province of Kweichow, where the poppy is so extensively cultivated as *to leave no space for the production of cereals.*"

From *Newchwang*[5] in Manchuria, the consul writes, "the price of native drug has risen, in consequence of the exertions of the authorities, both here and in the adjoining provinces, to carry into execution the Imperial proclamation prohibiting its growth. A smaller quantity therefore has been produced, and the price is now nearly equal to that of foreign opium."

From *Tientsin*[6] Consul Mongan reports :—

"There can be little doubt that last year's deficit in this case was due principally to the excessive likin taxes of this province, and to the competition of native opium.

"The second great cause of the falling off in the importation of 1872 was, no doubt, the competition

[5] *Ibid.*, p. 80.   [6] *Ibid.*, p. 111.

of native opium, the increased consumption of which
here was indicated last year by the re-exportation,
not only of all the Persian opium which had been
imported in 1872 (amounting only to twenty-seven
piculs), but also by the re-exportation of twenty-six
piculs of the same kind of drug which had remained
on hand from 1871. The price of Persian opium
generally follows that of Malwa, and is from fifty to
sixty taels cheaper. Thus, in point of cheapness,
Persian competes much more than either that of
Malwa or Bengal with native opium, and its dis-
appearance from the Tientsin market in 1872 was
most likely due to the fact that it did not pay
shippers to import it at all, owing to the cheap
rates ruling for its native rival. These rates again
showed that there was a large supply of the latter
in the market, a supply sufficient to drive the
comparatively cheap Persian out of the field, and to
limit the sale of the more expensive Indian.

" Although the prohibition of poppy-culture by
Imperial edicts has in former years been practically
inoperative, still there are some grounds for anticipating that the Rescript of 17th December, 1872,
will prove more efficacious, for the orders given are
more explicit, and in October last Mr. Taintor,
Acting Commissioner of Customs at Newchwang,
reported that a similar edict, directing the destruction of the poppy-crop in the province in which
the port is situated, and the adjacent districts of
Mongolia had in many places been carried into
execution."

Shanghai.   Report by Consul Medhurst [7]—

" The increase in the cultivation of the poppy has had a most injurious effect on the consumption of the foreign drug, *the import of which during the last five years remained perfectly stationary, this year indeed showing a decrease,* whilst the production of the native drug during the same time has more than quadrupled.

" Exact statistics of the growth of the poppy cannot be obtained, but there is no doubt, as far as can be ascertained from the Chinese themselves and from the reports of foreign travellers, it is year by year increasing largely.   Dr. Legge, the well-known sinologue and missionary, lately made the overland journey from Peking to Chinkiang, and he reports that the country between the Yellow River and the Yangtzse is covered with poppy fields.   The temptations to its cultivation are at present very great, as on the lowest estimate of the peasants themselves it is twice as profitable as growing wheat, some saying even six times.   The spread of poppy cultivation all over China, has again attracted the attention of the Imperial Government, and lately a decree appeared forbidding it.   This, of course, will not have the slightest effect, as it would be against the interests of all the officials to put down such a useful contributor to their exchequer, both public and private.

" Under these circumstances I cannot but express my opinion, and I am borne out in it by the principal

[7] China, No. 3 (1873), Part II. p. 140.

opium merchants of Shanghai, that we may look forward to a gradual falling off in the demand for the foreign drug, and if the cultivation of the poppy continues to spread, as it is now doing, to the virtual extinction of the trade in Indian opium."

Mr. Malet [8] in his general review of the Chinese trade, in a report to Mr. Wade, expresses himself thus : "The kind of danger to the Indian revenue arising from the increasing use of native opium may be likened to the danger to which our excise revenue would be exposed if the taste for light wine in preference to spirits were to become general in England."

He shows that the danger is not imaginary by a table [see Appendix] which gives only 8,261,381*l.* as the total net value of opium imported in 1872, against 8,695,592*l.* in 1871.

Now, if any one will take the trouble to compare the above two reports, that of the Customs for 1869, with that of the Consuls for 1872, he will see signs of a steady progress of opium-cultivation in China. But, if instead of comparing 1872, with 1869, we compare it with 1863, the contrast is startling. Mr. Hart, the Inspector-General of Chinese Maritime Customs, collected in 1864, from all the offices under his superintendence, replies to the question : "Has native opium been in use at the port in 1863 ?" To this question Newchwang, Chinkiang, Kiukiang, Ningpo, Foochow, Swatow, returned the brief reply,[9] "No." Chefoo replied,

---

[8] *Ibid.*, p. 223.

[9] Papers relating to Opium. Calcutta, 1870, p. 208.

"consumption so small that it may be stated as *nil*." In Canton, "some native opium had been used." Hankow reported an import of native opium from Szechuen of 500 peculs weight. Shanghai and Amoy also report imports of 500 peculs in each port. Thus in 1863, native opium hardly existed side by side with the Indian drug, whereas in 1872, it seriously threatens to oust it from the market!

The memorandum of the Financial Department of the Indian Government, dated 23rd of February, 1871, sums up the results of wide inquiry, in terms which fully support our views; particularly stating (1) that up to 1817, native opium was produced only in Yunnan; (2) that between 1817 and 1840, the cultivation was introduced into Szechuen, Kwangsi, and Kweichow; (3) that up to 1848, the Imperial Government strenuously opposed the cultivation, so that in some places, even bribes to the mandarins failed to secure the fields, and in other places the poppy was destroyed by an enraged populace; (4) that after 1848, a great increase of the poppy took place, so that in fifteen years from 1848 to 1864, the whole of Western China became an opium-producing region.

But information of a later date than that embodied in the memorandum shows a marvellous spread of the poppy within the last few years in Eastern China also, in Manchuria, in Shantung, Kiangpeh, Chekiang, Foh-kien. These provinces have all been referred to in the Customs and Consular reports above, but we may add here an extract from a leader in the *North China Herald* of 7th of June, 1873. " Most unexpected was the account given by the two travellers (Dr. Legge and Mr. Edkins) of the enormous extent of the cultivation of opium in Shantung and Kiangpeh, and the equally startling fact that the wide introduction of the cultivation of the poppy *only dates some two years back.*"

The case then stands thus. There is now an immense production of opium in China. In 1869 we have seen it estimated at 40,000 chests in three provinces. In 1872 nearly 100,000 chests in Szechuen only. It is probable that in the last case Szechuen is used rather as the designation of *all* western opium, than for that of one single province ; and even so, it may be an exaggeration. Nevertheless it is clear that the native production is already vast, and that it increases with rapid development. There are signs, also, that the quality of the native drug is improving, and more than that, that the *taste* for it, in preference to the stronger foreign article, is growing. The prices of the two may be compared in Shanghai in 1872, in Consul Medhurst's report. Indian ranged from 425 taels to 510 taels ; native from 250 to 300 taels. These East-coast prices would gradually rise for foreign, and fall for native opium, as one went from the coast towards the west. This very serious rivalry has sprung up whilst the cultivation of the poppy is *still illegal* in China. While some foreign witnesses declare that in most localities the illegality is no practical hindrance to the cultivation, there are indications that the present state of the law has a restraining influence, though, perhaps, not to a great extent. In this state of affairs, Prince Kung and his colleagues seriously debate the question whether it would not be well to revoke all edicts against the cultivation, on purpose to undersell and drive out of the country the opium imported from abroad. We hear, too, of one of the most influential of the great satraps of China, Li Hung Chang, positively encouraging the growth all through his jurisdiction.

If we do not seize time by the forelock our Indian opium revenue may die a natural death within a few years, and we may have to bear the inevitable loss, as well as to carry the stain upon our escutcheon to the end of time.

One method of countermining the Chinese and saving the revenue for India, at least in part, is patent enough to every one who regards the state of affairs with the eyes of a merchant or political economist prepared to ignore all considerations of morality and philanthropy; but the suggestion is so frightful, that no right-minded person will hear it stated without pain. We might deliberately set to work to double or treble our Indian production, and swamp the Chinese market by an inundation of cheap opium, which should render the native drug unsaleable. Our Indian monopoly profits leave a terrible margin to work

upon.   In 1871-2 the Bengal opium cost about
Rs. 360 per chest, and sold in Calcutta for Rs. 1387
per chest : more than 1000 Rs. per chest clear
profit.   In that year 49,695 chests were sold for
export.   Now it is evident that if the export were
increased from under 50,000 chests to 100,000
or 200,000 chests, a profit of little more than one
half, or one quarter, of the present profit would bring
in the same revenue, allowing for some increase in
cost of production.   Rs. 360 equal about 108 taels.
With native opium fetching from 250 to 300 taels
in Shanghai, India might easily undersell the
Chinese opium and yet obtain more than double the
cost price of her opium.   But it is fearful to think
of such a competition.   The Chinese price includes
already irregular fees of various kinds to a large
amount, probably much over fifty taels per chest.
The grower's profit is stated as sometimes six times
as much as he would get from a grain crop.   The
Chinese therefore could lower their prices to a
large extent, and every year's production must
accustom new hands to the manufacture, and make
production cheaper.   The sure result of such a
strife between the two countries would be the
cheapening of the drug to an alarming point, and
the consequent great increase of its consumption.
That is almost the only sure result, for the increase
of production in India could not be attained in one
year, or in ten : and there is no reason, so far as
we can see, why in the end the Chinese should not
be able to produce quite as cheaply as India.   But

whatever the final issue, the process could not take place without a fearful acceleration of China's ruin. Although the national conscience seems almost insensible to the present evils of the opium trade we cannot believe that Britain would ever knowingly consent to enter upon such a fatal extension of the traffic.

CHAPTER VII.

THE immediate result of the opium policy initiated by the East India Company, and continued by the British Government, has been a great extension of poppy cultivation in India and China. The monopoly is responsible for this directly in the case of Bengal, partly directly and partly indirectly in the case of Central India, and indirectly in the case of China. For the proof of these assertions we refer to the historical facts already narrated at length in previous chapters. Defenders of the policy vainly strive to shelter it behind the ordinary operation of the trade laws of demand and supply. The operation of these economic laws does not divest of responsibility those who set them in motion at either end; for though it would be absurd to speak of supply as alone creative of demand, there is no question but that an abundant and constantly sustained supply increases demand, whenever the article is not one of absolute necessity. When silk came by caravans across Central Asia, and a single robe was worth its weight in gold in Europe, the shining fabric was reserved for emperors and nobles, and no demand could be said to exist for it among common people; whereas now the abundant supply creates a demand among all classes but the very poorest. The maid-servant who covets a silk dress may be literally said to have had the demand *created* in her case, by the ample supply of the material which places it constantly before her eyes, and renders it not impossible for her to obtain it. Only a few years ago there was no demand for newspapers amongst multitudes who are now daily or weekly purchasers of them. In this case the supply of penny and halfpenny journals may be fairly said to have almost alone created the demand. Such illustrations might be indefinitely multiplied, and no reasonable man can refuse to acknowledge that the demand for opium in China did not increase from a few hundred chests in 1766 to perhaps 200,000 chests in 1872 without the immense supply from India contributing to foster and develope the ever-increasing demand. Compliance with the ordinary operation of this natural law of trade is of course innocent, *if the article dealt in be innocent.* But what shall we say of it if the article be *known to be noxious?* And how shall we explain the conduct of the East India Company in at the same time *fighting against* the ordinary economic law in its own territories, and yielding itself voluntarily to be carried along with the current when it set towards China? Can the same fountain at once send forth sweet water and bitter?

But it is a glaring contradiction of the well-

known facts to justify the Indian exportation of
opium as a simple compliance with the laws of
supply and demand. The monopoly interfered
with the ordinary processes of trade, both inter-
nally and externally, both in production and in sale.
The influence of Government, the machinery of
Government, *the capital* of Government, have all
been employed in stimulating production,[1] while
British bayonets and cannon insured the con-

---

[1] The Calcutta Blue Book contains abundant evidence of this.
See Minute by the Hon. J. Strachey, Simla, 10th April, 1869, on
p. 86, in which he says : " There seems to me to have been for
some time past a constant and most wise desire on the part of the
Government of Bengal, to increase the production of opium."
. . . . The Benares Opium Agent has been urged by the Lieutenant Governor to extend the cultivation as much as can be
judiciously done. . . . . It seems to me, therefore, that immediate
measures of the most energetic character ought to be taken with
the object of increasing the production of opium. . . . . I think
that special inquiry should be made as to the possibility of profitably extending the cultivation of opium in the districts of the
North-Western Provinces, in which canal irrigation is available."
Letter from the Hon. W. Grey, Lieutenant Governor of Bengal
dated Barrackpore, 22nd April, 1869 (p. 88), says to Mr. Campbell :—I have a telegraphic message from Simla, urging " that
every possible expedient that you (I) approve should be used even
now to extend the opium cultivation next season to the utmost
practicable extent." Minute by Sir R. Temple, dated 27th April,
1869, (same page): " I am clear for extending the cultivation, and
for insuring a plentiful supply. If we do not do this, the Chinese
will do it for themselves. They had better have our good opium
than their own indifferent opium. There really is no moral
objection to our conduct in this respect." Add to these the statement in Sir W. Muir's Minute (1868): " A few years ago the
Government of Bengal was straining every nerve to extend the
cultivation of the poppy."
Other proofs are given in the Appendix.

tinuance of the sale. When a Government advances
millions to cultivators to secure a crop, when it
sends an agent to Indore with millions more to buy,
how can it pretend to leave the laws of trade to
fulfil themselves? When it first connives at
smuggling, and then fights for smugglers, how
can it plead a wise obedience to the teachings of
political economy? We must therefore conclude
that the Government is directly responsible for
extension of poppy cultivation in Bengal, also
responsible, formerly by direct intervention, latterly
and always by its support of the trade, in Malwa;
and responsible also for the cultivation in China,
in so far as that cultivation has sprung out of
rivalry to the introduction of foreign opium.

Before considering the results of the opium policy
to India and China separately, it is desirable that
we should look at this extension of cultivation in its
relation to the food supply, a bearing of the question
important to both countries. Now we cannot say
that opium is to be condemned simply because it
occupies the soil which might otherwise grow grain.
That argument would require the condemnation
of indigo, tobacco, and every article which takes up
ground and labour that might be bestowed upon
edible products. The question of importance here
is *how much* land is taken up by opium? If opium
were a harmless luxury, it is still certain that men
and women would starve if all the land were planted
with the poppy. The degree, therefore, in which
this substance, useless for the nourishment of life,

takes the place of cereals, is a question of great importance.

The proportion of land and labour which may be given to the poppy without detriment to the food-supply depends upon the existing means of inter-communication between the poppy district and other grain districts. The poppy-grower may make by his opium twice or five times the money that wheat or rice would bring him : but if there is no grain to be bought by his silver, he cannot live upon the metal nor upon the drug. Now even in India, under British government, with its roads and railways, canals and steamers, we know that the means of transport in the country are far from adequate to all emergencies. The shocking memory of the Orissa famine,[2] in 1865-7, in which the total deaths were estimated at a million and a quarter, about one-fourth of the population, in which parents ate their own children, and horrors we cannot bear to transcribe were witnessed,[2] has been almost oblite-rated from the public mind by the heroic efforts of the Government to meet the necessities of the recent terrible famine in Bengal. Upwards of 500,000 acres of the richest land in the very districts in which this last famine was most severely felt, and this land largely enjoying the benefit of artificial irrigation, was devoted to the poppy. The lavish expenditure of Government having averted the worst results of the famine, we are not likely to hear how far the opium cultivation was detrimental to the

[2] *Vide* Fraser's Magazine, September, 1867, p. 373.

food supply.   But these two recent famines are only the latest of a long series.   Dr. Wilson, giving evidence[3] before the Select Committee of the House of Commons, said that the poppy cultivation in Malwa cut off from Rajpootana its natural source of supply in time of famine, and that "lately, according to Government accounts, if I have read them correctly, 1,200,000 people died of famine, and the diseases induced by it."   This proves that the danger of opium production leading to the starvation of the people is not merely hypothetical, even in India.

Turn now to China.   If the relations between the number of mouths, the food supply, and the means of transport are such in India that a single season's drought over a limited area produces such serious results, think how momentous this matter becomes to China, destitute of railways, of good roads, with very few steamers upon her inland waters: in a word, with means of transport inadequate to a degree almost inconceivable to our western ideas.   Famines recur periodically, though at irregular periods, in the vast, mountain-divided provinces of China.   Chinese history abounds in records of most awful seasons of dearth.   Even within the last ten years, dwellers on the coast have been repeating to one another the horrible rumour that, while they were enjoying cheap rice, in Kansuh human flesh was being sold for food! It is clear that in such a land the spread of poppy cultivation becomes, or may become, a question of life or death to multitudes.

[3] Report, East India Finance, 1871, p. 340.

Putting together the information of the Customs Report, and that given by Mr. Edkins in the *North China Herald*, we arrive at these conclusions. One *mow*[4] of land will produce about eight catties of opium annually. A regular opium smoker, consuming his tael[5] a day, will require 22¾ catties in a year—that is, nearly the produce of three *mow*. Three *mow* of land, it is calculated, will produce grain-stuff sufficient for one person for one year. But the poppy only occupies the soil for half the year, and another crop may be taken off the ground as well; therefore it only absorbs one-half of the food-producing power of the land. Every two smokers, who consume each a tael a day, do therefore deprive the country of food for one person, or thereabouts. Sir R. Alcock reports, in 1869, that " about two-thirds of the province of Szechuen, and one-third of Yunnan," are devoted to opium.[6] Szechuen is the larger province : but say one-half of the land in these two provinces together is laid down in opium. This will deprive the people of an annual amount of grain equal to one quarter of the whole possible production ! Allowing for exaggeration in the figures —allowing that the poppy may partly displace sugar, cotton, tobacco, and other products not cereals—the statement, after every deduction, is formidable, and it is not surprising that Chinese

---

[4] About three-fifths of an acre.

[5] The *tael*, or Chinese ounce = 580 grains troy. This is probably much above the average usually consumed.

[6] Calcutta Blue Book, p. 235.

statesmen view the progress of the poppy with alarm. The memorial of Yau Pehchwan,[7] which led to the last edict against the cultivation, says that "the poppy deprives hundreds of thousands of people of grain-food, and *that many have committed suicide under pressure of starvation*, with money in their hands to buy food when none was to be had." If smoking were to become universal in China, putting together the enormous increase of poppy growth and consequent decrease of grain supply, with the effect of opium in diminishing physical power for labour, and in producing sterility, one might speculate as to the number of generations which would succeed before the entire extermination of the Chinese people. Happily, smoking *cannot* become universal, because such considerations put a natural check upon it, besides the moral check. Yet while such an extremity of evil is not to be apprehended, the amount of poppy cultivation in Szechuen and Yunnan alone is already great enough to render the prospects of those provinces truly pitiable in the event of a time of scarcity.

The results of the British Opium Policy in respect to India itself are two : injury to our national reputation, and the imperilling of our Indian finances. Wherever there is wide increase of cultivation, there can hardly fail to be also an increase of consumption. It would appear, then, that we ought to place this increase of consumption in the forefront of the evils

[7] *Ibid.*, p. 222, and Appendix.

resulting to India. But we will not insist upon this : for, on the one hand, the intention and actual effect of the monopoly, as we have seen in our chapter on the policy of the Company, was to restrict the consumption in India; and, on the other hand, although several witnesses attest the fact that the cultivators of the poppy do themselves consume part of their produce, we have no definite information upon this head. The Bengalees do not appear to be generally inclined to the vice of opium-eating. In the native states of Rajpootana and Central India, the habit of opium-eating is said to be almost universal; but though the stimulus which the Company gave to opium production there, by opening the China market to those states, very probably had a considerable influence in stimulating the home consumption, here again we lack such clear information as would justify us in charging the Company with the extension of the practice among the Rajpoots and Sikhs. We confine ourselves, therefore, to the two articles specified below.

(1) The injury to the good repute of the British Government and people among the natives of India which has resulted from our Opium Policy.

Dr. Wilson testifies to this before the Parliamentary Committee : being asked, " What opinion do you think the natives generally hold regarding the Government connexion with the opium traffic ?" he replied,[3] " I have frequently heard the natives referring to it as indicating that the Government had

---

[3] Report, East India Finance, 1871, p. 344.

not proper regard to the well-being of the different oriental nations; that it was accessory to the injury of China, and to the injury of India by what it did in favour of opium. I am in the way of hearing them bring forward objections to Government, but generally I must say that in those districts with which I am acquainted, *with the exception of the opium matter*, they are very much inclined to speak well of the Government." Again, Mr. Geddes[9] delivers this pointed opinion : "No rajah under a purely native system could administer the opium revenue as we do. The Brahmins would very soon starve him out." That is, the moral sense of heathens would be strong enough to compel the cessation of a system which the moral sense of Christians permits ! This can easily be credited by those who have had personal acquaintance with Asiatics. The Christian has a much stronger sense of individual accountability than the heathen, but, as respects the action of government, his views are apt to be more lax. Political expediency is allowed to condone for moral obliquity. The known inability of government to secure virtuous conduct by legislation brings with it an impression that government and virtue have two independent spheres. To the oriental, government is a very simple idea : despotic authority on one side, absolute obedience on the other. Hence the Asiatic admits no considerations of expediency to interfere, but visits the Government with the same moral judgments he would pass upon an individual. This

* *Ibid.*, p. 454.

opium monopoly business is of ill odour among Englishmen: English statesmen, adverting to it in the House of Commons, treat it as an unhappy necessity, a puddle which we cannot clean out, and, therefore, should not stir up. We may be sure that through the length and breadth of India, as education advances, as the native press spreads wider and wider, so the conduct of the British Government will be more and more the subject of popular criticism. To some persons it may seem a matter of small import what our black-skinned subjects think of their masters. But every thoughtful man who ponders the future prospects of British sovereignty in India will see that the opinion the natives have of us is of the very gravest importance to the stability of our Government: and the philanthropist, who regards our rule in India as of far less import for the share it contributes to our national glory than as a means of benefiting and elevating the native races, will deem it no small matter that the confidence of the natives should be weakened, and their respect for us impaired, by witnessing a line of policy they cannot but condemn as unjust.

(2) The dependence of our Indian Empire upon this precarious opium revenue is so startling a result of the policy under which it has gradually swelled to its present dimensions, that one almost hears the silent footfall of Nemesis approaching to strike us down with the very weapon we have forged ourselves. Already the anxieties of those statesmen who have been compelled to face the question have

been a foreboding of calamity. Thirty-two years ago the House of Commons Committee declared, when the revenue was under 1,000,000*l*., that "it would be highly imprudent to rely upon the opium monopoly as a permanent source of revenue." But the "high imprudence" being profitable for the moment, they put off the day of reverting to sounder principles of finance; and it has been put off from that day to this, until the revenue has increased to such a vast sum that now it appears impossible to make any change. Our British Government has run a course parallel with that of the Chinese opium-smoker. He begins with a few whiffs, very pleasant, very refreshing, suggesting no thought of peril. Presently he is consuming his three or four pipes every day, and then a sudden qualm seizes him. He reflects "it would be highly imprudent to get to depend entirely upon opium for health, happiness, even life itself." But he postpones the day when he must abandon his favourite indulgence. A few years more, and now he takes his daily ounce as an absolute necessity. There is no longer a thought of relinquishing it. The only anxiety now is to get a constant supply. At last the day arrives when his supply fails, and he perishes miserably. Our Government has got to the stage of *confirmed opium-revenue consumer*. It has long ago passed the stage when the income of a few hundred thousands from the poppy might have been regarded as a luxury of revenue; now it clings with desperate tenacity to its millions of profit from the poppy as a necessity. And now, when our dependence upon it seems a matter of life and death to our Indian Empire, the supply threatens to dry up. Is the opium-smoker's end to be that of the British Indian Empire also?

The opium revenue, which was under one million when the House of Commons sanctioned it in 1832, had grown to about a million and a half when the House, by rejecting Lord Ashley's attack on the system, again undertook full responsibility for it in 1843. It had grown to five millions by 1862. When Sir Wilfrid Lawson again in 1870 led a gallant assault upon it in the House, the revenue had swelled to 6,733,215*l.* In 1871-72, the latest year of which we have printed parliamentary returns, the opium income was 7,657,213*l.*![1]

In 1871-72 the total revenue of India was 50,110,215*l.*; expenditure, 48,614,512*l.*; leaving a surplus of 1,495,703*l.*

What do these figures import? That out of our Indian revenue of fifty millions, seven millions and a half, nearly one-sixth of the whole revenue, accrue from opium. That if this source of revenue had not existed, the surplus of one and a half million would have been changed into a deficit of six millions!

The year 1871-72, however, is an exceptionably favourable specimen of Indian finance. During a

---

[1] Since then the revenue has been less: the latest returns are,—

1872-73	6,870,423*l.*
1873-74	6,333,599*l.*

long series of years Indian finance ministers have
had to face a succession of deficits.   In 1869 Sir
Richard Temple, in his speech on the Income Tax
Bill,[2] said,—" Sir Charles Trevelyan, speaking in
1863, expressed a fervent hope, *not yet realized*, that
the deficit of 1861-62 would prove to be ' the last of
a long series of Indian deficits.' . . . . But now for
two years past the deficits have reappeared, and
for the current year I shall have to tell the old tale
of deficit."   In the same speech he informs us that
in eight years, from 1860 onward, three only were
years of surplus, while five were years of deficit.   A
writer in the *Quarterly Review* in 1871 represents
the Indian financial condition as one of normal
deficit : the expenditure being about three millions
more than the income.[3]   Difficult of comprehension
as this subject is to those not experts in Indian
affairs, the discussions about the Income Tax in
India have made some thoughts pretty familiar to
the English mind.   One is the expensiveness of the
British government of India—an expensiveness which
seems steadily increasing.   Another thought is the
very slight elasticity of Indian resources.   In what
might be called the romantic age of our connexion
with India, our mighty dependency, mysterious by
its distance, vastness, antiquity, and by the wide
gulf which divides the Oriental mind from the
English, was regarded as an El Dorado of wealth, a
land to which Englishmen went out poor and

---

[2] *Vide* East India Finance, 1871, Appendix No. 3.
[3] *Vide* Appendix.

returned nabobs, a land able to supply inexhaustible spoils to conquering Clives, and practically illimitable revenues to courts of directors. But the age of romance has passed, and is succeeded by an age of prosaic reality, when the purse-strings are in our own keeping, and we have to balance the income and expenditure ourselves. The hard facts of actual experience have taught us that a population of 200,000,000, of whom the vast majority live in a condition of poverty hardly understood in England, getting little more than a bare subsistence of rice and vegetables from the soil they till, cannot, in spite of their immense numbers, supply revenues equal to the requirements of our expensive system of government, without difficulty, and in some cases even distress. When we are informed that we cannot govern India without exacting from the very poorest of the people a tax of 700, in some places 600,[4] per cent. on such a necessary of life as salt, we can hardly help wondering whether, after all, British government can really be on the whole so great a boon to India, whether perhaps the natives do not pay a price for the boon which takes all the gloss off it. This at least is certain, that so far from being able at will to change the nature of our taxation, every authority on Indian finance agrees that we are living in a dependence upon the opium revenue, which may be described as abject. It is about as difficult to suggest any other object or direction of taxation which could take the place

[4] Report, East India Finance, 1871, pp. 183 and 453.

of these seven millions, as to indicate any method
of economizing expenditure which would save the
seven millions. Even with the seven millions we
are embarrassed by a deficit which may almost be
called chronic, and are at our wit's end to keep
things going. As to giving up the opium revenue,
Indian financialists would think it equivalent to proposing political suicide. To this pass has our opium
policy brought us! Forty, and again thirty years ago,
we deliberately elected to serve mammon rather than
God, and now we find ourselves the chained bond-
slaves of the evil one, absolutely compelled to persist in a course from which extrication seems hopeless. No wonder that advocates of the *status quo*
close their eyes desperately to the facts of the case,
deny resolutely that there is any immorality in the
opium revenue at all, take refuge in such miserable
shifts as that, if *we* did not poison the Chinese,
some one else would. British opium policy has
brought us to this, that we cannot afford to keep a
conscience.

What will be the issue of it all? God alone
knows. Optimists flatter themselves that, as the
opium revenue has grown for three quarters of a
century, so it may last on for an indefinite time; or,
if it decrease, the decrease will be gradual, and
therefore easily borne. Pessimists foretell a fatal
derangement of our Indian finances. All we know
for certain is that this opium policy has brought us
to a shameful and dangerous position, and we can
see no way of escape from it. A way there is

indeed, as we shall try to show in the next chapter; but it seems almost as unlikely that the British nation should take that way, as it is unlikely that the confirmed opium-smoker should renounce his pipe and regain his original state of freedom.

We now turn our eyes to China. What have been the results of the British opium policy there?

(1) The physical and moral deterioration of an unknown, but certainly large number of victims of the opium-pipe.

We have no wish to exaggerate the case against ourselves. Of course no man becomes an opium sot without having to blame himself more than any other person or institution. If he blames those who brought the temptation to his door, he must first of all inveigh against his own people, the opium dealers, who buy and distribute the drug all over the country; the native smugglers, who used to introduce it in defiance of the laws, and the venal officials who connived at their misdeeds. We know that native cultivation has for a long time shared with foreign commerce the odium of the supply of the drug. British policy is not solely responsible for the demoralization of the people by opium; but neither can we clear our country of a grave share of the responsibility. We have been accomplices in the injury of the people. We cannot get rid of that fact. The particular manner and measure of our responsibility for all the evil opium has wrought in China, the reader may deduce for himself from the record presented in the earlier portion of our work of the actual facts of that policy. But to repudiate responsibility altogether, because the Chinese need not have bought opium unless they chose, or because they at last consented to its introduction under a duty, reminds us of Pilate's washing his hands.

(2) The same remarks as to England's share in the matter apply also to the impoverishment of the country through the use of opium. This indictment is something over and above the direct noxiousness of the drug. Even were it a harmless luxury, China *could not afford* the land, the labour, the time, the money which indulgence in it costs her. We need no Puritanical aversion to enjoyment in order to be convinced of this. On the contrary, we may contend that every innocent gratification is of itself a clear gain to the human race, and to be encouraged and supported by the philanthropist. But no one will dispute that necessaries must be placed before luxuries. Flowers are beautiful and fragrant, but we cannot afford to attend to floriculture until the food supply is secured. China is a poor country, densely populated, the people closely pressing upon the means of subsistence. The nation cannot spend its annual millions upon opium without multitudes being deprived of food and clothing. This, which is true in the general, is visible in innumerable particular cases. Opium-smoking prevails among the poor as well as the rich, and the poor supply the pipe at the expense of their backs and their bellies; and not their own only, but those of their wives and

children. In round numbers, a pound weight of
foreign opium costs China a pound sterling in money.
In 1872 the importation was 8,039,246 lbs., for
which China paid 8,261,381*l*.[5] Even this does but
represent a fraction of the loss to the country; for
there must be added to it all the loss of vigour and
inclination for useful labour which are the consequences of smoking.

(3) The "opium" war directly, and our subsequent wars indirectly, must be attributed to our
British opium policy. There were other causes of
irritation between the two Governments, and we
cannot acquit the Chinese of blame for unreasonable
and unjust behaviour in their dealings with foreigners.
But throughout all our intercourse with them this
baneful trade has been one of the chief causes of
animosity. The damage, immediate and indirect,
caused by these wars to the Chinese Government and
people cannot be calculated.

(4) As a consequence, the influence of the Chinese
Government has been greatly weakened, and its
power to preserve order and avert anarchy greatly
lessened. After our "opium" war came the terrible
ravages of the Taepings, which laid waste a large
portion of the land and destroyed millions of lives.
The prestige of the existing dynasty is shattered.
An impression widely prevails that its years are
numbered. People anticipate a change, and yet
know not from what quarter to look for it. Past
history teaches that revolutions in China are not

[5] China, No. 3 (1873), Part II., Commercial Reports, p. 222.

the affair of a few months or a year or two, but
that generally a long period of anarchy and distress
has marked the downfall of one dynasty and rise of
its successor.   For recent political troubles in China
foreign influence is in great part accountable, and of
that influence no item has been so mighty, so baneful as opium.

(5) Lastly, the British opium policy has supplied an unanswerable argument for hostility to
foreigners.

No one can estimate the degree to which this
hostility is prejudicial to the welfare of China itself,
and also to foreign intercourse with China.   Among
the records of intercourse between the civilized
nations of Europe and the semi-civilized kingdoms
of the East there is nothing to compare with the
wonderful adoption by Japan of western ideas,
western science, education, manufactures, industries,
and all within the space of a few years.   China
perhaps would not have been as Japan, had there
been no opium in the case.   It might have taken
decades or generations to accomplish in vast China
what was effected in little Japan in a few years.
But the same process, though differing in rate of
progress, might have taken place in China, if from
the first the intercourse of foreign nations had been
conducted on the liberal and enlightened principles
which have characterized our relations with Japan.
Notwithstanding all obstacles, some measure of
progress has taken place in China through her
intercourse with Europe.   But the hindrances have

been great, and the greatest has been, and still is, opium. The literati, the leading governing classes, fear us and hate us, and one of the chief causes of their hatred and their fear is opium. This animosity is a constant hindrance to progress, a constant source of danger.

In the first place it is an absolute barrier to a truly peaceful intercourse. We are not at war with China only because China does not think the time ripe for war with us. But at the back of all our intercourse with the Chinese lies the " inevitable gunboat." Opium and Manchester goods go in, tea and silk go out; the traders bargain, the missionaries preach,—and the gunboat renders all possible. Meantime the Chinese devote the increased resources they acquire through foreign trade to building arsenals, casting cannon, laying up stores of shot and shell. English residents in China, and those who have friends in the country, receive the news of every trifling local disturbance with anxiety—for Europeans there are living on the edge of a volcano, and no one can tell when the next eruption may break out.

This animosity is a barrier to the progress of trade and introduction of improvements. Our merchants ask for increased facilities of trade and they are refused. They propose to place steamers on the inland waters and meet with a rebuff. Railways, telegraphs, coal-mining, gold-mining—everything is persistently opposed. A line of railway is offered as a gift to the Emperor and is refused.

This unreasonable antagonism to all introduction of foreign methods and appliances for the development of the resources of China is an injury to us, but it is a thousandfold injury to China itself. The civilization of the country, the increased knowledge, comfort, happiness, of three hundred millions of the human race are retarded, and many generations to come may be defrauded of them—and why? The proximate cause is Chinese hostility to us; but what is the cause of that hostility? Let any one read Williamson's " Travels in North China," and he will gain some notion of the magnificent natural capabilities of the country, of its inexhaustible mineral resources. The loss to China, the loss to the world, through the neglect of these is beyond all power of estimating. Our coal supply in England threatens to come to an end: yet we ship cargo after cargo every year to the far East, employing our vessels and our sailors in carrying more than half round the world the mineral which exists already stored up there in the soil. And this is but one small item in the altogether incalculable total loss which results from an animosity we have done our best to deserve.

Finally, this anti-foreign animus of the Chinese is an almost insuperable barrier to their reception of the Gospel. Some measure of opposition to Christianity for its own sake was only to be expected. Old faiths, old prejudices, will not submit to be overthrown and swept away without a struggle. If the Chinese followers of Confucius cannot bear to

hear his supremacy assailed by a strange name unknown to their fathers, without impatience and
wrath, this is only analogous to the course of human
nature in general.   But, besides all this, opium has
created an immense obstacle to the patient hearing
of the claims of Christianity.   " By their fruits ye
shall know them," the heathen cry : and the better-
educated class, those who take a more intelligent
interest in national affairs, stop their ears against
the sound of the Gospel, and, as far as their authority
extends, prevent every one else from hearing it.[6]

Such are the results of British opium policy.   Our
pitiful dependence upon a dishonourable traffic for
the support of our empire, and the encouragement
of a destructive vice among the Chinese, alone condemn the policy past all defence.   But to the
thoughtful mind contemplating the great world-
drama of Humanity, slowly enacting through the
ages, perhaps the ulterior consequences will seem
altogether to surpass in magnitude of evil these
direct visible results.   Great Britain, by its sovereignty of India and pre-eminent influence in China,
wields a mighty influence over the destinies of more
than half the human race.   For a little while (who

---

[6] In 1869 Dr. Schereweseky, of the American Episcopal
Mission, visited Kaifengfu, the capital of Honan, to inquire into
the condition of the remnant of the Jews residing there.   A mob,
collected by the literati, drove him from the city, shouting after
him, "You killed our Emperor ; you destroyed our summer
palace; you bring poison here to ruin us ; and now you come to
teach us virtue!"   This was a forcible expression of objections
familiar to every missionary.

can say for how long ?) the hegemony of the world is ours.   For the time being we are peaceful, rich, and powerful—better fitted than any other people to meet the demands of this vast empire and influence upon our resources.   Never since mankind began has any nation had so splendid an opportunity as that which is now put into our hands.   We are summoned to pour the new life-blood of our religion, our liberty, our commerce, our science, our education, into the stagnant veins of the dying East.   A right and noble discharge of our national duty now would go far towards regenerating the world, and bringing in the golden age.   What then can be comparable in importance to this, that Great Britain should have a clear conscience and an unselfish aim ?   We have the material resources, we have the physical force : what we want is the moral character, that we may use our unexampled opportunity for the welfare of mankind.   But what avails our profession of desire to wield our sceptre in the highest interests of humanity, whilst this opium-scandal remains ?   While British supremacy rests upon the opium revenue, our national glory is rotten at its foundation ; our national character is a hindrance to the progress of truth, righteousness, and peace among the vast nations of the East, and our national bad repute fearfully counteracts the efforts of private individuals amongst us to do good to our oriental fellow-creatures.   Perhaps the worst result of our opium revenue is, that it chains us to the low standard of political morality which suffered its growth.

CHAPTER VIII.

If any clear lesson is derivable from our retrospect of British opium policy, it is this, that we have been led astray by the golden lure of an abundant and easily-gotten revenue. We must demand, therefore, both as proof of repentance, and as indispensable basis for a new line of policy that the revenue must be abandoned, so far as it interferes with our doing justice to our own people and to China. We say so far as justice demands, because free trade in opium would be a worse evil than the present state of things, and unless the cultivation of the poppy be absolutely interdicted throughout our empire, taxation, in some form, would be a simple necessity. In a previous chapter we contended that the true principle on which such articles should be made subjects of taxation is that taxation limits consumption, and so tends to check the abuses consequent upon it. According to this principle, the aim of Government is to diminish, not to multiply consumption, and the income accruing from taxation is not its primary object. If, then, we would rectify the errors of our opium policy, we must be prepared to sacrifice a portion, if not the whole, of our present gains from it. Unless we start with this honest determination, it is vain to seek expedients for improvement. While the cry is, "We cannot do without the revenue," no proposal of change will get an impartial hearing, or every attempted reform will be but a change of form, not a substantial remedy. We must come to the firm resolve that we will consent no longer to maintain our Indian empire by a revenue derived from the vices of mankind, and upheld by our physical force against the claims of justice. Let us do right, and let the revenue go. When this is our sincere language; when we are prepared to abolish an unrighteous trade, and to bear the loss; then we may, without hypocrisy, take in hand to consider what is actually required of us, and how we may best set our house in order.

It would be folly to disguise the fact that this sacrifice would involve serious difficulty. This is not an essay on Indian finance, nor is the writer an expert on that subject. But the Parliamentary Reports make it quite clear that to do away with, or only to cripple, the opium revenue would be cutting off the right arm of Indian resources. Seven millions out of a revenue of 50,000,000*l.*; the boldest financier will hesitate before he lightly tampers with such a sum as that. A source of income of such magnitude would be treated with the greatest solicitude even in an English budget; in India, it seems like proposing self-destruction to suggest interference with it. And now, at this point of our discussion, we find that the old recommendation of the opium revenue, " that it is drawn from foreigners," cuts our own fingers. If we were advocating the abandonment of our excise revenue in England, by some measure that contemplated the extinction of the drinking customs of the country, the immediate loss to the revenue would be immense, but the saving to the country by the cessation of wasteful and injurious expenditure would be so much vaster, that it could easily bear some new form of taxation to replace the abandoned excise. Not so in this case; for the opium, which produces all but a mere fraction of the revenue, is consumed out of India. The loss would fall upon the Indian treasury; the material and moral gain would be enjoyed by the Chinese. The inhabitants of India are not responsible for the opium policy, although they have enjoyed its proceeds. To distress India in order to relieve China, would be to inflict undeserved hardship. Thus we are placed in a grave dilemma.

The present writer frankly confesses that he has for long regarded England's connexion with opium with a feeling of hopelessness. Nations, like individuals, may bring upon themselves evil consequences of their follies and crimes, from which even repentance seems to hold out no way of escape. Strenuous exertion may break the chain of evil habit, and yet its consequences linger on long after it is broken. England paid twenty millions to clear her-

self from the blood-guiltiness of Negro slavery; but
we are not clear of its consequences to-day. It seems
but a little while since the savage outbreak of the
negroes in Jamaica, and the deplorable excesses of
our own officers, demonstrated that the melancholy
legacy of slavery is not yet paid up in full. Do we,
then, think that our noble effort to atone for the
wrong was in vain?

For answer, look at the United States. Contemplate the fearful penalty they had to pay for obsti-
nate adherence to the wicked system. Agonies of a
gigantic civil war, the blood of her best and bravest
poured out like water, treasure that would have
purchased the liberty of every slave in the Union
squandered in devastating its provinces and slaugh-
tering its citizens; and after all was over, dis-
organization and distress, internal anarchy in the
conquered states, and smouldering embers of fierce
hatred which even now send up their flashes of
wrath and bloodshed. Truly to do right, however
late, at whatever cost, is always safest, wisest, best.
Let us face our difficulty manfully; let us shake off
the palsying influence of despair, and endeavour to
see what is the right course to take, prepared to
endure whatever sacrifice may be required of us,
assured that to do right is always and in every
sense the only right thing to do.

It seems to be accepted as an axiom by our
Government that India must bear her own burdens,
must pay for all the expenses of her own administration. The wisdom and justice of this axiom cannot

be disputed. During the recent famine in Bengal some voices pleaded for a grant of British money as a befitting exhibition of Christian philanthropy towards our perishing fellow-subjects. Our legislature, supported by a large share, if not the unanimous concurrence, of public opinion, was deaf to this plea, as unnecessary, and not in the true interests of India. How much more unreasonable it would be to propose that any of the ordinary burdens of the Indian Government should be defrayed by the British tax-payer. We govern India for the good of India, and whatever were the faults of our fathers in the acquisition of that country, whatever the blemishes and imperfections of our administration now, there is no doubt that not only do we desire that British rule should be a benefit to India, but that it actually is so, and that to an extent not easily calculable. As an ordinary rule, therefore, every principle of righteousness and fair-dealing demands that India should support the expenses of her own Government, and that they should not fall upon the already heavily-burdened inhabitants of the British Isles.

Is this tantamount to saying that the opium revenue must on no account be disturbed, at the peril of Indian national bankruptcy? At first sight it would seem so, but a closer scrutiny gives us a gleam of hope. Since the failure of the Indian income-tax, no new tax remains to be proposed in India.[1] But if the loss of the opium revenue cannot

[1] Since the above was written, the *Spectator* has suggested that

be replaced by additional taxes, there is no such absolute impossibility of diminution of expenditure. The English mind is getting familiar with the suspicion that our Indian Government, though very good for the country, is expensive; too expensive for its resources. This is not the place to enter upon a minute inquiry into Indian expenditure; but if the opium revenue is to be touched, it will necessitate a thorough, searching scrutiny of every item of the accounts, which of itself would be a great boon to India, and perhaps in the long-run more than indemnify her for the loss of opium profits. There is an old saying which says, "Necessity is the mother of invention." While these annual millions of opium revenue continue on the books, reduction of expenditure may appear impossible; but let the opium revenue be boldly struck out of the account, and we may indulge a sanguine expectation that retrenchment may go a long way towards meeting the deficiency. Besides retrenchment, it is possible that a Committee of the House of Commons instructed to discover ways and means to deal with Indian finance *minus* the opium revenue, might light upon certain payments now saddled upon India, which properly ought to come out of our Exchequer. India ought to bear her own burdens; but are we sure that she is not now bearing part of ours? An extract from a speech by

if the opium revenue had to be abandoned, a tax upon tobacco might supply the deficiency, though at the risk of great unpopularity.

Mr. Fawcett, at the Mansion House, on 14th April, 1874, will explain what we mean. Mr. Fawcett was speaking about the proposal to assist India to bear the heavy burdens of this present famine by assistance from the English Government and objecting to a grant of our public money, or a guarantee; he remarked, "But there is a pecuniary assistance which at the present time—and not only at the present time, but in all succeeding years—the English Government can render to the Indian people. If Lord Salisbury, one of the most influential members of a powerful Government, will insist that the pecuniary relations between England and India should be revised, if he will utilize the interest which is now felt in India, by insisting that India should bear no charge improperly—that no burden should be cast upon her improperly by the British Government—then, without any of the disadvantages of a grant of public money or the guarantee of a loan, he will render a signal and permanent service to India; he will alleviate the pressure on her finances, he will provide her with funds which will prevent the recurrence of these unfortunate famines. He will do something more; he will knit the two countries more closely together, because he will make the Indian people feel that our government over them is henceforward to be placed upon a more just and equitable basis. The present would scarcely be the occasion to enter into any detailed description of charges which are improperly thrown upon India by the English Government. No fact, however, was more clearly brought out in the evidence given before the Indian Finance Committee, which sat for three years. I am now going to quote to you the opinions—two very remarkable opinions. I could multiply them indefinitely. The language is strong, but it is not my language; it is the language of men speaking with official experience. One who held one of the highest official positions in India has declared that Indian finance is constantly being sacrificed to the wishes of the Horse Guards and the exigencies of English estimates. Another official, with thirty-five years' experience of Indian office, has declared that he never knew a single instance where the pecuniary interests of England and India came into contact, in which India had the slightest chance of obtaining fair play. Let this now be done; let the Government and the House of Commons carefully go through all the financial relations between England and India; let the English Government understand that it is the wish of the English people, that because India is weak, unrepresented, and powerless, she should not bear a single charge which we would not venture to cast upon our colonies, and then I am as confident as I can be of anything that India would derive a pecuniary assistance, which would be of the utmost importance to her in this time of severe financial pressure." [2]

[2] Compare with these statements of Mr. Fawcett, the Report of the East India Finance Committee, 28th July, 1874. This Report deals with the military expenditure alone, and with respect to this states, " Your Committee have received an impression that

The report of this meeting states that loud applause frequently interrupted Mr. Fawcett's remarks, and that at the close of his speech loud and continued applause attested that he had touched the right chord, in appealing to every Englishman's desire to do justice to India. May we take that influential gathering at the Mansion House, in the heart of the City of London, to represent the true feeling of Britain on this matter? Mark well what Mr. Fawcett meant. He meant that now at this time we are doing injustice to India, in plain terms robbing India, by imposing upon her charges which ought fairly to be borne by England. He meant that henceforth certain charges, not a small sum, a sum great enough to be of the utmost importance to a country whose revenue is fifty millions, should be transferred from the Indian account to our own account. Is England prepared to do right in this matter at the expense of her own pocket? If so, then there is hope that even so serious a difficulty as the loss of the opium revenue may be encountered and overcome.

For if once our country's sense of justice is fairly awakened, determined to do right by India, we may be sure that it will not stop at a bare readjustment of burdens. If we once for all adopted a firm resotion to get rid of the opium scandal at any cost, and to plant our Indian Empire on the secure basis of justice

charges have, in some instances, been imposed upon India, which ought to have been borne by England." The report indicates that our financial relations with India require re-examination.

to all, we should then remember that India is encumbered with this huge opium difficulty through the fault of another, and not through her own. Granted that it is a just and sound principle that India should pay her own Government expenses, this opium revenue occupies an exceptional position. British policy made it what it is, and brought India to be dependent upon it. If the conscience of Britain cannot abide the opium revenue any longer, and demands its abrogation, then it seems only just and reasonable that Britain should come to the help of India if any temporary embarrassment should befall her, in consequence of interference with this source of income. After all, it must be remembered that however much to the advantage of India our Government of that country may be, we were not invited to assume that Government. We did not consult the will of India, but possessed ourselves of the sovereignty by right of conquest. We are bound therefore to govern the country within its means. If we cannot rule India without availing ourselves of a revenue condemned by the first principles of morality, or except by the imposition of burdens which would be more injurious to the people than anything they might have to suffer under native rule or misrule, then we had better retire from India altogether. There is, however, no reason to apprehend that we shall find ourselves pushed to that humiliating extremity. Economy and readjustment will meet all the demands of the case. India can afford to pay for all the Government she really needs, and we must learn to restrict the machinery and operations of Government within the limits that she can afford to pay for. But it is quite probable that the loss of the opium millions might bring on a temporary state of insolvency, when the help of her rich and powerful sovereign might be needed for awhile to sustain her credit, and bear her safely through the crisis. This we must be prepared to give. Until this is laid down as settled, it is waste of time to discuss any plans for amending our opium policy. But if it be granted that we are prepared to give up the revenue, so far as necessary, and to undertake the consequences, we may go on to consider the plans which have been proposed to relieve us from our dependence upon opium.

The first plan, and the simplest, is the short and sharp method of entirely interdicting all cultivation of the poppy within British India, and stopping all exportation from the native states by the refusal of a passage for the drug through our territory to the coast. Dr. Lockhart says, " The far better plan would be for the Government directly to prohibit the growth of opium in all its territory, except for direct medical use, and also not to allow it even to pass through its territory from the independent states. Whether this could be carried out as a political measure cannot be discussed here." Several years later, in the pages of the *Nonconformist*, the Rev. Griffith John, of Hankow, reiterated the same demand, " But what is wanted is *absolute* prohibition.

England should not allow this poisonous plant to be grown in or pass through any part of her territories, save for medicinal purposes. Whether this can be done consistently with our constitutional laws I must leave others to discuss. I only maintain that the laws of justice, honour, and fairness demand that England should wash her hands clean of this foul trade as soon as possible. She owes this to herself, and she owes this to China."

This missionary demand for total prohibition is natural enough, because it is the Chinese demand. We have heard Prince Kung and Wen Seang urge it upon Sir Rutherford Alcock, and, through the ambassador, upon the British Government and the British public. The Chinese demand it because they are used to treat such matters in this way. Whenever anything appears to be injurious to the health, welfare, or morals of the people, the Chinese Government at once attacks it by direct prohibition. So thoroughly accustomed are they to this mode of thought and action that the Chinese Government and people cannot easily conceive that any other Government could see any objections, except selfish ones, to this course. But it is noticeable that Dr. Lockhart and Mr. John urge adoption of their root-and-branch remedy under an expressed doubt as to its practicability : though they do not indicate wherein the impracticability may be supposed to lie. Now to suggest a remedy which is either impossible, or contrary to our constitutional laws, is equivalent to suggesting no remedy at all. But let us consider it for ourselves, and see if we can detect the practical difficulty.

One may dispose at once of the counter argument that to prohibit the poppy in India would be utterly useless, because if we do not supply the Chinese with opium, others will. They will get it from Turkey, from Persia, they will grow it themselves. They must and will have opium, and therefore we may as well have the profit of supplying them. To this we reply in a word, that we are not now planning to save China, but to save England; we are not consulting how the Chinese may be cured of an enslaving vice; but how we may extricate ourselves from an unjust and dishonourable policy. If the missionaries have shown us *the right* course to take, let us take it, in God's name, even though never a single Chinese should smoke a single ounce of opium the less. But, besides this, the argument is unsound. It is true that if the Indian supply were abolished next year, it would not annihilate the opium-smoking of China. But it would certainly deal the vice a grievous blow. Nearly the whole foreign supply is from India. If this were suddenly cut off, the remaining supply from outside would be insignificant, and years must elapse before it could swell to the dimensions of our Indian export. The effect on China would be electrical. The native opium would remain; and that would meet the difficulty urged by Mr. Cooper and others, that, if the Chinese were suddenly deprived of opium, multitudes of them would die. No doubt an utter lack of opium would kill off a portion of the confirmed smokers. Far be any thought of cruelty from us, but we cannot but think that if the nation could be delivered finally, once for all, from the vice of opium-smoking, through the somewhat earlier death of a proportion of the more besotted smokers who are killing themselves already, the price paid for emancipation would not be too high. But there would not be a total lack. The native opium is there, and the Turkish opium would be still in the market. The price would be enhanced, of course, and the very poor smokers would die, because they could not afford to buy it. They do die now, however, and this is a very serious reason for objecting to the opium trade altogether. It is strange to notice how the defenders of the monopoly contend in the same breath, that it would be cruelty to the Chinese to deprive them of our Indian opium, and that if we give up the trade, others will soon fill up the gap. If, however, the Indian Government were to abandon the trade, the Chinese proposition made to Sir R. Alcock, that both countries might simultaneously limit the cultivation, and abolish it gradually, deserves serious consideration. Determined supporters of the monopoly will ridicule the notion of the Chinese being actuated by good faith, or, if so, having the slightest power to carry their part of the compact into execution. But those who look at the case impartially will see no reason to doubt the sincerity of the Chinese Government, and though their confidence in the administrative capacity of that Government may not be without misgivings, it will at least be sufficient to make them willing to give it a fair trial. The objection, therefore, that the utter extirpation of the poppy in India would not extinguish opium-smoking in China, goes for nothing. It would do all that _we_ could do towards attaining that desired result; it would certainly have an immense effect, and probably would lead to a very great permanent diminution of the vice, if not to its actual extinction.

Another objection, that to prohibit the poppy cultivation would be unjust and oppressive to our own subjects, and to those of the native princes of India, may also be easily disposed of. As to our own province of Bengal, the monopoly has been at the absolute disposal of the Government from the beginning of the century. Not a single private individual has been allowed to cultivate an acre of poppy at his own will and pleasure, nor have the ryots enjoyed the profits where they did cultivate it. The Government has bought the opium at its own fixed price, calculated so as to allow them a fair return for their labour, sufficient to make the toil popular generally, though not, it would seem, always. But the Government has always reserved the _profits_ of the monopoly for itself, and injustice would be done to no individual by its relinquishing and prohibiting the trade altogether. The case of Malwa opium is more difficult. There the cultivation has been in private hands, and the native princes have obtained certain advantages from it. But our Government has always had and exercised the right to impose what duty it pleased on the opium passing through its territory to the sea, and if a prohibitory duty were imposed, no one could question the legal right. It might seem hard to the native that he could no longer enrich himself at the expense of the Chinese; but he would soon see that it would be unreasonable to expect the British Government to allow him to continue the trade after it had been stopped in Bengal. And, as in Calcutta, so in the west, our Government has all along taken the lion's share of the profit by the enormous duty, and would itself be the chief loser. A short notice given would satisfy all vested interests, and, after a little while, no one in India would be the worse. What, then, hinders the adoption of this simple and effectual way of ridding ourselves once for all of the opium difficulty? What is it that made the missionaries doubtful about their project? Simply, we believe, the practical impossibility of getting the mass of the English nation to see that this is the right course to pursue.

We say the practical impossibility of getting Englishmen *to see* that it is their duty. We do not say that it is not the duty of our Government, but that it is hopeless to convince our people of it. It may seem strange that we hesitate to give a decided negative to the question whether it is our duty; that we regard it as quite possible that it may be the right thing, and yet despair of getting our countrymen to see it. Are Englishmen, then, so

obtuse, or so biassed by self-interest, that the right
has no chance of gaining the day among them ? An
immense amount of obtuseness of perception, and of
reluctance to sacrifice personal interest, would
undoubtedly have to be encountered by advocates of
extirpation; but it is not that which daunts us,
The right and the true have triumphed in England
over all such antagonism often and often before, nor
should we fear to attempt the struggle again. But
the difficulty here inheres in the nature of the case.
Without trying to define what is the limit of Government action, all will agree that it will be considerably modified by the wishes and expectations of the
governed. A law which would be arbitrary and
unjust if enforced upon a reluctant people, may be
righteous and good, if the sentiments of the governed
approve or even demand it. In England, for the
Government to say, you shall not make malt, you
shall not distil spirits, would be regarded by the
majority of the people as an oppressive interference
with the liberty of the citizen. Englishmen, therefore, naturally suppose that a similar legislation
about opium in India would be oppressive to the
people there. But would it ? We think not. In
India, as in China, the people believe in arbitrary
government; they expect their rulers to support
morality by legal enactments; they not only would
not murmur at restrictions upon their freedom of
action which Englishmen would not bear, but they
positively regard it as the duty, as the *raison-d'être*
of Government to enforce such restrictions. With

regard to China, we have no doubt that it is the clear duty of the Emperor to prohibit the cultivation of the poppy, not only because opium is a terrible blight to the physical and moral welfare of his subjects, but because the moral sense of the people demands this prohibition. The Chinese believe in arbitrary government and paternal legislation. " The Emperor," they think, "is placed over us by Heaven, is Heaven's visible vicegerent, to carry out Heaven's laws. It is his duty, his province, to prevent our injuring ourselves with opium, just as in every family the father ought to prevent his children from injuring themselves with it. As the father is clothed with authority to compel his children for their good, so has the Emperor a divine right and duty to compel us all in such matters." In China, therefore, the edicts ordering extirpation of the poppy no more offend the moral sense of the people, than do the edicts intended to repress brigandage.

What is the difference between India and China in this respect ? We doubt if there is any. Let any one read the evidence given by persons well acquainted with India to the Select Committee, and he will see abundant reason to conclude that the arbitrary paternal idea of Government is much more natural to the Hindoo mind than our English notion of representative Government, and non-interference with individual liberty. A Maine Liquor Law would probably be highly popular in India, and if we could see the Hindoo or the Mussulman's mental interior, we should most likely discover that he believes the British Government does not pass such a law, not from any respect for individual liberty, but because the Sahib himself likes his brandy-pawnee too well; and because the excise is profitable to the treasury. Extirpation of opium might be very unpopular, for a brief time, among a very small minority who now make profit out of it, but probably would receive the emphatic approval of the millions. Now this concurrence of the people is a most essential element in considering the duty of a Government: if our Government could confer a great moral benefit upon the people committed to their charge, and check or annihilate a vicious practice, and if the people themselves would give their moral support to legislation towards such ends, it seems difficult to assign reasons why it is not *the duty* of Government to do so.

But the moment we pass out of the oriental atmosphere of despotism into the free air of English individual liberty and responsibility, one perceives the practical impossibility of convincing John Bull of this. It is not now a Board of Directors meeting in Leadenhall Street which we have to convince, nor is it her Majesty's ministers for the time being, nor even the two Houses of Parliament. If the opium monopoly were a mere matter of detail in Indian administration, if it involved only a few hundreds of thousands which India would hardly miss out of her fifty millions, all we should have to do would be to convince those leading Indian officials whose counsel

in such matters the British Government would be
sure to respect and adopt.   But the question is far
too important to be settled by any cabinet council,
or even by a momentary expression of opinion in the
House of Commons.   No Government could venture
to touch it, unless assured that popular opinion in
England demanded the change, and would support
the Government in the searching investigations, the
great financial reforms, and the possible transfer of
a portion of the Indian burdens to English shoulders
which would be required to carry out a legislative
prohibition of the poppy.   We believe that the
heart of England is sound, and that the nation
would support a just and right policy towards India
and China, even at the cost of personal sacrifice.
But then the nation will demand to have it clearly,
overwhelmingly, *proved* that this is the right course
to take, before it will consent to reconstruct the
whole system of Indian finance, and take upon
itself pecuniary burdens from which it is now free.
Who is there that entertains the faintest hope of
convincing the great majority of the English people
that we ought absolutely to prohibit poppy-cultiva-
tion in India?   We cannot *prove* that opium is a
greater curse abroad than alcohol is at home.
Englishmen pride themselves upon logical consistency, and they think that if they allow themselves the liberty of dealing in, and intoxicating
themselves by ardent spirits, then logical consistency
requires them to allow Asiatics full licence to
narcotize themselves with opium if they please.

Then there is the real difficulty of defining what are the proper limits of Government interference in such matters. The majority of Englishmen do not believe in the attempt to create virtue by Act of Parliament. If we say that as regards India, we, the British nation, exercise despotic sovereignty, occupying to them a position analogous to that which the Emperor of China holds towards his subjects, we shall be met with the reply, that as we do not believe in despotic Government in morals and religion, it is not reasonable to expect us to apply it to India, that it is rather our desire to train the Indian people up to our standard of self-government, than to descend to their lower political level: moreover, objectors will point to the failure of the paternal despotism in China in its effort to put down this very vice. In fine, the proposal to extirpate the poppy for the preservation of morality in and outside of our own territory, is but a particular instance of a general principle which is strenuously advocated by a number of excellent men, but at present has found comparatively small favour with the nation at large. When we are generally agreed that it is within the province and duty of Government to guard the people from temptation by the absolute removal of exciting causes, then we may expect that opium will be included among the articles prohibited as noxious to public virtue. At present, however, we have not got so far as to concur in the advisability of passing the Permissive Bill, and no one ventures so much as to suggest a Maine Liquor Law for Great Britain. Until some such measure as at least the milder of these two has attained the support of a majority of the British nation, it would be hopeless to expect the nation to legislate for the extirpation of the poppy in India. Such a proposition, therefore, can only be regarded as a protest against an evil, not as a step towards practical remedy.

The proposition we must next consider comes to us with the recommendation of the great name of Lord Lawrence, than which higher authority on Indian affairs could hardly be adduced. Not having succeeded in procuring his original letter, we quote Dr. Lockhart. " Sir John Lawrence has given advice which, if adopted, would at least relieve the Government from the odium of being an opium merchant. Let it withhold the advances to the cultivation, break up its opium godowns, have no part in the monopoly; and instead of the profit arising from trading in the drug, charge it with a heavy export duty as it passes through Calcutta, doing in Bengal what is done in Bombay in this particular. The Government would thus be freed from the anomalous position which it now occupies before the world, and the entire responsibility rest on the opium merchants, and others who engage in the opium traffic."

Sir William Muir, in a Minute [3] dated 22nd February, 1868, advocates an inquiry into the desirability

[3] Calcutta Blue Book, 1870, p. 1.

of giving up the monopoly for the Malwa pass-
system, on these grounds :—

" *Primâ facie* the change proposed would remove
a blemish from the Administration without imperilling the finances. That cannot be an edifying
position for the Government to occupy, in which it
has to determine year by year the quantity of opium
which it will bring to sale, in which there is a
constant inducement for it to trim the market, and
in which its haste to secure wider harvests and
larger returns has repeatedly recoiled upon the
trade, stimulated baneful speculation and gambling
in Central and Western India, and ended in much
misery. I do not speak of the undignified aspect of
the British Government growing, manufacturing,
and selling the drug—performing, in fact, all the
functions of producer and speculator. I will merely
ask what the impression is upon the mind when we
see Holkar performing the functions of opium trader,
which are now discharged by the Government of
Bengal.

" The change would relieve the British Government from the odious imputation of pandering to
the vice of China by over-stimulating production,
over-stocking the market, and flooding China with
the drug, in order to raise a wider and more secure
revenue to itself—an imputation, of which at least
on one occasion, I fear that we are not wholly guilt-
less. A few years ago, when the Government of
Bengal was straining every nerve to extend the
cultivation of the poppy, I was witness to the

discontent of the agricultural population in certain districts west of the Jumma, from which the crop was for the first time being raised. Where the system of advances has long been in vogue, and the mode of preparing the drug well understood, no doubt the poppy is a popular crop; though even there the system of Government monopoly gives to Government officers a power of interference over those who have once taken their advances, which must be liable to abuse. But the case to which I allude was that of new districts where the poppy had not hitherto been grown, and into which the Bengal Board were endeavouring to extend the cultivation by the bait of large advances among an unwilling peasantry, and at the risk of inoculating them with a taste for a deleterious drug, and all this with the sole view of securing a wider area of poppy cultivation, and thus a firmer grasp of the China market. Witnessing this when on circuit in 1864, the impropriety of the position was to my mind so painful that, as the Governor-General may perhaps recollect, I ventured at the time to address his Excellency directly on the subject.

" By retiring from the monopoly the Government of India will avoid these and all other unseemly imputations. China wants opium : our traders and merchants are ready to supply it. The licence duty will support the revenue, and thus the action of Government will be that of check, and no longer of stimulus. The fluctuations in the demands of China will be met, in the ordinary course of trade, by

corresponding variations in the supply from India.
The area of cultivation will be adjusted by the direct
action of the Chinese themselves, upon speculators
and producers, and will no longer depend upon the
arbitrary will of the Government."

Sir William Muir's recommendation is that the
Government should retire gradually from its opium
business, giving facilities to private capitalists to
purchase the buildings and stock, so that no sudden
shock would affect the trade. He calculates that a
tax of Rs. 700 per chest, both on Bengal and
Bombay opium, would bring in a revenue of six
millions, half a million more than the average of the
five years preceding his Minute. The Government
would not throw the trade entirely open, but still
retain a restrictive power by permitting manufacture
only under a system of licences, and he also suggests
a licence fee of three or five rupees per acre for
cultivation.

Nothing could more palpably exhibit the impossibility of any proposition whatever receiving a fair
and impartial consideration from bigoted supporters
of the monopoly, than the various replies to this
temperate and well-considered proposal which are
on record in the Calcutta Blue-books. It is curious
that while " the Governor of *Bombay* in council can
only see that the reasons advanced for the change
appear to be of the greatest weight :" [4] and Mr. L.
Reid, Commissioner of Customs in *Bombay*, writes,
" the disadvantages of the Government monopoly

Calcutta Blue Book, 1870, p. 13.

are so clearly pointed out that its further retention will surely find no advocacy, and its death-knell may well be sounded :" [5] the officials on the *Bengal* side can see nothing whatever but misapprehension and absurdity in all the objections brought against the monopoly. Arguments have been brought forward by Bengal civilians in defence of the monopoly which, to ordinary minds, would tell powerfully against it. One is that if the Government cease to make advances, " a very large portion of the hereditary cultivators will abandon the cultivation of the poppy plant, and take to other remunerative crops ; and after the cultivation of the poppy has been once abandoned, it will be most difficult to re-establish it." [6] And the very people who advance this argument, in the very same paper, are astonished at Sir W. Muir and others for proposing to abolish the monopoly, because then the poppy " will be grown in small patches for local consumption in almost every village and hamlet in Bengal," and the whole population of India will be exposed to the evil of an unrestricted supply of the drug. But when we find persons gravely arguing that " the drug, which in its pure state is not pernicious, if not used to excess, will be rendered so by adulteration with all sorts of deleterious ingredients," we can only marvel at the pitch of fanatic admiration of their profitable system to which these gentlemen have arrived. It is quite intelligible that opium merchants like Messrs.

[5] *Ibid.*, same page.
[6] Report East India Finance, 1871, Appendix, p. 525.

Jardine, Matheson, and Co., should regard their beloved drug as heaven's chief blessing to China; but
it is almost past belief that any men not biassed by
direct pecuniary considerations should put forth such
arguments as these.

Most surprising of all is the apparent inability to
see the immorality of the monopoly. Its advocates
are too blind to be called wilfully blind; they must
have become actually blind. Sir R. Temple, "does
not see the moral objections to the monopoly, and,
if there be such, the change proposed would not set
them right." Mr. H. S. Maine expresses himself
more forcibly still : " the true moral wrong, if wrong
there be, consists in selling opium to the Chinese,
and the only way of abating it would be absolutely
to prohibit the cultivation of the poppy in British
India, and to prevent the exportation of opium from
the Native States. The British Government is sufficiently despotic to effect this; and, *for moral purposes, there is no distinction between what a despotic
Government does itself, and what it permits its subjects
to do.*" [7] It really is a fine psychological study, to
hear such men produce such arguments, and
evidently in perfect good faith. It proves what we
said before, that while the revenue is allowed to
remain, it is vain to expect clear moral vision about
opium. A mighty shower of gold is continually
falling around these otherwise able and keen-sighted
men, and it blinds them as completely as ever snow-
storm blinded bewildered traveller. Nothing wil

[7] Calcutta Blue Book, 1870, p. 9.

enlighten them; but we may try the effect of an illustration or two. The British Government is sufficiently despotic in India to close a considerable number, if not all the idol temples: therefore its not doing so is exactly equivalent to its building and endowing those temples. Here in England, our Government is sufficiently despotic to put down horse-races, therefore, until Parliament interferes with the turf, our Government is in fact equally responsible as if it supported the races by grants of public money and conducted them by Government salaried jockeys. But why accumulate illustrations? The fallacy of these arguments is obvious. There is a vast deal of difference between what a Government does, and what it merely tolerates. Whether it is right to permit private individuals to grow opium for sale to the Chinese is one question; whether our Indian Government ought itself to grow it is quite another. There may be, in fact there is, considerable difference of opinion about the first question: there is none whatever about the second, except among those suffering from gold-blindness.

"But," in effect, say Sir R. Temple and Mr. Maine, " Sir William Muir promises us as good a revenue under his system as we enjoy now with the monopoly. It's as broad as it's long. India grows the opium ; China smokes it: our Government gets the money. Where is the practical difference?" This hits the blemish of Sir W. Muir's scheme. It is permeated by far too tender a concern for the revenue. Granted that if such a scheme had been carried on from the

first, our Indian Government would be free from the
shameful reproach under which it now labours; we
must remember that the monopoly has been an
existing fact during the whole of this century, and
for the Government to place all the results of its
long years of application of capital and talent to the
drug-business at the disposal of private capitalists
is something more than mere permission of private
enterprise.   One may confidently affirm that if the
Indian Government had from the first left opium
alone, except as an object to be taxed as heavily as
it would bear, the opium revenue would never have
become what it is.   To withdraw now in such a
cautious gradual manner, as to invite, even assist,
private capitalists to enter into all our business, and
secure to us an equal return, though in another form,
is not an honest and thorough abandonment of the
monopoly.   It would be morally a slight improvement
of our position, and would demand some degree of
sacrifice for the sake of principle; because the
change could not be effected without risk, and, once
effected, the Government's direct responsibility would
cease, and with it would cease its direct power to
raise a revenue from opium.   However slowly and
cautiously the transfer of the trade from public to
private hands might be effected; when once transferred, it might languish for want of capital, from
dislike of the ryots to their new employers, from
other unforeseen reasons; and the Government would
then be unable to interfere, but would be left to the
risks of the market.   But on the other hand, the

transfer of the trade to private speculators *might* be attended with opposite results. In principle the change would be admirable, but if in practice the result should turn out to be an increase of the production, it would be a calamity. The last state would be worse than the first. We must scrutinize the plan more narrowly.

Does Sir William Muir's proposition entirely satisfy the demands of justice? We think not. Are we then shut up to Sir R. Temple's *reductio ad absurdum* of total prohibition? Again, we think not. Justice and morality demand that Government should withdraw altogether from encouragement to the opium manufacture; and, if it takes revenue at all, take only that amount which accrues from taxation honestly meant to have a restrictive force. The interference of Government hitherto has been twofold, first in production, then in the sale of the article produced. The Government has devoted capital, the service of its own agents, and its influence among the people to produce opium, and it has devoted its military and naval force and the influence over China acquired thereby to sustain the sale of opium. Both of these illegitimate interferences with the course of trade should be at once abandoned. What would be the result? In India the withdrawal of Government capital, energy and influence would, in all probability greatly diminish the area of land devoted to the poppy, and at once reduce the production. Having resolved that our object is not to save the existing revenue, there is no reason for any gradual relinquishment of the business. When existing contracts are fulfilled, the Government should at once divest itself of its association with the manufacture, by summarily disposing of the buildings and implements, careless whether or not they be purchased by persons intending to use them for their former purpose. It can hardly be doubted, that this withdrawal of the Government from the opium trade would for a time seriously lessen the producing power of the Bengal poppy districts, and lead to a considerable extent of the land being reclaimed from the poppy for the production of other crops. This diminished production in Bengal would of course raise the price of Malwa opium. The Government has the power of meeting this advanced price by an increase in the duty, which would prevent the abandonment of the monopoly being attended by an augmented production in the native states. When the shock of the transition had passed, the Government would have nothing more to do with opium except to levy the highest duty possible, compatible with the prevention of smuggling. The Malwa opium is under control already. In Bengal the taxation might take the three forms, of a licence for cultivation at so many rupees per beegah, a licence for manufacture, which should bring the private factories under Government inspection, and a pass-duty on each chest, before it began its passage to the coast, or was taken up for internal consumption. When all these changes were fairly established, the Government would be free from its anomalous connexion with the production and traffic in a deleterious article, not without a temporary loss of revenue, possibly with a permanent diminution of it.

This would remedy one side of the Government's opium error, but the other still remains, the support of the sale by undue influence upon the Chinese Government. We cannot pretend to make amends for the past without restoring to China that full autonomy in respect to opium of which we have deprived her. We must give to the Chinese Government its natural right of imposing any amount of import duty upon Indian opium, or of prohibiting its introduction altogether. Not only must we withdraw from the coercion hitherto put upon China, but must take precautions in future that our subjects do not infringe the Chinese laws as in times past. If the introduction of opium is again made illegal, we must no longer permit British ships and merchants to violate Chinese laws with a high hand.

This last suggestion, reasonable as it is, will be received with intense disgust by those who would revive the old smuggling trade, if let alone. They will visit the proposition with contempt, and accuse him of Sinophobia who thinks that China ought to be treated with real equity, and not cheated by the mockery of a mere semblance of upright dealing, who sincerely desires to act to an inferior power on the principle "do as you would be done by," instead of snatching at all the advantages which the material and moral inferiority of China places within the reach of a strong and unscrupulous nation. The contempt which such people would express for our intellect and patriotism, we can bear with equanimity, regarding it indeed as an honour. To disinterested and impartial judges it will be easy to establish the simple justice and indispensable necessity of our proposal. Those who have attentively perused the historical part of this essay, cannot fail to have been struck with the strange fact that English merchants and shipmasters on the coast of China occupied a position from 1833 to 1842, which was practically independent of all law. Previous to 1833 the East India Company had the control of the trade, and their superintendent stationed at Canton had power to expel any trader from the port who should infringe the regulations, or so misconduct himself as to provoke a breach of the peace between the nations. The Company acted the part of King Log, so far as smuggling was concerned ; but they had the power if they liked to use it. They withheld their own agents and ships from engaging in the illicit traffic, and might also have restrained all others who only enjoyed the privilege of entrance into the trade by their permission. But after the British Government succeeded to the Company's management of the commerce, even this power of expelling unworthy traders was withdrawn from the new superintendents. The Sovereign under his own royal sign manual authorized his representatives to give good advice in any amount and of any kind he might think proper ; but carefully abstained from clothing him with any power to insure obedience to his instructions. The consequence was that when the critical period arrived, Captain Elliot occupied the undignified position of a hen cackling to her brood of young ducklings who will take to the water. When the power of a simple police magistrate to arrest those who threaten to provoke a breach of the peace, might have saved England and China from a long, bloody, and expensive war, disastrous to China's prosperity and to England's reputation, H.M. Representative found himself deserted by his own Government, and compelled to solicit the Chinese officials to support *his* orders, by *their* physical force.

After the Pottinger treaty, the opium smugglers were practically more independent of law than before. The Chinese now dared not touch them: the English Government would not. If an indiscreet official thought that his country's honour required that the treaty should be carried out on both sides in good faith, he was removed to a distant station, to " teach him not to interfere with the enterprises of British subjects." Consuls and naval officers quick to resent any Chinese infraction of the treaty were applauded for their zeal; but while British subjects openly violated Chinese laws, they must stand by with folded arms. All this of course was necessary while the British Government manufactured and sold the drug which these law-breakers were introducing into China. And if we were going to revive the miserable spectacle of those shameful years, it would be better to continue as we are; a legalized trade based upon armed force is hardly so bad as an illegal trade winked at by our Government, and enjoying its moral, more properly its immoral, support. An outcry would be raised against the *absurdity* of the British Government's doing custom-house duty for the Chinese. 'Surely it is their business to defend their own revenue, not ours;' and so forth. Yet we have done internal military duty for the Chinese, by lending them substantial aid towards putting down the Taeping rebellion. We have done water-police duty for the Chinese by despatching our gun-boats against pirates. We have actually done custom-house work for the Chinese by lending them the men for an Imperial customs' service composed principally of English subjects. All this we have done, and no one saw any absurdity in it; but to prevent Englishmen from continuing an open, notorious violation of Chinese law would have been "absurd," *while an opium revenue had to be collected out of Chinese pockets for India.* But if only we are honestly determined that that opium revenue is to be abandoned to its fate, if we are prepared to pay for the loss of it, if need be, there will be no difficulty in showing the essential rectitude of our coercing all would-be smugglers of our own nation.

First, the obligation rests upon us in common fairness, because we know the inability of the Chinese Government in former times to cope with the wealth and the daring of English opium-smugglers. The intercourse between Great Britain and China is not the equal intercourse of two great nations which have attained to the same degree of civilization. As between England and France, or England and Germany, it is fair enough to say to the other party, we will protect our coasts and our customs, do you protect yours. It would not be fair to China, because the weakness of its Government and the venality of its officials would make it mockery to leave her a helpless prey to the practices of our illicit traders. The Chinese Government did not invite us to China, does not want us in China. We have forced our commerce upon an unwilling people, and the least we can do is to enforce upon our own citizens the observance of the stipulations of those treaties which we extorted from China on their behalf. It would be more decent at once to demand an annual tribute of seven millions sterling from the Chinese than to force them to a commercial intercourse, and, while pretending to recognize their rights, to exact the annual millions through the medium of illicit transactions connived at by our Government.

Not only common fairness would demand this restraint of our own people, but the obligation may be logically deduced from the very text of our treaties. We have said there was a period of several years when British subjects on the coast of China were practically outside the pale of law, at least so far as opium was concerned. But now we have treaty regulations by which the British Government claims and exercises exclusive jurisdiction over its own citizens throughout the remotest districts of the Chinese Empire. These are what are popularly referred to as the ex-territoriality clauses. By these all British subjects, whether resident in the ports, or travelling in the interior, are as independent of all Chinese laws as if they were walking the pavement of Regent-street. The one sole right allowed to the Chinese Government, even to the Emperor himself, is that of handing over the offender against Chinese law to the nearest Consul for trial. This exemption from Chinese jurisdiction entailed the necessity of clothing British officials with authority over residents and travellers in China, and considerable powers have been given to the Consuls and the Judicial tribunal at Shanghai for this purpose. The responsibility for the good conduct of British subjects has therefore been openly assumed. True, Lord Elgin inserted an article into the treaty,[*] implying that the Chinese Government would be left to take care of itself so far as the revenue was concerned. But this exception in favour of British smugglers, necessary when the introduction of opium had not yet been legalized, and our policy was to preserve the opium revenue at any cost, ought surely now to be treated as obsolete. If we honestly determine to give up the opium revenue, there no longer exists a reason for keeping in the treaty a clause so utterly out of harmony with its spirit. Let the clause be erased, and let Britain engage to do

[*] Article xlvi. *Vide* Correspondence relating to Lord Elgin's Mission, p. 353.

her utmost to control British subjects in Chinese waters.

Without a distinct provision of this kind it would be hypocrisy to pretend to allow China her natural right to prohibit opium. The great wealth of the trade, the enterprise and unscrupulousness of those engaging in it, the corruption of a vast number of the Chinese petty officials, the inefficiency of the Chinese police, would render the renewal of smuggling on the most extensive scale probable. If bribery failed, the traders could and would employ armed steamers, the swiftness and armament of which would set Chinese naval cruisers at defiance; unless, indeed, the employment of foreign appliances, and the engagement of foreigners in their service, should render the Chinese more of a match for the smugglers than they used to be.

If the moral sense of the British nation does not demand the absolute interdiction of the poppy in India, it certainly would not support any proposal to compel China to receive the drug against its will. The Chinese Government, as a friendly Government living in peaceful intercourse with us, is entitled to expect our full, explicit assurance that henceforth we will respect its natural right to legislate, according to its conscience and political views, not according to ours, in this matter. Our past conduct makes this necessary, although it carries with it the painful necessity of self-condemnation. Appeal has already been made to us, in the very form we ourselves fixed. We made it our object for

years to get a representative of the British crown
settled at Peking, in order that he might be the
means of communication between the Chinese
Government and our own. After our last war we
succeeded in obtaining the fulfilment of our long-
cherished aim. Our ambassador has lived in Peking,
and the Chinese Government made use of the opportunity of his presence, to bring this matter formally
before his notice. Not satisfied with personal conversation, they put their demand in writing. That
demand is not couched in ambiguous terms. It
plainly seeks the annulling of those regulations
which bind the Chinese to admit our opium under
duty. If we refuse the demand, we are actually
still forcing opium into China at the sword's point,
and perpetuating the grievous wrong of which we
were guilty in the Opium War. If we persist in our
present system, we are not only supporting our
Indian Empire by the proceeds of a dishonourable
traffic, but we are maintaining that traffic in plain
violation of the rights of nations.

Supposing that the Chinese Government should
enter upon a new crusade against opium, having the
hearty support, instead of the armed opposition of
the British Government, their struggle might have a
very different issue from the former one. If England
engaged to do what she could to repress smuggling
on the part of her own subjects, the other Treaty
powers, the United States, France, and Germany
would doubtless do the same. Everything leads to the
belief that if the Chinese Government were assured

of the co-operation of the Treaty powers, it would make a splendid attempt to eradicate the poppy and extinguish opium-smoking from the Great Wall to the Southern ocean, from the Pacific to the mountains of Thibet. Having the moral support of its own people, it might succeed. On the other hand, through the venality of its own officials it might fail. The result would not be our responsibility, and no prognostication of the result can affect our duty.

Let us review the practical conclusions to which we have arrived.

(1.) In any scheme for reform of our relations with opium, the first requisite is a readiness to relinquish, in whole or in part, as may be necessary, the revenue derived from the drug, and a determination to treat it henceforth on considerations independent of, even hostile to, the raising of revenue from this source. At this point we part company with our numerous well-wishers who deplore the history of British connexion with opium, who acknowledge that our present position is indefensible on moral grounds, and assure us that if we will only point out some other mode of raising the revenue which shall not inconvenience anybody, they will support us with all their might. There is many a man getting his living by dishonest courses, who would gladly abandon them at once, in exchange for an equal income from an unexceptionable source, if only he could make the exchange without risk or inconvenience. But repentance is not to be had on such cheap terms. Our argument against the opium revenue is that as hitherto and now collected and defended, it is *morally wrong*, and on this ground we urge its relinquishment. To those who admit the validity of the argument, the conclusion is imperative.

(2.) Having formed this righteous resolution, we might easily jump to the conclusion that the only consistent course is to suppress the cultivation and exportation altogether. In favour of this course powerful arguments may be alleged, but we can not but admit a certain measure of doubtfulness attending them. In the present condition of public sentiment it appears extremely improbable that such a course will commend itself to the judgment of the nation. Another generation which has solved our difficulties in connexion with alcohol, may be relieved from our hesitation in respect to opium; but we cannot wait for another generation to abandon the unrighteous treatment of China which our fathers commenced and we are continuing.

(3.) Therefore we urge on India an instant return to the principle of employing taxation as a *bonâ-fide* method of repression. In order to carry out this change of policy, we urge the abandonment of the monopoly, not only to relieve the Government from the appearance of having a direct interest in the promotion of vice, but because in the present system the Government has, in reality, a direct interest in the promotion of vice, and because we have seen that the moral instincts of Government have not been proof against the temptation involved in this.

(4.) Such a change, however, would by itself be little more than formal, because the bulk of our revenue comes from China. Our great demand is justice for China. We urge that we must cease altogether from coercion of the Chinese. We must leave them free to prohibit the entrance of our opium altogether, or to tax it as high as they think fit, even prohibitively. This alteration of behaviour towards China could not be effected without acknowledgment on our part of error in the past, and we should not shrink from full and candid confession of our fault. On the other hand, such acknowledgment would afford a fair opportunity for pointing out the share which the misconduct of China has had in bringing about the evils of the past; and our change of policy at so great a cost would enable us to urge upon China the importance of repressing the growth of opium within her own borders. In this way the progress of the vice of opium-smoking would be at once arrested, and we have good reason to hope that the Chinese Government could and would reduce it to a minimum. At all events, we should have done all that as a political power we can do to retrace our steps, and make amends for the past.

(5.) As such an altered policy could not be carried out without great diminution, or total loss, of the opium revenue, and as the inhabitants of India are not responsible for the growth of this revenue, it appears that justice requires the English nation to guard the interests of the

Indian Empire in effecting this reform. As a rule, India is bound to pay her own charges; but in this case, the fault lying at our door, we are under obligation to take care that our repentance does no injury to the innocent.

Such are the conclusions we arrive at. If we lack the courage of our convictions; what then? Possibly the opium revenue may slip away from us, and fail us when we are in a worse position than we are now. Possibly we may be forced again to fight for it, and rebaptize our drug profits in Chinese blood. In one way or another the inevitable Nemesis will come. But it is our desire to accomplish the aim of this essay by begetting convictions of duty, not by appealing to motives of expediency. If the British public resists the appeal to its sense of right, it will hardly be moved by attempts to frighten it.

APPENDIX A.

TESTIMONIES AS TO THE EFFECTS OF OPIUM-EATING AND OPIUM-SMOKING.

I.

William Lockhart, F.R.C.S., F.R.G.S., of the London Missionary Society. In the "Medical Missionary in China," chap. xiv :—

"When a smoker first commences the use of opium it is a pleasant and refreshing stimulant, an artificial vigour and tone are given to the system, followed by a corresponding relaxation and listlessness; after which an effort is made to remove the latter by a return to the pipe. This stage in the smoker's progress may be prolonged for some years without the health being interfered with; but he soon becomes a victim to the habit thus formed, which cannot easily be shaken off; the strength, however, is not impaired, and attention can be paid to business as usual; indeed, the stimulus of the drug enables him to enter with vivacity upon any pursuit in which he may be engaged. At this time a little decision would enable him to throw off the habit, but this is seldom called for, and the smoker continues to use his pipe, thus accustoming himself more and more to dependence on his much-loved indulgence. By and by retribution comes; he cannot live comfortably without the stimulant; all the pleasure has gone, but he must obtain relief from the pain of body and dissipation of mind which follow the absence of the drug at any cost, the quantity of the drug called for being from time to time greater, and its use more frequent.

"Among the symptoms which present themselves are

griping pains in the bowels, pain in the limbs, loss of appetite, so that the smoker can only eat dainty food; disturbed
sleep and general emaciation. The outward appearances are
sallowness of the complexion, bloodless cheeks and lips,
sunken eye, with a dark circle round the eyelids, and altogether a haggard countenance. . . . In fine, a confirmed
opium-smoker presents a most melancholy appearance;
haggard, dejected, with a lack-lustre eye, and a slovenly
weakly, and feeble gait."

*   *   *   *   *   *   *

"There is, perhaps, no form of intemperance more seducing
than the use of opium, nor is there any more difficult to be
delivered from. To acquire a full acquaintance with the
effects of the agent, the consequences of which are now
being discussed, it is necessary to view it under two forms:
1st, As to its incipient effects in the stage of exhilaration,
while the individual is in good health, and the powers of life
are in full vigour; at this time the drug is a means of enjoyment. 2ndly, As to the effects produced by the drug when it
is employed as a means of relief from the distress and pain
resulting from the long-continued use of such a stimulant.
This may be called the stage of depression; in this condition
the individual soon becomes a martyr to his former vices,
and bitterly repents of his having submitted to the temptation.

"When the pipe is first taken, during the incipient stage,
a few grains are sufficient to produce the full effect. This
small quantity requires to be gradually increased to produce
a given result; the times of using it must become more
frequent, until the victim is soon compelled to use one
drachm, or sixty grains, in the course of twenty-four hours.
This quantity per day will supply the smoker for some years,
but it has at last to be augmented till two, three, four, or even
five drachms are daily consumed. This may be denominated
the second stage.

"Some are said to use ten drachms daily, but these are only
the superior classes, who have no need to attend to any

business or occupation, and can spend almost their whole time in intoxicating themselves with the use of the drug, or in recovering from its effects. The life of such persons is not prolonged, and the many complaints arising from the excessive indulgence soon put an end to their useless existence.

" Besides the cases of death arising from the excessive use of opium among the higher classes, who can afford to gorge themselves with their stimulant till they die, there are many more unhappy dissolutions arising from the inability to procure the accustomed and to them necessary quantity. In the case of those who are in middling circumstances, and are inured to the habit, the enervating effects are such that they become after a time unable to attend to their ordinary avocations. They then lose their situations, or their business fails, and they are reduced to necessity. Gradually they part with their little property, furniture, clothes, &c., until they come to the level of the labouring poor, without those energetic habits which might otherwise form the ground of support. Having no property, furniture, or clothes to dispose of, their wives and children are sold to supply their ever-increasing appetite for the drug, and when these are gone, with greatly diminished strength for labour, they can no longer earn sufficient for their own wants, and are obliged to beg for their daily bread. As to the supply of opium, they must depend on the scrapings of other men's pipes; and as soon as they are unable to obtain by begging the necessaries of life, together with the half-burnt opium on which their very life depends, they droop and die by the road-side, and are buried at the expense of the charitable.

" The writer once knew two respectable young men, the sons of an officer of high rank, who died in this part of the country. They were both well-informed men, had received a good education, were evidently accustomed to good society, and excited considerable interest in the minds of those with whom they came in contact. But they were opium-smokers; so inveterate was the habit, and so large the quantity necessary to keep up the stimulant, that their available funds were exhausted during their stay in this city. Friends assisted them to some extent, and relieved their necessities again and again; but it was impossible to give them bread and opium too, and they subsequently died one after another, in the most abject and destitute condition.

"Whilst these notes were preparing, the writer had occasion to go into the city, and just inside the north gate, in front of a temple, he saw one of such destitute persons, unable to procure either food or the drug, lying at the last gasp; there were two or three others with drooping heads sitting near, who looked as if they would soon be prostrated too. The next day the writer passed and found the first of the group dead and stiff, with a coarse mat wound round his body for a shroud. The rest were now lying down, unable to rise. The third day another was dead, and the remainder almost near it. Help was vain, and pity for their wretched condition the only feeling that could be indulged.

    *   *   *   *   *   *   *

"As to the moral evils arising from indulgence in opium, they are very patent. It blunts the moral sense, causes good men to waver in virtue, and makes bad men worse. Even Coleridge, with all his fine sensibilities and acquaintance with religious truth, was tempted to prevaricate and deceive in order to conceal his indulgence in the habit, and elude the vigilance of those who were engaged in watching him. How much more, then, may we expect a lying nation like the Chinese to lie so much the more in their attempts to conceal their vices from the eyes of observers. So invariably is it the practice of Chinese opium-smokers to deny their having any connexion with the drug, that it is never advisable to ask them any questions about it, lest one should induce them to tell unnecessary untruths. No confidence can be placed in the religious profession of an opium-smoker, unless he abandon the vice, and even then the missionary should have very good evidence of his having done so before admitting him into connexion with the Church. Not only is the moral sense weakened in opium-smokers, but the habits they have acquired naturally and necessarily lead them into associations where they are directly tempted to the most profligate vices. A man accustomed to the use of the drug, therefore, soon becomes worse in other respects, and having commenced the downward career, every step in the rake's progress is more and more deteriorating. Opium-smoking is thus the parent of numerous evils which are not originally chargeable upon it. When unable to procure the drug by honest means, such is the craving for it among its slaves, that fraud, peculation, and theft are resorted to in order to obtain it; insomuch that the Chinese themselves are in the habit of withdrawing their confidence from those addicted to the vile habit, unless they have other methods of tying them down to honesty.

*　　*　　*　　*　　*　　*　　*

" The writer cannot close without a few words of exhortation to those who deal in the drug in China. The principals are professing Christians, and justly pride themselves on being humane men. But Christianity and humanity both inculcate principles which, if carried out, would lead them to refrain from the traffic. Both of these would teach them that they are not to benefit themselves to the injury of others. Granting that a large quantity of the opium they sell is used only as a ' harmless luxury,' and that in those cases where harm ensues it is the abuse, and not the use, of the article which causes it; granting all this, they must admit that the use leads to the abuse, by a natural and necessary process, and that if they did not import the drug, neither the use nor abuse of it could possibly take place. We do not say that all the opium imported does harm, but much of it assuredly does so; and if every chest but killed its man, or shortened the life and happiness of a single individual, it cannot be denied that it does harm. And can any sit down contented with the thought that the gains they are acquiring are obtained at the expense of the diminished comfort or shortened existence of others; while the wives and children of the deluded victims are bitterly bewailing the hour when the head of the family ever came in contact with opium? Surely, if all the results of the traffic were known, humanity would lead them to recoil from any participation in it."

NOTE.

The essayist wrote to Dr. Lockhart for farther explanation of his opinion as to the possible moderate use of the drug, and received the following reply, under date 27th January, 1874 :—

" Opium is used as spirituous liquors are used, as a stimulant, and I have known many respectable Chinese who have used the drug for many years without apparent injury to their health; but the fascinating effect of opium seduces the larger number of smokers to use more and more of the drug, which then tells powerfully and injuriously upon health; and being once become slaves to this large need of the drug (one to two drachms, that is, one-eighth to one-quarter of an ounce), they cannot leave it off without great pain and dysentery, but go on to a still increased quantity, and thus they are dragged down to misery."

II.

J. Dudgeon, M.D., C.M., London Missionary Society, in the third Annual Report of the Peking Hospital, under his care, page 12 :—

" The opium patients are readily recognized by their emaciation, debility, sallow complexion, livid lips, and langour of the eye. The opium-smoking will, however, bear a favourable comparison with the drinking customs at home. It does not produce the intoxication of ardent spirits. The opium-smoker is not such a nuisance to the community and his family. Both are evils ending in loss of health, wealth, physical and mental powers, influence, and shortening of life. It leads to beggary, and is the cause of much crime. Thefts and robberies are committed to procure the drug or pay the opium bill."

This third report was the first issued by Dr. Dudgeon, the hospital having been for two years under Dr. Lockhart's care. In the fifth Report of the Hospital (1866), Dr. Dudgeon speaks thus of opium-smoking :—

"It is a powerful habit, a second nature, stronger and more insinuating than strong drink. I have had numerous professions of cure, but I have learned to receive such with great caution, and the more so the longer the period in which the drug has been used. To give up the fascinations and associations of the pipe, and to overcome and hold out against the agonies, pains, discomforts, even with the aid of foreign medicine, which are induced by attempts at reformation, require great strength of will. After abstinence for months, perhaps, the victims relapse into their old habits. During the last three years I have had four different applications from the same person for medicine to effect a cure."

Dr. Dudgeon being now (February, 1876) in Scotland has kindly written for me the folllowing statement of his opinion as to the effects of opium-smoking. After some remarks as to the probable number of smokers, which will be found in Appendix B., the Dr. says:—

"Opium-smoking gives no immunity from disease, except, perhaps, in the case of shock or severe operations. The Chinese, smokers or non-smokers, are not subject to acute or inflammatory diseases, and the characteristics which we observe in many cases, and after surgical interference, are common to all classes, and are doubtless owing to their abstemious habits, and their well-known constitutional peculiarities. I must here enter my strong dissent, however, against the important but incorrect and misleading evidence laid before the Committee on Indian Finance (1871) in regard to the effect of opium on malaria, this being assigned by two of the most influential witnesses as the cause of the prevalence of the vice in China. Many of their diseases are rather aggravated by being addicted to the habit, and others in their initial stage, such as the various chest or pulmonary affections in the cold north, are benefited by the use, and life, if not in many cases lengthened, is at least made more comfortable and endurable. A large percentage of those who acquire the habit, do so, it is said, from the absence of skilled medical men for the cure of disease or the alleviation of suffering. It is curious that, although their disease does not go on improving as it did during the first two or three weeks of treatment, nor show the slightest signs of giving way in eighteen or twenty years, but is rather aggravated, and has superinduced upon it a more serious disease, no Chinese patient ever dreams of throwing his doctor (Dr. Poppy) overboard. The treatment of such cases is rendered much more difficult—our remedies which contain preparations of opium, and depend upon this drug for their chief remedial or palliative action, being quite inert. Some of the above patients came for diarrhœa, dysentery, spermatorrhœa, impotence, want of posterity, and such-like complaints, but the great bulk are for ordinary diseases, not depending upon the opium as a producing cause. You know I established a shop in the neighbourhood of the hospital for the sale of anti-opium pills, and thither the distinctly opium patients go, who come to be cured or relieved, or tided over difficulties. By confirmed I mean long-continued cases, in which the habit, appetite, or desire is so established that it has become, as it were, a very part of his constitution, and without which, or some equivalent, he could not exist. This looks as if it were impossible to give up the habit when once acquired. And generally speaking it is so. A very large number of criminals die annually in the prisons of China from deprivation of the drug. They are generally cut off by diarrhœa and dysentery. These deadly affections—for they prove quite intractable in the case of the opium-smoker; the Chinese designate these diseases in such cases by the appellation *yen*, or opium diarrhœa and dysentery—sometimes also attack the confirmed smoker, and then his case is hopeless. Opium, which is ordinarily a powerful remedy in these cases, seems to be quite inert. I have known a goodly number, however, who have given up the pipe : some had recourse to stimulants, and at each meal (twice daily) partook of a little samshoo; others made decoctions of Chinese tonic herbs, and added certain quantities of crude opium which were calculated to last a certain time, and in every subsequent decoction or preparation of the prescription, introducing gradually less and less opium until they got cured;—some, of whom about a dozen have been members of our church at Peking, gave up the habit by means of medicines furnished by me, being a combination of stimulants, sedatives, and tonics. These cases have extended from one or two years to twelve and and fourteen years. Spirits were not taken in their cases as a *quid pro quo*, although of course occasionally indulged in at meals, as is very common in N. China. And I have met with three or four cases in my experience, where the patients, by strength of will, or through intimidation from parents, masters, or superior officers, have given up the habit without any help whatever. I have been much struck with these cases, the poor smokers having suffered considerably by the great effort. I cannot recommend such a course. They complained of dyspepsia, derangement of the bowels, want of energy, but chiefly, and this is always present, and is what the smoker feels when the habit is not gratified at the proper period, pain all through his bones.

"Speaking generally, then, it may be asserted that it is next to impossible to give up the habit when once thoroughly established. The next question is, when is this habit formed; or in other words, how long can a man smoke before the habit becomes confirmed; or in other words, are there any 'moderate' smokers? The man that smokes five candareens or even one mace, will consider himself a 'moderate' smoker in comparison with other smokers who consume four or five mace, or one tael daily. I have been told by well-to-do patients that their *yin*, or habit, was not great, for they only smoked five or six mace, or eight mace, or one tael two mace, or in some cases more daily. I have often said in such cases that I would consider one candareen a large dose, at which they were always much astonished. If by moderate we

mean that a man can take a small dose, or what he considers
a moderate quantity, and adhere to that without further
increase, then my conviction from twelve years' experience
is that this is indeed rare. I have known cases—the parties
asserted it at least—where a similar quantity has been indulged in for years, without increase or diminution : the
quantity has been invariably increased from the time when
the smoker began, or when the habit got confirmed; to
obtain the same effect the dose must be from time to time
slightly increased. Time, money, and other circumstances
and conditions frequently modify it. I have seen vast
numbers of cases in which the quantity has been diminished
by a third or even a half. These cases have always been
confirmed smokers, and the reasons assigned have been want
of money chiefly, although a few have admitted self-interest,
or the preservation of their health. Those in the lower
and poorer ranks have taken to eating the ashes ; and those
in the middle class of smokers, with whom money is not
plentiful, half smoke and half eat the ashes. This, however,
is only an apparent diminution, for, as may readily be
imagined, a small and cheaper dose by the stomach will
produce the same effects as a larger dose by the lungs. I
ought to say that the eating is manifold more injurious than
smoking.

" With these explanations, is there then in our sense anything in China to correspond to our moderate drinking—
taking a little daily, and for years, without any effect upon his
constitution or life, nay, in some cases improving the one
and lengthening the other—letting it alone if desired without
feeling any the worse for it, and without any craving,
periodical or otherwise, for the beverage. In this sense I very
much doubt the existence of moderate opium-smoking.
Until the habit is formed, which may embrace a period of
from two to four months, the smoker *may* not find that
periodical imperious craving which *demands* satisfaction ; but
sooner or later he finds himself the slave to the appetite, and
then, whatever be the quantity, this man in this sense ceases

to be a moderate smoker. He must, sooner or later, increase his dose, and, sooner or later, the drug will breed its usual train of symptoms, physical, moral, social, intellectual, and commercial. I have met a few cases in which it was asserted that opium was only now and again had recourse to on the occasion of a feast, &c., but if the man has the means, and his work or service does not preclude him indulging, he will take to the pipe regularly, and soon feel that he cannot do without it. If, however, there were much moral and religious principle and a strong will, I believe it is possible to take a small dose of opium every two or three days over a long course of years without any appreciable habit being formed or injury to the system being sustained. After my experience I am inclined to think that the physical evils have been to some extent overrated, and that a very considerable dose, say one, two, or even three mace regularly taken by a man in good circumstances and with good living, will not materially or to any great extent shorten life; nay, for a short time, while the habit is forming, or once formed, requiring increase, but before it has had time to destroy the appetite for food, turning night into day, and causing various functional derangements of the brain, stomach, bowels, &c., the smoker may experience some benefit, just as a glass of wine or beer before or at dinner, to the delicate constitution, may give strength and appetite and power to digest, and enable the patient to take what before never could be taken, a hearty meal. It is not uncommon to hear smokers assert that their indulgence in the vice has extended over twenty, thirty, and even forty years. In this respect it is therefore not unlike spirits and tobacco. In practice, however, speaking generally, we do not find "moderate" opium-smoking, without its concomitant results of increase and injury. Some may say they could leave it alone, but in practice they do not. Some, doubtless, assert this, not wishing to acknowledge their slavery or their weakness. When it is understood that a man's moral character goes, that he loses his place, is suspected by all -

that no one can trust him—not only is the Chinese view of it evident, but there is here a reason for not acknowledging its power. It is unlike spirits in most particulars. In the latter, the injury is, as it were, the exception; whereas in the former it is the *rule*. The reader will be able to form his own idea of the moderate opium-smoker from these desultory remarks."

III.

W. H. Medhurst, H.B.M. Consul, Shanghai, in " The Foreigner in Far Cathay :"—

" The effect upon the individual, when indulged in habitually and to excess, is certainly debasing, and there is, perhaps, no vicious habit from which complete recovery is more difficult. At the same time I would caution the reader against an unqualified acceptance of the tales of horror one hears and reads of in connexion with opium-smoking in China. How that, for instance, every fifth, or tenth, or twentieth, or even fortieth man in the empire is a victim to the habit; how that the opium hells are as abundant as the provision shops, and crowded day and night with hundreds of infatuated wretches hurrying to their ruin; how that skeletons haunt the streets, and whole families, beggared by drugged husbands and fathers, may be seen dying in the highways and fields, and so on. There are opium-dens, no doubt, and quite numerous enough to sadden the philanthropic observer, and the victims which the drug drags to misery and death are also, alas ! beyond all counting. But what is the vice, and where is the country of which the same may not be said with equal or approximate truth ? Indeed, were I asked to state candidly in which part of the world I thought the effects of vicious indulgence are more outwardly observable, socially speaking, I certainly should not name China. Statistics on the subject cannot be relied on. It is known to a chest how much Indian drug is imported into the country, but there is no means of estimating the quantity

of native-grown opium produced, and I do not believe that
there is any person sufficiently informed on the subject to
be able to state with any approach to accuracy, what proportion the smokers of the drug bear to the general population. The most that can be asserted with truth is that the
vice is a general one, more especially in districts near the
sea-coast and great commercial centres, that a considerable
proportion of its victims indulge to an excess ruinous to
health and prospects, and that it has been gaining ground
upon the people with rapid strides during the last few
years."

IV.

Evidence of Mr. T. T. Cooper (the traveller, author of
" The Pioneer of Commerce," &c.), before Select Committee
of the House of Commons, 1871 :—

"5522. Do you think from your own experience in travelling
over China, and investigating these matters, that the use of
opium there causes as much public injury as the consumption
of drink in England, as far as you can see?—Yes. I think
that the effects of opium-smoking in China are worse than
the effects of drink in England, as far as my experience
goes.

"5523. But it does not cause the amount of crime that we
suffer from in this country as the effect of drink?—No. A
man when he commences to smoke lies down on his bed,
and does not get up till it is finished. It is very costly and
very dangerous in this way : that if a man has been in the
habit of smoking opium, and he has not money to supply
himself with opium, his constitution then receives such a
frightful shock that it shows very quickly; but as long as
he takes his regular quantity of opium every day he does
not feel anything ; he must have it, but it does not destroy
his health, because he eats and he works; but if he loses
his supply of opium on Monday morning, on Tuesday morning he will be ruined for work all the rest of the week ; he

will not pick up again, the system seems to fall so for want of opium.

"5524. And probably a man accustomed to it all his life would die?—They do die in China from that cause. In the more populous parts which I have gone through, generally after starting on my journey early in the morning, through the suburbs of the towns, before the watch have had time to go round, it is a very common thing to see half-naked men lying dead simply from want of opium.

"5525. I understand you that you think the evils which arise from the consumption of opium arise from the poverty that it causes, and not from any crime—that it does not lead to crime?—It leads to crime in this way, that men will do anything, they will sell their children, their wives, their mothers, and their fathers, to get opium."

NOTE.—Mr. Cooper's evidence is throughout interesting and important. See further quotations in Appendix B., especially as to "moderate" smoking.

V.

Assistant-Surgeon Impey, Government Examiner of Opium, in "Malwa Opium," published in Bombay, 1848:—

"Doubtless excessive indulgence in any propensity seldom fails to produce all the worst results which can ensue from a bad pursuit, and opium is not wanting in the most pernicious consequences or the most attached votaries. But it is hardly fair to condemn a practice from its evils. . . . . The baneful effects of intemperance are unfortunately but too well known, and few afflictions are exceeded by *delirium tremens* in horror and severity, while no vice is so ruinous to the constitution, mind, and morals, as addiction to drink . . . . still we would not stigmatize every one who indulges in these luxuries as drunkards. . . . . Opium has no doubt votaries among the voluptuous and the poor, though its price keeps it in some degree above the reach of the latter, yet upon them it produces its most calamitous effects; but, as with liquor, it would be rather too much to assert that every opium-smoker was irretrievably ruined in body and soul. The consumption of the quantity given up to the Chinese in 1839, viz. 20,283 chests, would amply and liberally satisfy thirty millions of smokers for twelve months, and surely the majority of these must use it in moderation, and more as a luxury than a vice. . . .

" The analogy which has been endeavoured to be drawn between opium and spirits, though true and just in most respects, is questionable, perhaps, in one important feature —the greater aptitude of the former to turn into an invete-rate habit, which it is to be presumed proceeds from its very seductive and pleasurable influence more than its stimulating property. . . . . Regarding the inveteracy of the habit, it is unfortunately but too true that, once formed, correction is next to an impossibility, and the commencement of the practice may be said to be synchronous with youth. Opium-smoking is not now, however, a mere luxury, but an essential to the very existence of the Chinese people, in whatever rank of life—from the humblest mechanic to the highest functionary and greatest dignitary; it forms the chief part, not only of their enjoyment, but their daily necessities. . . . . Yet, notwithstanding this repeated application to the pipe, and the apparent excess denoted thereby, it is in reality comparatively innocuous, and its effects cannot but be regarded as very *ethereal*, and its consequences much less injurious than are imagined. No sort of difference can be recognized, either in the personal appearance, gait, or manner of the professional testers in Bombay,—men who earn their livelihood by constant and repeated doses of it, as it were."

VI.

Dr. Eatwell, First Assistant and Opium Examiner in the Bengal Monopoly Service :—

" Having passed three years in China, I may be allowed

to state the results of my observation, and I can affirm thus far, that the effects of the abuse of the drug do not come very frequently under observation, and that when cases do occur, the habit is frequently found to have been induced by the presence of some painful chronic disease, to escape from the sufferings of which the patient has fled to this resource. That this is not always the cause, however, I am perfectly ready to admit, and there are doubtless many who indulge in the habit to a pernicious extent, led by the same morbid impulses which induce men to become drunkards in even the most civilized countries, but these cases do not, at all events, come before the public eye. It requires no laborious search in civilized England to discover evidences of the pernicious effects of the abuse of alcoholic liquors; our open and thronged gin palaces, and our streets afford abundant testimony on the subject, but in China this open evidence of the evil effects of opium is at least wanting. As regards the effects of the habitual use of the drug on the *mass* of the people, I must affirm that no injurious results are visible. The people generally are a muscular and well-formed race, the labouring portion being capable of great and prolonged exertion under a fierce sun, in an unhealthy climate. Their disposition is cheerful and peaceable, and quarrels and brawls are rarely heard amongst even the lower orders; whilst in general intelligence they rank deservedly high amongst orientals.

"I will, therefore, conclude with observing that the proofs are still wanting to show that the moderate use of opium produces more pernicious effects upon the constitution than does the moderate use of spirituous liquors; whilst at the same time it is certain that the consequences of the abuse of the former are less appalling in their effect upon the victim, and less disastrous to society at large, than are the consequences of the abuse of the latter.

" Board of Customs, Salt, and Opium,
" 1st November, 1850."

VII.

Pareira. *Materia Medica*:—

"Opium-smoking.—In the first edition of this work I stated that although the immoderate practice of opium-smoking must be highly detrimental to health, yet that I believed the statements of Medhurst and others applied to cases in which this practice was carried to excess; and I observed that an account of the effects of opium-smoking by an unbiassed and professional witness was a desideratum. My opinion was founded on the statements of Botto and Marsden. The latter, a most accurate writer, observes that ' the *Limun* and *Batang Assei* gold-traders, who are an active and laborious class of men, but yet indulge as freely in opium as any others whatever, are, notwithstanding, the most healthy and vigorous people to be met with on the island.' This desideratum has been supplied by Mr. Smith, surgeon, of Pulo Penang, whose statements fully confirm my opinion. For although the practice is most destructive to those who live in poverty and distress, and who carry it to excess, yet it does not appear that the Chinese in easy circumstances, and who have the comforts of life about them, are materially affected in respect to longevity, by the private addiction to this vice. ' There are many persons,' observes Mr. Smith, ' within my own observation who have attained the age of sixty, seventy, or more, and who are well known as habitual opium-smokers for more than thirty years past.' The first effect of this drug on the Chinese smokers is to render them more loquacious and animated. Gradually the conversation drops, laughter is occasionally produced by the most trifling causes, and to these effects succeed vacancy of countenance, pallor, shrinking of the features, so that the smokers resemble people convalescing from fever, followed by deep sleep for half an hour to three or four hours. An inordinate quantity causes head-ache, vertigo, and nausea. The Malays are rendered outrageous and quarrelsome by the opium-pipe.

" It is extremely difficult to discontinue the vice of opium-smoking, yet there are many instances of its being done. The continuance of this destructive practice deteriorates the physical constitution and moral character of the individual, especially among the lower classes. Its powerful effects on the system are manifested by stupor, forgetfulness, deterioration of the mental faculties, emaciation, debility, sallow complexion, lividity of lips and eyelids, languor and lack-lustre of the eye, appetite either destroyed or depraved, sweetmeats or sugar-cane being the articles that are most relished. 'In the morning these creatures have a most wretched appearance, evincing no symptoms of being refreshed or invigorated by sleep, however profound. There is a remarkable dryness or burning in the throat, which urges them to repeat the opium-smoking. If the dose be not taken at the usual time, there is great prostration, vertigo, torpor, discharge of water from the eyes, and in some an involuntary discharge of semen, even when wide awake. If the privation be complete, a still more formidable train of phenomena takes place. Coldness is felt over the whole body, with aching pains in all parts. Diarrhœa occurs; the most horrid feelings of wretchedness come on; and if the poison be withheld, death terminates the victim's existence.' The offspring of opium-smokers are weak, stunted, and decrepid."

VIII.

Evidence of Sir R. N. C. Hamilton, Agent in Central India, before Special Committee, 1871 :—

" 4986. It (opium) is not used by the population (of Malwa)?—A very small quantity is consumed in the country.

" 4987. Then opium consumers are rare there?—Yes.

"4988. Does it affect their health injuriously?—Certainly.

" 4989. Whether it is either eaten or smoked, it generally produces very serious effects on the health?—Certainly: opium-eaters are very soon unfit for any active pursuits.

" 4990. And it shortens their lives?—Yes."

IX.

Sir Benjamin C. Brodie :—

" However valuable opium may be when employed as an article of medicine, it is impossible for any one who is acquainted with the subject to doubt that the habitual use of it is productive of the most pernicious consequences, destroying the healthy action of the digestive organs, weakening the powers of the mind as well as the body, and rendering the individual who indulges himself in it a worse than useless member of society. I cannot but regard those who promote the use of opium as an article of luxury as inflicting a most serious injury on the human race."

(Quoted in *Nonconformist*, 14th Dec., 1870.)

X.

Dr. J. Carnegie, formerly of Amoy:—

" Chesterfield, April 12th, 1874.

" My views, I fear, would, in the eyes of Quakers, appear heterodox. I have no hesitation in pronouncing opium a great curse to the Chinese, as alcohol is to the English ; but I am not prepared to say that the moderate use of the drug is either impossible or injurious, any more than the analogous beverage in our own country. I have seen it used in moderation with no apparent injury to mind, body, or estate, and I have seen it used in excess to the utter ruin of all three. Undoubtedly, the latter mode of using the drug vastly preponderates."

XI.

De Quincey's " Confessions of an English Opium-eater:"—

[It being impossible to give a fair account of this author's teaching about the effects of opium by a few brief quotations, we have thrown our impressions in the form of a critique.]

This work is but of slight, if any, value in a scientific

point of view. The object of the brilliant *littérateur* is
evidently, first of all, artistic, as he himself avows. He
meant to write, and has written, an intensely interesting
composition which should live among the classics of our
language. Second, or co-equal with that, was his desire to
present his own conduct in as favourable a light as possible.
Whatever the public judgment shall be upon the practice of
opium-eating, he is determined that the public shall not visit
with severe moral censure Thomas De Quincey, the opium-
eater. Apart from these drawbacks, his work helps us but
little in forming a judgment, because it is careless in giving
dates, amounts, and collateral information. He tells us very
little about the effects of opium on his physical health,
nothing as to whether he succeeded in reducing his consumption with or without medical aid. But these facts may be
gleaned from his case, if we can place faith in the statements of an opium-eater :—

(1.) He resorted to opium for relief from physical torture
of the severest description.

(2.) He used it intermittently, "about once in three
weeks" for eight years, before he became a daily opium-
eater. During this time he perceived no injurious result.

(3.) He reached at one time a daily ration of "eight, ten,
or twelve thousand drops of laudanum." According to his
calculation, 8000 drops = 320 grains of opium. His highest
consumption, therefore, viz., 480 grains, was less than that
of many confirmed Chinese smokers, who use one tael and
more per day. One tael = 580 grains. But opium taken
into the stomach has a much more powerful effect than when
only the fumes of it enter into the lungs.

(4.) Under the influence of the larger quantities he suffered indescribable mental agonies, and sank into mental
imbecility, which made him dread loss of reason, or of life.
"The Circean spells of opium" brought on "intellectual
torpor." "But for misery and suffering I might, indeed,
be said to have existed in a dormant state." "Nothing
short of mortal anguish in a physical sense, it seemed, to

wean myself from opium ; yet, on the other hand, death through overwhelming terrors—death by brain-fever or lunacy—seemed too certainly to besiege the alternative course."

(5.) He succeeded more than once in greatly lowering his consumption, to forty daily grains, and at last to five or six grains daily. But the effort was terrible.

" I triumphed. But infer not, reader, from this word *triumphed* a condition of joy or exultation. Think of me as one, even when four months had passed, still agitated, writhing, throbbing, palpitating, shattered, and much, perhaps, in the situation of one who has been racked. Meantime, I derived no benefit from any medicine whatever, except ammoniated tincture of valerian. The moral of the narrative is addressed to the opium-eater, and therefore, of necessity, limited in its application. If he is taught to fear and tremble, enough has been effected. But he may say that the issue of my case is at least a proof that opium, after an eighteen years' use, and an eight years' abuse, of its powers, may still be renounced."

De Quincey, malgré his purpose to defend himself and opium-eating as a part of his existence, is constantly adduced as condemning the habit. And no wonder. He used opium, off and on, for more than fifty years, and therefore proved an opium-eater need not be short-lived. He did his best, with his enchanting style, to free opium from the stigma of inducing mental stagnation. But no one can miss the *moral* of his Confessions, viz. that opium is pre-eminently seductive and dangerous. Few of his readers will be encouraged by his example to adventure on such a slippery incline.

XII.

Sir. D. F. McLeod, Lieutenant-Governor of the Punjaub, in evidence before Select Committee, 1871 :—

" 4649. I understand that opium was extensively used by the population of the Punjaub ?—By the Sikh population.

They form a very small portion of the Punjaub, but they use it largely.

"4650. And what is the effect upon them ?—They sometimes become almost torpid for a time, and then seem to be cheered by it. I have seen some of the small Sikh chiefs, who have been in the habit of using it, when debarred from it at the proper time, become almost imbecile and helpless until they got their quantity of opium, and then they got lively after a short time; and I do not think in the end it produced any very injurious effects.

"4654. You think that opium does not shorten life ?—I am not aware that it does. Probably it does when carried on to a great extent. I have seen some very fine specimens of Sikhs who have been all their lives taking opium."

XIII.

Lieutenant-Colonel James Todd, Political Resident at the Court of the Rana of Oodipore :—

"This pernicious plant (the poppy) has robbed the Rajpoot of half his virtues; and while it obscures these, it heightens his vices, giving to his natural bravery a character of insane ferocity, and to the countenance, which would otherwise beam with intelligence, an air of imbecility. Like all stimulants, its effects are magical for a time; but the reaction is not less certain, and the faded form, or amorphous bulk, too often attest the debilitating influence of a drug which alike debases mind and body."

Tucker's Memorials, page 154.

XIV.

" Opium-eating in Turkey and Persia." Dr. Oppenheim, quoted in Pareira's *Mat. Med.*:—

" The habitual opium-eater is instantly recognized by his appearance. A total attenuation of body, a withered, yellow countenance, a lame gait, a bending of the spine, frequently to such a degree as to assume a circular form, and glossy, deep-sunken eyes, betray him at the first glance. The digestive organs are in the highest degree disturbed, the sufferer eats scarcely anything, and has hardly one evacuation a week; his mental and bodily powers are destroyed—he is impotent. By degrees, as the habit becomes more confirmed, his strength continues decreasing; the craving for the stimulus becomes even greater, and, to produce the desired effect, the dose must constantly be augmented. . . . After long indulgence, the opium-eater becomes subject to nervous or neuralgic pains, to which opium itself brings no relief. These people seldom attain the age of forty, if they have begun to use opium at an early age. . . . When this baneful habit has become confirmed, it is almost impossible to break it off ; the torments of the opium-eater, when deprived of his stimulant, are as dreadful as his bliss is complete when he has taken it ; to him night brings the torments of hell, day the bliss of Paradise."

XV.

Rev. Griffith John, London Missionary Society, Hankow :—
" I would observe that it is a great mistake to refer opium to the same category as tobacco and spirits. On this point there is a wonderful unanimity of opinion among those who are capable of forming an opinion on the matter. Tobacco, beer, and wine may be taken in moderation, and are generally believed to be harmless if so used, but even the *moderate* use of opium is baneful, and, what is worse, it is impossible to take it in moderation. The smoker is never satisfied with less than the intoxicating effects of the drug. He smokes with the view of making himself drunk, and his cravings are never appeased until he gets drunk. If time and means permit, he lies in a state of ecstatic trance or intoxication, from which he desires never to be waked up. Opium-smoking cannot be compared with moderate drinking, but with drunkenness itself. This habit is more

insidious in its approach than that of drinking, and holds its victim with a far more tenacious grasp."

(*Nonconformist*, 1870.)

" Opium-smoking affects the population by producing sterility. The excessive use of the drug for three or four years deprives the victim of the power *liberos procreare*."

Ibid.

XVI.

Dr. J. H. Bridges, author of Essay on China in " International Policy :"—

" I say then, first, that every medical man in Europe knows that whereas the use of beer or wine in small quantities is in most cases not injurious, the constant use of even small doses of opium, except in certain cases of disease, is injurious exceedingly. Secondly, whereas beer or wine can easily be taken in moderation, like tea or coffee, from year to year, without increasing the quantity, opium cannot. It requires constant increase to produce its pleasurable effects. This is a practical distinction of the greatest moment. In large manufacturing towns especially, where mothers of children work in factories, the physician sees its baneful effects on children to whom it is given by the tired nurse. The dose must be constantly increased. Two drops of laudanum— that is one-tenth of a grain of opium—are enough to kill an infant of a month old. But under the sedulous ministrations of the nurse, a dose of sixty drops, equal to three full doses for an adult, is at last tolerated and demanded. In Bradford the rate of mortality for all classes is high, 25 to 28 per 1000, as compared with the average in the community of 22. But the mortality of children under five years is out of proportion even to that high standard, 230 per 1000, as compared with the general English rate of 150. This I know from personal experience to be largely due to opium. But it would be entirely erroneous to measure the mischievous effects of opium merely or mainly by its effects in shortening life. Nor is it on the intellectual faculties that its worst evils primarily and directly fall. It is the manhood, the energy, the will, the concentration of purpose that in the first place are attacked and undermined. The life-long suicide of Coleridge and De Quincey is painful evidence of this."

XVII.

Mr. Fortune, botanist and traveller in China:—

"From my own experience, I have no hesitation in saying that the number of persons who use opium to excess has been very much exaggerated. . . . . I have often seen the drug used, and I can assert that in the great majority of cases it was not immoderately indulged in. At the same time, I am aware that, like the use of ardent spirits in my own country, it is frequently carried on to a most lamentable excess."

XVIII.

Abbé Huc:—" With the exception of some rare smokers, all others advance rapidly towards death, after having passed through successive stages of idleness, debauchery, poverty, the ruin of their physical strength, and the complete prostration of their intellectual and moral faculties. Nothing can stop a smoker who has made much progress in the habit."

XIX.

Dr. Medhurst, of the London Missionary Society:—
" Calculating the shortened lives, the frequent diseases, and the actual starvation which are the result of opium-smoking in China, we may venture to assert that this pernicious drug annually destroys myriads of individuals."

XX.

Mr. A. Wylie, agent of the British and Foreign Bible Society in China, says :—" Any one who has lived for ten years among the Chinese can scarcely have a doubt as to the destructive effects of opium, physically, mentally, and morally. Undoubtedly this is one of the greatest evils with which China is affected, and unless some means be found to check the practice, it bids fair to accomplish the utter destruction, morally and physically, of that great empire."

XXI.

Dr. Johnston, of the Chinese Hospital at Shanghai, says :— " It is believed by many that the evils resulting from opium-smoking are much exaggerated. I do not think so. On the contrary, I believe that very few people have the slightest conception of the mischief done to the constitution by opium-smoking. Unfortunately the principal sufferers are the working classes. In their case rapid deterioration of health, with loss of muscular power, soon follows the use of the drug, and at no late date, disease, starvation, and death."

(*North China Herald*, June 7, 1873.)

XXII.

Dr. Anstie, in " Stimulants and Narcotics," pp. 79 and 147, and 243 :—

" With regard to opium, there is difficulty in coming to a decision, because the mental phenomena which are caused by its use are less familiarly known. In the great majority of European constitutions, opium produces nothing resembling mental excitement; the effect on myself, for instance, of a large dose, is mere depression and misery. But with most Orientals, and with some Europeans, whose constitutions or habits of life are peculiar a condition is produced by taking a large but not fatal dose, which is very remarkable, and very difficult to analyze. These persons are able, sometimes without any previous practice, to take large quantities of opium, without suffering stupefaction; on the contrary, they appear much exhilarated in spirits, and their minds work with much freedom; in some cases muscular power and the disposition for exertion seem to be increased, but more frequently there is great indisposition to locomotion or hard work of any kind. These effects last for a period varying from eighteen to forty-eight hours; they are succeeded in some cases by a heavy, semi-comatose sleep of long duration, in other cases no particular after-effects are noted."

* * * * * * *

" In the countries where opium is indigenous, it is an article in daily use with the great majority of the population, by whom it is employed for a very different purpose than that of procuring sleep—in fact, as a powerful and rapidly acting stimulant; and in those localities far larger quantities can be taken without producing any other effect than this, than in the countries of Europe, where the poppy is only a transplanted growth. Taken in still larger quantities even, by the natives of Syria and the East, it proves as decidedly and poisonously narcotic as would much smaller doses taken by an Englishman; and this kind of effect is, doubtless, often seen as a consequence of the *abuse* of opium by Orientals. But its *use* is an important and a genuine one; it acts as a powerful food-stimulant, enabling the taker to undergo severe and continuous physical exertion without the assistance of ordinary food, or on short rations of the latter—a fact to which numerous Eastern travellers testify. . . . To a certain extent, and in certain circumstances, the same remarks would apply to natives of this country, although the doses taken are, as a rule, much smaller than in the East. De Quincey mentions the fact that many poor over-worked folk in towns like Manchester, consume regularly a moderate quantity of opium; not using it as the means of a luxurious debauch, but simply to remove the traces of fatigue and depression: and the experience of physicians who know the poor of London would testify to the considerable prevalence of this custom among that class. It has frequently happened to me to find out, from the chance of a patient being brought under my notice in the wards of a hospital, that such patient was a regular consumer, perhaps of a drachm of laudanum, or from that to two or three drachms *per diem,* the same dose having been used for years, without any variation. And I am assured that the practice is very extensively carried out in many parts of this country by persons who would never think of narcotizing themselves, any more than they would of getting drunk; but who simply desire relief from the pains of fatigue endured by an ill-fed, ill-housed body, and a harassed mind. These instances appear to me inexplicable, except upon the supposition that they depend on a kind of food-stimulant effect, similar to that which is certainly experienced by the majority of Orientals in taking opium; and they must be carefully distinguished from that kind of narcotic delirium which is sometimes sought for by the literary dilettante, and of which so vivid an account has been left us in the ' Confessions of an Opium Eater.' "

*   *   *   *   *   *   *

" By degrees the nervous centres, especially those on which the particular narcotic used has the most powerful influence, become degraded in structure; this is not merely from the direct repeated action of the poison, but also from another cause, viz. the small amount of common nutriment taken. This is, at least, the case as regards opium and alcohol, towards which the digestive system seems to have a tolerance, as yet not explained, in virtue of which large quantities of them are at last easily accepted, and have the effect of satisfying appetite without causing nausea or disgust. The habitually immoderate opium-eater, or alcohol-tippler, most commonly takes very little food; but life is supported, in a considerable number of such cases, with little apparent diminution of vigour. The result, however, of this abnormal mode of nutrition is still further disastrous to the nervous system. Deprived of the proper nutriment, which it can only derive from an active supply of blood of the richest and purest quality, the nervous matter tends more and more towards degeneration, and the results of such degeneration are very varied. They may tend to shorten life, or they may not so tend. The changes induced in the nervous matter may be such as may lead to a sudden catastrophe (such as rupture of brain fibres) which may put an end to life at once; or they may consist merely in the gradual shrinking of the brain or spinal cord, or both, in bulk, and the degeneration of a certain amount of their vesicular matter; and this is probably a more frequent issue of chronic narcotism than any positive shortening of life by a sudden overwhelming lesion of the nervous centres."

*   *   *   *   *   *   *

" In all cases where degradation of the elements (especially the vesicular) of the nervous centres takes place, it is easy to understand that narcotic effects could not so easily be induced as before. A certain quantity of nervous tissue has in fact ceased to fill the *rôle* of nervous tissue, and there is less of impressible matter upon which the narcotic may operate; and hence it is that the confirmed drunkard, opium-eater, or *coquero* (coca-eater of Peru), requires more and more of his accustomed narcotic to produce the intoxication which he delights in."

APPENDIX B.

ON THE PROBABLE NUMBER OF OPIUM-SMOKERS IN CHINA.

Dr. Lockhart (Medical Missionary, p. 386), says:—

"As to the probable number of smokers, we have only approximate calculations. Innes, writing on the subject in December, 1836, supposed that a tael or an ounce a day is the proper allowance for a confirmed opium-smoker. A writer in the *Repository* for October, 1837, gives only three candarens, or seventeen and a half grains a day for a moderate smoker. Both estimates seem to be in error, the one being excessive, and the other defective. On inquiry of the Chinese in Shanghai, in the present day, the invariable answer is a mace, or a dram, a day for moderate smokers, adding that there are few who confine themselves to this amount; the most of them consuming two, three, and five mace a day, in order to keep up the stimulus once excited by a single mace. Assuming the proportion of a mace a day as the average amount of daily consumption of each person to be correct, we can easily arrive at the number of smokers throughout the empire. Proceeding upon the statement of the *China Mail* that 67,000 chests were delivered in China last year, and that each chest contained seventy catties of smokeable extract, allowing to each smoker one mace a day, we have little more than two million smokers for the whole empire! .... Supposing the native-grown opium to be one half the amount of the imported, it would then raise the amount of smokers to somewhere about three millions, about one per cent. of the population."

This was in 1854. A proportional calculation for 1874 would make the number under four millions. This tallies with Sir R. Alcock's evidence before the Committee, as follows :—

"My own opinion is that we very much exaggerate the area of consumption, because we know very well what is brought to China from abroad; and that it does not exceed 80,000 chests; although we do not know equally certainly what amount is now grown in the provinces. It is roughly estimated that about half that amount is grown. We know also that the ordinary consumption of a Chinese, who can afford it, is from half a mace to a mace a day, and a great many of them smoke more. Supposing that you have 120,000 chests of opium, and that every man smokes, say, his mace a day, you will see that you have not got above three or four millions of people who can consume it at all." (Report, East India Finance, 1871, p. 275.)

Dr. Dudgeon, in his seventh Peking Hospital Report, says :—

"The following figures may be taken as approximately true, drawn from a careful inquiry and comparison of the statements submitted to me.

Class.	Per cent.
Among small officials	40
„ Agriculturists and field labourers	4 to 6
„ Ditto in drug-producing provinces	40 to 60
„ Merchants in Peking, about	20
„ Mercantile community at the ports	30
„ Followers and servants of mandarins	70 to 80
„ Female attendants	30 to 40
„ Soldiers	20 to 30
„ The literary class	20 to 30
„ Eunuchs of the palace	50
„ Manchu bannermen	30 to 40
„ Male population in China generally, probably	30 to 40
„ The general city population	40 to 60

In this table it is estimated that the average among agriculturists is four to six per cent., among the whole population thirty to forty per cent. Now as the agriculturists form the great bulk of the population, these two estimates appear inconsistent, even though we allow for the increased estimate among the labourers of the drug-growing provinces. Such statements being, of course, mere conjectural estimates by Chinese, and not based on any actual numeration, while they are probably not far from the truth when they refer to small and well-known classes, such as the mandarins, and to particular localities, decrease in reliability when they cover vast areas, of which individuals can have but slight personal knowledge. Dr. Dudgeon adds in his letter, dated February, 1876 :—

"I have nothing new to add to what I have already published about the numbers of smokers. I don't think I have estimated the number too high. About ten per cent. of all the male patients seen at our hospital are confirmed opium-smokers, recognized, by the foreign practised eye and every Chinaman, at once, and without the least difficulty, by their peculiar appearance, and without the necessity of asking them a direct question.[1] To this number, however, must be added at least five per cent. more for incipient cases. And even then it is a question how far the above percentage of patients at a foreign hospital in China would be a fair criterion from which to judge of the extent of the vice. In this country, hospital and dispensary practice would afford a better and safer index to our intemperate habits. Such an estimate would be too high for the province, and yet too small for the city. Generally speaking, and in

[1] Opium smokers are easily recognized by their emaciated, consumptive appearance—stooping gait, raised and bent shoulders, dark yellow-greyish complexion, and blue lips, caused by imperfectly arterialized blood, contour of the mouth, projecting and pouting, caused by the large opium pipe—the sunken cheeks, greatly caused by the constant inhalation and inspiration of the pipe ; the small contracted pupil ; the unnatural lustre and blackness of the eye, and the dirty forefinger, caused by manipulating the drug over the lamp.

the absence of other data, it may be taken as a fair average."

Mr. T. T. Cooper's evidence as to the amount smoked per day, agrees with what we have already adduced; but its bearing upon the "moderate" use should not be overlooked.

"5460. Have you any idea what quantity an individual who is ordinarily fond of opium consumes?—About an ounce of raw opium a day is a very good allowance; that is to say, between fifteen and twenty pipes of opium is a large allowance for a man. The generality of men that I have seen and smoked with, have not taken more than six to ten pipes a day.

"5461. Is that carried on every day in the year?—Yes. If they once become habituated to the use of opium, that is, if they smoke for a week or ten days a pipe of opium every day, it becomes almost impossible to leave it off without some medical assistance.

"5462. But is there no intermediate stage between the confirmed smokers that you have described, and the people who use it slightly?—I have seen in the case of many Chinese, and in fact have experienced it myself, that if you smoke a single pipe of opium once or twice a week, it has very little effect on you; but if you smoke for three or four days steadily, a pipe or two a day, it begins to affect you so seriously, that before you can rouse your energy sufficiently to go about your daily work, you have to take your quantity of opium, a pipe or two pipes.

"5463. I want to understand from you what would be about the consumption of a person who might be said to smoke moderately and reasonably as compared with the con-sumption of a confirmed smoker, such as I understand you to describe?—I should say that the average smoker smokes from a half to three-quarters of an ounce of opium, and a very great smoker would smoke from an ounce and a half to two ounces and over. In fact there is scarcely any limit to what the old men who have smoked all their lives will do.

" 5544. I suppose that about three pipes of opium a day would be rather beneficial than otherwise, if a man could keep to that ?—No, I think not; because if a man is in the habit of smoking three pipes a day, and by any misfortune he could not get his supply of opium, he would be very ill." (Report, East India Finance, 1871, p. 253.)

In respect to the number of smokers, Mr. Cooper has what I cannot but look upon as an exaggerated notion. He says, " You would destroy one-third of the population of China if they were deprived of opium;" and again, " I should say that one-third of the adult population would die for the want of opium." If so many as one-third of the adults are opium-smokers, where does all the opium come from ? Probably Mr. Cooper has judged of the whole population by the chair-coolies who carried him, and the traders he met with at inns. In Southern China the passengers on board the steamers and native passage-boats indulge their habit freely on board the vessels. If one might judge of the proportion of smokers to the whole adult male population, from what is commonly witnessed among these passengers, it would probably fall short of one-tenth instead of reaching to near one-third. In country districts, out of the track of commerce, it might be found that opium-smoking is rare. It is not equally distributed over the whole empire; at least, there is every reason to suppose the contrary. In the treaty-ports and districts adjacent to them, and in the provinces growing native opium, it will be found most frequent.

This view is supported by the memorial of Choo-Tsun to the Emperor, in 1836, in opposition to the proposition to legalize the trade, and only to prohibit the officers and military to smoke. He says :—

" It is said, indeed, that when repealing the prohibitions, the people only are to be allowed to deal in and smoke the drug, and that none of the officers, the scholars, and the military are to be allowed this liberty. But this is bad casuistry. It is equal to the popular proverb, " Shut a woman's ears before you steal her earrings." The officers, with all the scholars and the military, do not amount to more than one-tenth of the whole population, and the other nine-tenths are all the common people. The great majority of those who at present smoke opium are the relatives and dependents of the officers of Government, whose example has extended the practice to the mercantile classes, and has gradually contaminated the inferior officers, the military, and the scholars. Those who do not smoke are the common people of the villages and hamlets."

The Rev. Joseph Edkins, of the London Missionary Society, Peking, says :—

"At Shanghai, fifty-five per cent. of men smoke. In Shantung, fifteen per hundred in towns. None in many villages. The practice is still spreading."

APPENDIX C.

ACTION OF THE INDIAN GOVERNMENT IN INCREASING THE SUPPLY OF OPIUM FOR THE FOREIGN TRADE.

It is difficult to get the English public to realize the fact that, as regards the production of opium for the foreign trade, the British Government of India is a commercial firm, animated by the spirit of trade. The Viceroy and his Council in Calcutta, the Secretary of State for India and his Council in Parliament-street, are, when they come to deal with opium, in a position exactly similar to that of Messrs. Jardine, Matheson, and Co., and Messrs. Sassoon and Co. There is one difference, viz., that the private merchants put the profits in their own pockets; the public merchants trade for the public treasury. But it is to be feared this difference is far from guaranteeing in our statesmen-merchants that indifference to the pecuniary result of their commerce which would insure an impartial verdict on its moral character. Moreover, the Secretaries of State and Viceroys are but temporary chiefs of an enormous bureaucracy, the permanent officials of which are the practical Government of India, and their interests are directly as well as indirectly concerned in the affluence of the Indian Treasury. If any one will only read their own published documents, it will convince him that, with a few honourable exceptions, Indian officialdom has been as much biassed in favour of the opium trade as the private opium-dealers have been, and by a similar cause—its profitableness.

Our first witness is Mr. St. George Tucker, Finance Minister in the Indian Government, and afterwards twice

Chairman of the Court of Directors. He wrote to Sir Robert Peel : [1]—

" When I was connected with the finances of India, the policy pursued in the management of the monopoly was to draw the largest revenue from the smallest quantity of the drug . . . But when the province of Malwa came under our dominion, it occurred to some of our functionaries that an opium revenue might be obtained at Bombay analogous to that derived from the monopoly of the manufacture in Bengal, and every possible stimulus was given to the cultivation of the poppy. . . . From this time an entire change in our policy took place, and it became the object of the Government to crush the competition from other quarters, which high prices might engender, and to draw the same revenue from a large quantity at lower rates."

And in a similar strain to Mr. Marjoribanks : [2]—

" For the last twenty years we have been *encouraging* the production by all possible means, and we now export to China alone the enormous quantity of 27,000 chests. This I have always considered an intolerable evil."

He also addressed an earnest remonstrance to the Court of Directors :—

" Ever since I had the honour of being a member of this Court I have uniformly and steadily opposed the encouragement given to the extension of the manufacture of opium ; but of late years we have pushed it to the utmost height, and disproportionate prices were given for the article in Malwa. We contracted burdensome treaties with the Rajpoot States to introduce and extend the cultivation of the poppy. We introduced the article into our own districts, where it had not been cultivated before, or where the cultivation had been abandoned, and we gave our revenue officers an interest in extending the cultivation in preference to other produce much more valuable and deserving of encouragement. Finally, we established retail shops, which brought it to every man's door. How different was the policy of Lord

[1] Kaye's Administration.　　　　[2] Ibid.

Cornwallis, Lord Teignmouth, Lord Wellesley, and Lord Minto, who circumscribed the produce within the narrowest limits, confining the cultivation of the poppy to two of our provinces, and actually eradicating it from districts where it had been previously cultivated! How fatal have been the consequences of a departure from this wise and humane policy! Is there any man still so blind as not to perceive that it has had a most injurious effect upon our national reputation? If a revenue cannot be drawn from such an article otherwise than by quadrupling the supply, by promoting the general use of the drug, and by placing it within the reach of the lower classes of the people, no fiscal consideration can justify our inflicting upon the Malays and Chinese so grievous an evil." [3]

This appeal to the Company's nobler instincts fell on deaf ears. They and their successors, the British Government, deliberately resolved to make as much money by the trade as they could, regardless of its consequences. Witness the avowal of Sir Cecil Beadon, K.C.S.I., formerly Lieutenant-Governor of Bengal, to the House of Commons Committee : [4]

" 3329. *Mr. Fawcett.*]—I understand you to say that opium is grown in India simply for purposes of revenue ; no moral considerations at all influence the Government?—The Government only regard opium as a means of obtaining revenue.

" 3330. That if, for instance, they thought they could obtain more revenue by doubling the cultivation of opium in India, they would do so, and would not be deterred from adopting such a course by any considerations as to the deleterious effect which opium might produce on the people to whom it was sold?—Probably not."

Sir William Muir, in his Minute recommending the abandonment of the monopoly, indicates the commercial spirit of the Government in these words: [5]—

---

[3] Papers relating to the Opium Trade, 1842−1856, London, p. 54.
[4] Report, East India Finance, 1871, p. 161.
[5] Calcutta Papers, 1870, p. 6.

"That cannot be an edifying position for the Government to occupy, in which it has year by year to determine the quantity of opium which it will bring to sale, in which there is a constant inducement for it to trim the market, and in which its haste to secure wider harvests and larger returns has repeatedly recoiled upon the trade, stimulated baneful speculation and gambling in Central and Western India, and ended in much misery."

The utterances of the Indian Government, through its officials, contain abundant proofs of a systematic determination to treat opium simply and solely as a source of gain, and to push the trade to the utmost. Take the following as illustrations.[6]

Extract from Minute by the HONOURABLE J. STRACHEY, *dated Simla, 20th April,* 1869.

"It seems to me, therefore, that immediate measures of the most energetic character ought to be taken with the object of increasing the production of opium. No doubt this may lead to present expense, and it is possible that, if we take no extraordinary measure now, the fortunate recurrence of two or three good seasons may relieve us from our difficulties. But the risk that we are running seems to me too serious a one to be accepted. I think that the very least which we ought now to do is to endeavour with the least possible delay to bring up the total area under opium cultivation to 790,500 beegahs, the extent declared by the Lieutenant Governor of Bengal to be necessary for the production of 54,500 chests. I believe myself that we might, with propriety, go much further, but anything less than this will, I think, be certainly too little. I observe that in the three years ending with 1861-62 opium cultivation was extended from 435,000 to 832,000 beegahs. The provision of opium in 1860-61 was 29,358 chests; it was 39,656 in 1861-62; 49,727 in 1862-63; and 64,269 in 1863-64. If it

_____
[6] Calcutta Papers, 1870, p. 85, *et seq.*

S

was possible a few years ago to make so immense an increase of production in so short a time, I should hope that it might be found practicable to make the far smaller increase that is now required in a much smaller space of time than now appears to be contemplated. Whether very much can be done during the present year is unfortunately doubtful, for the season is now far advanced. Still it may not be too late to do something more than has been already proposed. I recommend that the Lieutenant-Governor be immediately addressed on this subject, and that he be requested to consider whether measures might not still be taken with advantage, which would increase the area of opium cultivation in the season of 1869-70 to something like the full amount necessary to give an average annual production of 54,500 chests. Even if it be too late now to accomplish this altogether, any increase of cultivation which can be brought about without excessive expenditure will be a clear gain.

" 626. I think that special inquiry should be made as to the possibility of profitably extending the cultivation of opium in the districts of the North-Western Provinces, in which canal irrigation is available. It seems not improbable that we might thus diminish to some extent the precariousness of production which now causes so much difficulty."

Demi-official, from the Honourable W. Grey, *Lieutenant Governor of Bengal, dated Barrackpore, 22nd April,* 1869.

To C. H. Campbell, *Esq.*

" 639. I have a telegraphic message from Simla, urging ' that every possible expedient that you (I) approve should be used even now to extend the opium cultivation next season to the utmost practicable extent.'

" 640. From all accounts it is not practicable to do anything more in the Behar Agency. The figures you sent me the other day show the area of cultivation to have been larger in 1867-68 than in any previous year, and Abercrombie seems positive that it cannot be further stretched without taking up altogether new fields of operation.

" 641. But are you quite satisfied that the fullest possible extension (that is, of course, under existing circumstances, and without an increase of price) is being pushed in the Benares Agency? I see from the figures you sent me that the cultivation of that agency was in 1863-64 358,000 beegahs, which gave the large yield of 51,542 maunds, an average of 5-11¾ per beegah. In 1867-68 the cultivation was 265,572 beegahs. If Carnac should see his way to doing anything more than he has done already to extend the cultivation for next season, you need not hesitate to sanction it at once."

Minute by Sir R. Temple, *dated 27th April,* 1869.

" 642. On the general question of the opium supply I do not wish to controvert anything which Mr. Strachey has written in his Minute of the 20th.

" 643. In the general principles on which his opinion is based, I concur.

" 644. I am clear for extending the cultivation, and for insuring a plentiful supply. If we do not do this, the Chinese will do it for themselves. They had better have our good opium than their own indifferent opium. There really is no moral objection to our conduct in this respect.

" 645. I, therefore, quite agree with Mr. Strachey in the general policy of increasing the cultivation.

" 646. But I think that even here caution is required. If we suddenly increased it in every direction, and if after that there ensued a 'bumper' harvest, we might have more opium on our hands than we could dispose of, and, inasmuch as we must pay for all that is brought by our ryots, the *expenditure* would be great."

(*Extracts from*) No. 533, dated 14th May, 1869.

From R. B. Chapman, Esq., *Offg. Secy. to the Govt. of India,*
Financial Dept.,
To the Secretary to the Government of Bengal.

" 687. I am directed in continuation of my letter No. 2069,

s 2

dated 17th ultimo, to address you on the subject of the arrangements that are necessary for insuring an increased supply of opium. . . . .

"695. (9.) It is impossible not to regard with anxiety the possibility that in consequence of the deficiency of supply, the price next year will increase to such an extent as to furnish a dangerous stimulus to competition with the Indian drug in the China market. If, unfortunately, the crop of next season should be again deficient in quantity, the consequences to our opium revenue might be permanently disastrous.

"696. (10.) It is true that a succession of favourable seasons may extricate the Government from its present difficulties, but his Excellency in Council considers the risk of depending upon such a fortunate contingency too great to be accepted. His Excellency in Council is therefore of opinion that the most energetic measures should be taken to increase the cultivation, with the least possible delay, to not less than 790,500 beegahs, as estimated by the Lieutenant Governor, or to 800,000 beegahs.

" 697. (11.) The Governor-General in Council observes that in the three years ending with 1861-62, the opium cultivation was extended from 435,000 to 832,000 beegahs. The provision of opium was :—

In 1860-61 .	.	.	.	. 29,358 chests.
„ 1861-62 .	.	.	.	. 39,656 „
„ 1862-63 .	.	.	.	. 49,727 „
and „ 1863-64 .	.	.	.	. 64,269 „

" If it was possible then to bring about so immense an increase of cultivation and production in so short a time, his Excellency in Council thinks that it may be found practicable to effect the far smaller increase that is now required in a shorter time than now appears to be contemplated. It may not be too late to do something more than has been proposed even for the coming season.

"698. (12.) Any increase of cultivation that can be obtained without excessive expenditure will apparently be a clear gain. The Government of India thinks that special inquiry should be made as to the possibility of profitably extending the cultivation of the poppy in the districts of the North-Western Provinces in which canal irrigation is available. It seems not impossible that in this way the precariousness of production which causes so much difficulty might to some extent be diminished."

These extracts make it abundantly evident that our Indian Government does not hold the calm, indifferent position of a superior authority laying a heavy tax upon an injurious article, the consumption of which it cannot prevent; but, on the contrary, that it enters into the trade with the same eager desire for its increase that a private capitalist would feel. Who does not blush to think that a British Government should be engaged in the sordid pursuit of profits raised from Chinese opium-smoking dens?

But the most painful evidence is found in the result of Sir Rutherford Alcock's visit to Calcutta, in 1870. Our ambassador went from Peking to the capital of our Indian empire with the revision of the Treaty of Tientsin in his hands, in which revision he had agreed to grant to the Chinese an increase of duty on opium of about two and a half per cent., in return for certain privileges to be granted to English commerce. Sir R. Alcock laid the matter before the Indian Council, urging them not to oppose this concession, and setting forth the strong moral objections to the trade. The whole account of this interview and its sequences may be read in the Calcutta Opium Papers.[7]

"In answer to questions put by his Excellency the Viceroy and others, Sir Rutherford Alcock said that he had no doubt that the abhorrence expressed by the Government and people of China for opium, as destructive to the Chinese nation, is genuine and deep-seated; and that he was also

[7] Papers relating, &c., 1870. Addendum to Appendix IV.

quite convinced that the Chinese Government could, if it pleased, carry out its threat of developing cultivation to any extent. On the other hand, he believed that so strong was the popular feeling on the subject, that if Britain would give up the opium revenue and suppress the cultivation in India, the Chinese Government would have no difficulty in suppressing it in China, except in the province of Yunnan, where its authority is in abeyance.

" He then read extracts from his despatch (copy is in the office) to Lord Clarendon upon the question, and he dwelt upon the fact that the additional import duty was largely nominal, as the Chinese could impose what transit duties they pleased upon opium, and did impose upon it *very heavy* duties of this kind.

" Sir R. Temple inquired whether the Chinese Government would be willing to enter into an agreement for repressing the growth of the poppy in China, upon condition that the Government of India would fix a limit to the amount of opium to be sent to China; also, whether they would have the power and the will to observe their side of any such agreement. Sir Rutherford Alcock thought that they would be ready to adopt any reasonable proposition, and would be able to carry it out more or less effectually.

" He repeated that the Chinese Government did certainly hope and desire that the British Government would agree to some arrangement for giving effect to the wish of China for the discouragement of the consumption of opium by the Chinese people."

The Viceroy and his Council discussed the matter, and came to the conclusion that the Government could not protest against the additional import duty; but adopted the following resolution :—

No. 2090, dated 25th March, 1870.

RESOLUTION.—*By the Government of India Financial Department.*

" Resolution.—The Government of Bengal shall be informed that the Supreme Government has resolved to increase the annual provision of opium in Bengal for export to China to 60,000 chests, gradually indeed, but still with as much promptitude as may be conveniently practicable, and will be prepared to sanction any expenditure that, on full consideration, may appear necessary for this object. It is not deemed needful at present to raise the price paid to the cultivators to 5 Rs. a seer, but the Supreme Government recognizes the probability that this concession must soon be made, and will be prepared to consider favourably any recommendation made by the Government of Bengal for such an increase if it be found by experience that effect cannot otherwise be given to this Resolution.

" Ordered, that the foregoing Resolution be communicated to the Government of Bengal for information and guidance."

After reading this, who will have the face to assert that the Bengal monopoly is simply a mode of taxation?

APPENDIX D.

HISTORICAL.

EXTRACTS FROM "CORRESPONDENCE RELATING TO CHINA," 1840.

No. 61.

SIR G. B. ROBINSON TO VISCOUNT PALMERSTON.

> "His Majesty's Cutter 'Louisa,'
> "Lintin, Feb. 5, 1836.

"I SEE no grounds to apprehend the occurrence of any fearful events on the north-east coast, nor can I learn what new danger exists. I am assured from the best authority that the scuffles between different parties of smugglers and mandarins, alike engaged and competing in the traffic, are not more serious or frequent than in this province. In no case have Europeans been engaged in any kind of conflict or affray; and while this increasing and lucrative trade is in the hands of the parties whose vital interests are so totally dependent on its safety and continuance, and by whose prudence and integrity it has been cherished and brought into its present increasing and flourishing condition, I think little apprehension may be entertained of dangers emanating from imprudence on their part. Should any unfortunate catastrophe take place, what would our position at Canton entail upon us but responsibility and jeopardy? from which we are now free.

"On the question of 'smuggling opium' I will not enter in this place, though, indeed, smuggling carried on actually in the mandarin boats can hardly be termed such. Whenever his Majesty's Government direct us to prevent British ships engaging in the traffic, we can enforce any order to that effect; but a more certain method would be to prohibit the growth of the poppy and manufacture of opium in British India; and if British ships are in the habit of committing irregularities and crimes, it seems doubly necessary to exercise a salutary control over them by the presence of an authority at Lintin."

No. 82.

CAPTAIN ELLIOT TO THE FOREIGN OFFICE.

" Macao, July 27, 1836.

" It has been a confusion of terms to call the opium trade a smuggling trade; it was a formally-prohibited trade, but there was no part of the trade of this country which had the more active support of the local authorities. It commenced and has subsisted by the hearty connivance of the mandarins, and it could have done neither the one nor the other without their constant concurrence."

No. 110.

CAPTAIN ELLIOT TO VISCOUNT PALMERSTON.

" Canton, Nov. 19, 1837.

" The native boats have been burned, and the native smugglers scattered; and the consequence is, as it was foreseen it would be, that a complete and very hazardous change has been worked in the whole manner of conducting the Canton portion of the trade.

" The opium is now carried on (and a great part of it inwards to Whampoa) in European passage-boats belonging to British owners, slenderly manned with Lascar seamen, and furnished with a scanty armament, which may be rather said to provoke or to justify search, accompanied by violence, than to furnish the means of effectual defence.

*　　*　　*　　*　　*　　*　　*

" In fact, my lord, looking around me, and weighing the whole body of circumstances as carefully as I can, it seems to me that the moment has arrived for such active interposition upon the part of her Majesty's Government as can properly be afforded, and that it cannot be deferred without great hazard to the safety of the whole trade, and of the persons engaged in its pursuit."

No. 116.

Viscount Palmerston to Captain Elliot.

" June 15th, 1838.

" With respect to the smuggling trade in opium, which forms the subject of your despatches of the 18th and 19th November, and 7th December, 1837, I have to state that her Majesty's Government cannot interfere for the purpose of enabling British subjects to violate the laws of the country to which they trade. Any loss, therefore, which such persons may suffer in consequence of the more effectual execution of the Chinese laws on the subject, must be borne by the parties who have brought that loss on themselves by their own acts."

No. 137.

Captain Elliot to Viscount Palmerston.

" January 2nd, 1839.

" . . . . I have now to inform your lordship that Mr. Innes applied to the provincial government for a passport, and left this place for Macao on the 16th ultimo, having previously forwarded a declaration to his Excellency, confessing that the opium was his, that it came from his boat, and not from the American ship, and absolving the two coolies from all artful participation in the offence, upon the ground that they were ignorant of the contents of the boxes. The difficulty which remained to be removed before the trade could be re-opened, was the illicit traffic in opium carried on in small craft within the river, a considerable number of which were stationary at Whampoa, receiving their supplies from time to time in other vessels of a similar description, from the opium ships at Lintin or Hong Kong.

"The senior Hong merchants, on the evening of my arrival in Canton (the 12th ult.), complained in bitter terms that they should be exposed to the cruel and ruinous consequences which were hourly arising out of the existence of this forced trade, not merely at Whampoa, but at the factories themselves, of which they were the proprietors, and, therefore, under heavy responsibility to the Government. And they insisted that they would not carry on the lawful commerce (having the governor's sanction for their conduct) till effectual steps were taken for the suppression of this dangerous evil. . . . .

"Carefully considering the critical posture of those momentous interests confided to me, I resolved, as a preliminary measure, upon an appeal to the whole community; not only with some hope that such a proceeding might have the effect of clearing the river of these boats, but because (if the case were otherwise) I felt it became me distinctly to forewarn her Majesty's subjects concerned in these practices of the course which it was my determination to pursue. On the 17th ultimo, therefore, I convened a general meeting of all the foreign residents at Canton in this hall, and addressed them in the manner your lordship will find reported in the accompanying note,[1] taken at the

---

[1] *Vide infra.*

moment by my secretary. On the 18th I promulgated the enclosed notice,[1] and having ascertained that the smuggling boats were still at Whampoa on the 23rd (some of them wearing British ensigns and pendants), I addressed the accompanying note [2] to his Excellency the governor."

*   *   *   *   *   *   *

"Having now drawn the statement of these proceedings to a close, I may turn to a more particular explanation of the motives and the manner of my interposition. It had been clear to me, my lord, from the origin of this peculiar branch of the opium traffic, that it must grow to be more and more mischievous to every branch of the trade, and certainly to none more than to that of opium itself. As the danger and shame of its pursuit increased, it was obvious that it would fall by rapid degrees into the hands of more and more desperate men; that it would stain the foreign character with constantly aggravating disgrace in the sight of the whole of the better portion of this people; and lastly, that it would connect itself more and more intimately with our lawful commercial intercourse, to the great peril of vast public and private interests.

"Till the other day, my lord, I believe there was no part of the world where the foreigner felt his life and property more secure than here in Canton, but the grave events of the 12th ultimo have left a different impression. For a space of near two hours the foreign factories were within the power of an immense and excited mob, the gate of one of them was absolutely battered in, and a pistol was fired out, probably without ball, or over the heads of the people, for at least it is certain that nobody fell. If the case had been otherwise, her Majesty's Government and the British public would have had to learn that the trade and peaceful intercourse with this Empire was indefinitely interrupted by a terrible scene of bloodshed and ruin. And all these desperate hazards have been incurred, my lord, for the scrambling and, comparatively considered, insignificant

[2] Ibid.

gains of a few reckless individuals, unquestionably founding their conduct upon the belief that they were exempt from the operation of all law, British or Chinese."

* * * * * * *

" I should observe in this place that the remarkable vigour, not merely of the local, but of the general Government, for some months back, furnished additional causes to apprehend some exceedingly serious dilemma. And regarding the subject in every point of view, I could not but perceive that a person in my station should lose no time in taking such a position as would give weight to his representations in any moment of emergency."

Inclosure 7 in No. 137.

CAPTAIN ELLIOT'S ADDRESS AT A GENERAL MEETING OF ALL FOREIGN RESIDENTS AT CANTON.

" 17th December, 1838.

" . . . . Seeking, however, for the immediate source of this critical interruption of the usual course of events, he felt bound to say that he found it in the existence of an extensive traffic in opium, conducted in small boats upon the river. The present results of that traffic should be shortly stated and considered ; the actual interruption of the legal trade, the seizure and imminent jeopardy of innocent men, the daily exposure of every native connected with the foreigners to similar disastrous consequences, the life and property of the whole foreign community at the mercy of an immense mob for the space of at least two hours, the distressing degradation of the foreign character, the painful fact that such courses exposed us more and more to the just indignation of this Government and people, and diminished the sympathies of our own; of its futurity it might safely be predicted that it would fall into the hands of the reckless, the refuse, and probably the convicted, of all the countries in our neighbourhood. Attentively considering all these points, Captain Elliot felt that it became him to explain the course which it was his purpose to pursue with the view to the re-establishment of a safer and more creditable condition of circumstances. He should forthwith serve a notice upon the boats in the river to the effect that, if they were British-owned, and were either actually or occasionally engaged in the traffic, they must proceed outside within three days, and cease to return with any similar pursuits ; that failing their conformity with those injunctions, he should place himself in communication with the provincial Government, and frankly and fully express the views of his own, upon the necessary and perfectly admissible treatment of so serious an evil. He could not, however, help indulging the hope that the general reprobation of the whole community would have the effect of relieving him from the performance of a duty on many accounts extremely painful to him."

Inclosure 8 in No. 137.

PUBLIC NOTICE TO HER MAJESTY'S SUBJECTS.[1]

" I, Charles Elliot, Chief Superintendent of the trade of British subjects in China, moved by urgent considerations, immediately affecting the safety of the lives and properties of all her Majesty's subjects engaged in the trade at Canton, do hereby formally give notice and require that all British-owned schooners, cutters, or otherwise rigged small craft, either habitually or occasionally engaged in the illicit opium traffic within the Bocca Tigris, should proceed forth of the same within the space of three days from the date of these presents, and not return within the said Bocca Tigris being engaged in the said illicit opium trade.

" And I, the said Chief Superintendent, do further give

[1] Correspondence, 1840, p. 334.

notice and warn all her Majesty's subjects, engaged in the
aforesaid illicit opium traffic within the Bocca Tigris, in such
schooners, cutters, or otherwise rigged small craft, that if
any native of the Chinese empire shall come by his or her
death by any wound feloniously inflicted by any British subject or subjects, any such British subject or subjects, being
duly convicted thereof, are liable to capital punishment, as
if the crime had been committed within the jurisdiction of
her Majesty's courts at Westminster.

" And I, the said Chief Superintendent, do further give
notice and warn all British subjects being owners of
such schooners, cutters, or otherwise rigged small craft,
engaged in the said illicit opium traffic within the Bocca
Tigris, that her Majesty's Government will in no way inter-
pose if the Chinese Government shall think fit to seize and
confiscate the same.

" And I, the said Chief Superintendent, do further give
notice and warn all British subjects employed in the said
schooners, cutters, and otherwise rigged small craft, engaged
in the illicit opium traffic within the Bocca Tigris, that the
forcible resisting of the officers of the Chinese Government
in the duty of searching and seizing, is a lawless act, and
that they are liable to consequences and penalties in the same
manner as if the aforesaid forcible resistance were opposed
to the officers of their own or any other Government in their
own or any foreign country.

" Given under my hand and seal of office at Canton, this
eighteenth day of December, in the year of our Lord one
thousand eight hundred and thirty-eight.

(Signed)   "CHARLES ELLIOT, &c., &c."

Inclosure 14 in No. 137.

OFFICIAL NOTICE TO HER MAJESTY'S SUBJECTS.

31st December, 1838.

*   *   *   *   *   *   *

" After the most deliberate reconsideration of this course

of traffic (which he heartily hopes has ceased for ever), the Chief Superintendent will once more declare his own opinion, that in its general effects it was intensely mischievous to every branch of the trade, that it was rapidly staining the British character with deep disgrace, and, finally, that it exposed the vast public and private interests involved in the peaceful maintenance of our regular commercial intercourse with this empire, in imminent jeopardy.

" Thus profoundly impressed (and after the failure of his own public entreaties and injunctions), the Chief Superintendent feels that he would have betrayed his duty to his gracious sovereign and his country, if he had hesitated beyond the period he had formerly fixed, effectually to separate her Majesty's Government from any direct or implied countenance of this dangerous irregularity." . . . .

Inclosure 9 in No. 137.

CAPTAIN ELLIOT TO THE GOVERNOR OF CANTON.

December 23rd, 1838.

" . . . . Seeking for the immediate source of this dangerous state of things, he finds it in the existence of an extensive opium traffic, conducted in small craft within the river." . . . .

" The Government of the British nation will regard these evil practices with no feelings of leniency, but, on the contrary, with severity and continual anxiety : in proof of this, the undersigned has now to acquaint your Excellency that he has already, on the 18th day of this month, formally required all boats (owned by British subjects) engaged in this traffic, to leave the river within three days.

" He cannot faithfully declare that these injunctions have been fulfilled, and he has, therefore, now to request that your Excellency will signify your pleasure through the honourable officers, the Kwang Chowfoo and Kwanghee, so that all those concerned in these pursuits may know that he has received your Excellency's authority for this notice.

" . . . . It is further to be desired that your Excellency would command the honourable officers, who may be employed on this occasion, to proceed to the station of the boats, with the undersigned, in order that the peaceful and the well-disposed may not be involved in the same consequences as the perverse.

(Signed) " CHARLES ELLIOT, &c., &c."

Inclosure 10 in No. 137.

THE PREFECT AND COMMANDANT, JOINTLY, OF CANTON TO CAPTAIN ELLIOT.

*   *   *   *   *   *   *

" The said superintendent came, I find, to Canton in obedience to commands received from his sovereign to exercise control over the merchants and seamen, to repress the depraved, and to extirpate evils. Having such commands given him, he must needs also have powers. It is very inexplicable, then, that these boats, having in violation of the laws entered the river, he should now find it difficult to send them out again, owing to his not having the confidence of all."

No. 141.

CAPTAIN ELLIOT TO VISCOUNT PALMERSTON,

" 30th January, 1839.

" The stagnation of the opium trade at all points, however, may be said to have been nearly complete for the last four months. And it is now my duty to signify to your lordship the expected arrival of a very high officer from the court, of

T

equal rank with the Governor, and specially charged, as I am this day informed by Howqua, with the general conduct of the measures lately determined upon at Peking for the suppression of the opium trade. It must also be stated that the Emperor has recently been advised to command a total interruption of the foreign trade and intercourse, till the introduction of opium shall be effectually stopped, and an edict of great moment, evidently founded upon that policy, has been issued to the foreign merchants, but not yet to myself. It shall be transmitted to your lordship as soon as Mr. Morrison has translated it. . . . There seems, my lord, no longer any occasion to doubt that the court has firmly determined to suppress, or more probably, most extensively to check the opium trade. The immense, and it must be said, most unfortunate increase of the supply during the last four years, the rapid growth of the east coast trade, and the continued drain of the silver have, no doubt, greatly alarmed the Government: but the manner of the rash course of traffic within the river has probably contributed most of all to impress the urgent necessity of arresting the growing audacity of the foreign smugglers, and preventing their associating themselves with the desperate and lawless of their own large cities."

Inclosure 1 in No. 145.

EDICT FROM THE IMPERIAL COMMISSIONER, ADDRESSED TO FOREIGNERS OF ALL NATIONS.

" Lin, High Imperial Commissioner of the Celestial Court, a Director of the Board of War, and Governor of Hoo-kwang, issues his commands to the foreigners of every nation, requiring of all full acquaintance with the tenour thereof.

" It is known that the foreign vessels, which come for a reciprocal trade to Kwangtung, have derived from that trade very large profits. This is evidenced by the facts, that, whereas the vessels annually resorting hither were formerly reckoned hardly by tens, their number has of late years amounted to a hundred and several times ten, and that whatever commodities they have brought, none have ailed to find a full consumption ; whatever they may have sought to purchase, never have they been unable readily to do so. Let them but ask themselves whether, between heaven and earth, any place affording so advantageous a commercial mart is elsewhere to be found ? It is because our great Emperors, in their universal benevolence, have granted you commercial privileges that you have been favoured with these advantages. Let our ports once be closed against you, and for what profits can your several nations any longer look ? Yet more,—our tea and our rhubarb—seeing that, should you foreigners be deprived of them, you therein lose the means of preserving life—are without stint or grudge granted to you for exportation, year by year, beyond the seas. Favours never have been greater !

" Are you grateful for these favours ? You must, then, fear the laws, and in seeking profit for yourselves must not do hurt to others. Why do you bring to our land the opium, which in your lands is not made use of, by it defrauding men of their property, and causing injury to their lives ? I find that with this thing you have seduced and deluded the people of China for tens of years past, and countless are the unjust hoards that you have thus acquired. Such conduct rouses indignation in every human heart, and it is utterly inexcusable in the eye of celestial reason. . . .

" I proceed to issue my commands. When these commands reach the said foreign merchants, let them with all haste pay obedience thereto; let them deliver up to Government every particle of the opium on board their store-ships. Let it be ascertained by the Hong merchants who are the parties so delivering it up, and what number of chests, as also what total quantity, in catties and taels, is delivered up under each name. Let these particulars be brought together in a clear tabular form, and be presented to Government, in order that the opium may all be received in plain conformity thereto, that it may be burnt and destroyed, and that thus the evil may be entirely extirpated. There must not be the smallest atom concealed or withheld.

" At the same time, let these foreigners give a bond, written jointly in the foreign and Chinese languages, making a declaration to this effect :—' That their vessels, which shall hereafter-resort hither, will never again dare to bring opium with them ; and that should any be brought, as soon as discovery shall be made of it, the goods shall be forfeited to Government, and the parties shall suffer the extreme penalties of the law, and that such punishment will be willingly submitted to.'

" I have heard that you foreigners are used to attach great importance to the word ' good faith.' If then you will really do as I, the High Commissioner, have commanded,— will deliver up every particle of the opium that is already here, and will stay altogether its future introduction,—as this will prove, also, that you are capable of feeling contrition for your offences, and of entertaining a salutary dread of punishment, the past may yet be left unnoticed. I, the High Commissioner, will, in that case, in conjunction with the Governor and Lieutenant-Governor, address the throne, imploring the great Emperor to vouchsafe extraordinary favour, and not alone to remit the punishment of your past errors, but also, as we will further request, to devise some mode of bestowing on you his imperial rewards, as an encouragement of the spirit of contrition and wholesome dread thus manifested by you. After this you will continue to enjoy the advantages of commercial intercourse, and as you will not lose the character of being ' good foreigners,' and will be enabled to acquire profits and gain wealth by an honest trade, will you not stand in a most honourable position ?" . . . .

Inclosure 2 in No. 145.

EDICT FROM THE IMPERIAL COMMISSIONER TO THE HONG MERCHANTS.

" With regard, too, to foreigners, such as Jardine and others, who have been in the habit of selling opium,—all of them most artful and crafty men,—when the Imperial pleasure was expressed two years ago, that their conduct should be inquired into, and that they should be driven forth, the said Hong merchants still strenuously defended them. Such language as this was used: " That when it could be discovered that there had been any concert in selling opium, any money taken, or orders given, punishment would then be willingly submitted to." Such a bond is yet to be found among the archives! Let them ask themselves, whether, according to this bond, punishment should or should not be inflicted ?

" Again, the opium on board Innes' vessel was seized within the river, showing that the bonds given even for vessels that have entered the port have been no less unworthy of confidence." . . . .

No. 146.

CAPTAIN ELLIOT TO VISCOUNT PALMERSTON.

"Canton, March 30, 1839.

" MY LORD,—I have considered that I shall most perspicuously perform my present duty to her Majesty's Government, by confining this despatch to a narrative of events, accompanied by the documents connected with them ; and, indeed, my imprisoned and harassed condition is not suited to a deliberately comprehensive exposition of the motives which have influenced some of the momentous proceedings involved in this report. . . . .

" I then assembled the whole foreign community in Canton, and reading to them my circulars issued at Macao, enjoined

them all to be moderate, firm, and united. I had the satisfaction to dissolve the meeting in a calmer state of mind
than had subsisted for several days past.

"The native servants were taken from us, and the supplie
cut off on the same night; but it was declared by the merchants that the orders had been issued in the course of the
morning, by reason of Mr. Dent's opposition to the High
Commissioner's summons.

"An arc of connected boats was formed, filled with armed
men, the extremes of which touch the east and west points
of the bank of the river in the immediate front of the factories, cutting off a segment of the stream from the main
body; the square and the rear of the factories are occupied
in considerable force, and before the gate of this hall the
whole body of Hong merchants and a large guard are posted
day and night, the latter with their swords constantly drawn.
In short, so close an imprisonment of the foreigners is not
recorded in the history of our previous intercourse with this
empire. . . . .

"Canton, April 2, 1839.

"The only incidents of interest affecting our general situation since I last wrote are the permission to purchase food,
and the entrance, from time to time, of Coolies under strict
surveillance, to remove the foul linen. In other respects,
the blockade is increasing in closeness. Scraps of intelligence, however, have reached us, brought up by Chinese, in
cigars and in other adroit modes, from Whampoa, to the
31st ultimo, and from Macao to the 30th. All was tranquil
at either point when these tidings left, but the painful anxiety
of our families and countrymen will be conceivable to her
Majesty's Government."

EXTRACT FROM CAPTAIN ELLIOTT'S LETTER TO THE EARL OF
ABERDEEN.

"January 19, 1842.

"The condition of the opium market at that time was one

of excessive glut. There were 20,000 chests on the coast of China, upwards of 20,000 in Bengal, nearly 12,000 in Bombay, making a total of upwards of 50,000 chests ready for the market, and the crop of the current year would soon have had to be added to this stock. The annual consumption at its highest mark had never exceeded 24,000 chests, and for the three months preceding delivery, it has already been observed that there had been nearly a total stagnation of the traffic. So far as the general opium trade and the Indian revenue were concerned, Commissioner Lin's measure was one of great relief."

LETTER TO THE QUEEN OF ENGLAND FROM THE IMPERIAL COMMISSIONER AND THE PROVINCIAL AUTHORITIES REQUIRING THE INTERDICTION OF OPIUM.

" [THE paper of which a translation is here given—purporting to be a letter addressed to the Queen of England—was permitted to obtain circulation among the people, in the same manner as many official documents commonly do, about three months since, when the Commissioner and Governor were about to leave Canton to receive the opium surrendered in the name of the British Crown. Presumptive evidence of its authenticity is afforded by the expression on the part of the Commissioner of an anxious desire to know how he should convey such a communication to the English Sovereign]."—Chinese Repository, vol. viii. p. 9, May, 1839.

"LIN, high Imperial Commissioner, a director of the Board of War, and Governor of the two Hoo; TANG, a director of the Board of War, and Governor of the two Kwang; and E, a vice-director of the Board of War, and Lieutenant-Governor of Kwangtung, conjointly address this communication to the Sovereign of the English nation, for the purpose of requiring the interdiction of opium.

" That in the ways of Heaven no partiality exists, and no sanction is allowed to the injuring of others for the advantage of one's self,—that in men's natural desires there is not any great diversity (for where is he who does not abhor death and seek life ?)—these are universally acknowledged principles. And your honourable nation, though beyond the wide ocean, at a distance of twenty thousand miles, acknowledges the same ways of heaven, the same human nature, and has the like perceptions of the distinctions between life and death, benefit and injury.

" Our heavenly Court has for its family all that is within the four seas : the Great Emperor's heaven-like benevolence, —there is none whom it does not overshadow. Even regions remote, desert, and disconnected, have a part in the general care of life and of well-being.

" In Kwang-tung since the removal of the interdicts upon maritime communication, there has been a constantly flowing stream of commercial intercourse. The people of the land, and those who come from abroad in foreign ships, have reposed together in the enjoyment of its advantages, for tens of years past, even until this time. And as regards the rhubarb, teas, raw silk, and similar rich and valuable products of China, should foreign nations be deprived of these, they would be without the means of continuing life. So that the Heavenly Court by granting, in the oneness of its common benevolence, permission for the sale and exportation thereof,—and that without stint or grudge—has indeed extended its favours to the utmost circuit (of the nations) making its heart one with the core of heaven and earth.

" But there is a tribe of depraved and barbarous people, who, having manufactured opium for smoking, bring it hither for sale, and seduce and lead astray the simple folk, to the destruction of their persons, and the draining of their resources. Formerly the smokers thereof were few, but of late, from each to other the practice has spread its contagion, and daily do its baneful effects more deeply pervade the central source, its rich fruitful and flourishing population. It is not to be denied that the simple folk, inasmuch as they indulge their appetite at the expense of their lives, are indeed themselves the authors of their miseries : and why then should they be pitied ? Yet in the universal Empire under the sway of the great and pure dynasty, it is of essential import, for the right direction of men's minds, that their customs and manners should be formed to correctness. How can it be borne that the living souls that dwell within these seas, should be left wilfully to take a deadly poison ! Hence it is that those who deal in opium, or who inhale its fumes, within this land, are all now to be subjected to severest punishment, and that a perpetual interdict is to be placed on the practice so extensively prevailing.

" We have reflected that this poisonous article is the clandestine manufacture of artful schemers, and depraved people of various tribes under the dominion of your honourable nation. Doubtless you, the honourable Sovereign of that nation have not commanded the manufacture and sale of it. But amid the various nations there are a few only that make this opium : it is by no means the case that all the nations are herein alike. And we have heard that in your honourable nation too, the people are not permitted to inhale the drug, and that offenders in this particular expose themselves to sure punishment. It is clearly from a knowledge of its injurious effects on man, that you have directed severe prohibitions against it. But what is the prohibition of its use, in comparison with the prohibition of its being sold—of its being manufactured,—as a means of thoroughly purifying the source ?

"Though not making use of it oneself, to venture nevertheless on the manufacture and sale of it, and with it to seduce the simple folk of this land, is to seek one's own livelihood by the exposure of others to death, to seek one's own advantage by other men's injury. And such acts are bitterly abhorrent to the nature of man—are utterly opposed to the ways of heaven. To the vigorous sway exercised by the

Celestial Court over both the civilized and the barbarous, what difficulty presents itself to hinder the immediate taking of life ? But as we contemplate and give substantial being to the fulness and vastness of the sacred intelligence it befits us to adopt first the course of admonition. And not having as yet sent any communication to your honourable sovereignty,—should severest measures of interdiction be all at once enforced, it might be said in excuse that no previous knowledge thereof has been possessed.

" We would now then concert with your honourable sovereignty means to bring to a perpetual end this opium, so hurtful to mankind : we in this land forbidding the use of it,—and you, in the nations under your dominion, forbidding its manufacture. As regards what has been already made, we would have your honourable nation issue mandates for the collection thereof, that the whole may be cast into the depths of the sea. We would thus prevent the longer existence between these heavens and this earth of any portion of the hurtful thing. Not only then will the people of this land be relieved from its pernicious influence, but the people of your honourable nation too (for as they make, how know we that they do not also smoke it ?) will, when the manufacture is indeed forbidden, be likewise relieved from the danger of its use. Will not the result of this be the enjoyment by each of a felicitous condition of peace ? For your honourable nation's sense of duty being thus devout, shows a clear apprehension of celestial principles, and the supreme heavens will ward off from you all calamities. It is also in perfect accordance with human nature, and must surely need the approbation of sages.

Besides all this, the opium being so severely prohibited in this land, that there will be none found to smoke it, should your nation continue its manufacture, it will be discovered after all that no place will afford opportunity for selling it, that no profits will be attainable. Is it not far better to turn and seek other occupation than vainly to labour in the pursuit of a losing employment ?

And furthermore, whatever opium can be discovered in this land, is entirely committed to the flames and consumed. If any be again introduced in foreign vessels, it too must be subjected to a like process of destruction. It may well be feared, lest other commodities imported in such vessels should meet a common fate,—the gem and the pebble not being distinguished. Under these circumstances gain being no longer acquirable, and hurt having assumed a visible form, such as desire the injury of others will find that they themselves are the first to be injured.

The powerful instrumentality whereby the Celestial Court holds in subjection all nations is truly divine and awe-inspiring beyond the power of computation. Let it not be said that early warning of this has not been given.

When your Majesty receives this document, let us have a speedy communication in reply, advertising us of the measures you adopt for the entire cutting off of the opium in every seaport. Do not by any means by false embellishments evade or procrastinate. Earnestly reflect hereon. Earnestly observe these things.

Taou Kwang, 19th year, 2nd month—day.

Communication sent to the Sovereign of the English nation."

COPY OF THE LEGAL OPINION taken by the EAST INDIA COMPANY, and dated the 5th of August, 1857, as to the MANUFACTURE and SALE of OPIUM.

Case for the East India Company.

On the 9th March, 1857, the Earl of Shaftesbury moved in the House of Lords, that the following questions be submitted for the opinion of her Majesty's judges:—

First.—Whether, having regard to the 4th section of an Act passed in a session of Parliament holden in the third and fourth years of the reign of his late Majesty King

William the Fourth, intituled "An Act for effecting an Arrangement with the East India Company and for the better Government of his Majesty's Indian territories, till the 30th day of April, 1851," and other the laws bearing on this question, it is lawful for the East India Company to derive a revenue from opium by the following system, that is to say,—by prohibiting and preventing the growth of the poppy from which opium is made within their territories, except as grown on their account, and under their licence and superintendency, advances of money being annually made by them to the cultivators of the poppy, by way of prepayment of the price of all the juice of the poppy of a specified consistence, to be produced from the land in respect of which such advances are made, such price being estimated according to a price fixed by the company for the district in which the land happens to be situated, the cultivators delivering to the Company as much of such juice as the cultivators can produce, such juice being afterwards sent by the Company to their factories, and there manufactured by them into opium, afterwards sent by them from those factories to Calcutta, and there sold by them by auction at their sales, the excess of the sale prices over and above the first cost constituting the revenue in question.

Second.—Whether, having regard also to the Supplemental Treaty between her Majesty and the Emperor of China, bearing date the eighth day of October, 1843, which contains the following words,—"A fair and regular tariff of duties and other dues having now been established, it is to be hoped that the system of smuggling will entirely cease," it is lawful for the East India Company to deal with such opium in the manner stated in the first question, with the full knowledge that it is so purchased at the above-mentioned sales for the purpose of being smuggled into China, in contravention of the laws of that empire, and so to cultivate and manufacture the same with a view principally to the China market, and to its being so purchased for such purposes as aforesaid, the Company with that view manufacturing the opium into the form which the Company consider best adapted to facilitate and promote that contraband trade.

After some debate, in the course of which the Lord Chancellor used the following language, viz.:—"These matters, however, having been called to their attention, he was prepared to say, on the part of the Government, that when they shall have ascertained clearly and distinctly what were the facts as to the manufacture of opium by the East India Company, how it was done, who were concerned in it, how it was disposed of, everything, in short, being distinctly stated as matter of fact, the Government would have no objection to submitting, though not in the terms in which his noble friend had drawn them up, the question to the highest legal authorities whom they could properly consult, the law officers of the Crown; and that with respect to the second question, which related to the construction of the treaty concluded with China in 1843, he would say that they would consult the law officers of the Crown, with the addition of the Queen's Advocate, *and their Opinion the Government would communicate to their Lordships.*" His lordship also reminded the House that there was a well-known distinction between a person dealing with the produce of his own land and the ordinary transactions of commerce. The motion was by leave withdrawn.

The President of the Board of Commissioners for the affairs of India has now requested the Court of Directors of the East India Company to obtain the opinion of the Queen's Advocate and of the Attorney and Solicitor General and the Company's standing counsel on the points raised in the questions proposed by Lord Shaftesbury.

*　　*　　*　　*　　*　　*　　*

Your opinion is requested,—

1st. Whether the manufacture and sale of opium by the East India Company, in the manner aforesaid, in the presidency of Bengal, is or is not in contravention of the Act 3 & 4 W. IV. c. 85?

2nd. Whether the legality of the manufacture and sale of

opium by the East India Company, in the manner aforesaid, is in any way affected by the Supplemental Treaty entered into by her Majesty with the Emperor of China, in October, 1843?

Opinion.

1st. The Stat. 3 & 4 W. IV. c. 85, s. 4, requires the East India Company to close their commercial business and sell the effects distinguished in their books as commercial assets, and to discontinue and abstain from all commercial business which shall not be incident to the closing of their actual concerns, and to the conversion into money of the property hereinbefore directed to be sold, *" or which shall not be carried on for the purposes of the said Government,"* thus clearly implying that the East India Company were, after and notwithstanding that statute, to be at liberty to carry on commercial business for the " Purposes of the Government;" and, as it appears by the accompanying " Supplemental Memorandum," that from the year 1813 (when the Stat. 53 Geo. III. c. 155, was passed) the Company's accounts have been kept (as therein directed) under three distinct heads, territorial, political, and commercial, and that the profits of the Company's commercial business in opium have always been placed to the account of the " territorial and political " branch, and never included in the " commercial " accounts, and that this was the state of affairs at the passing of the Act 3 & 4 W. IV. c. 85.: We are of opinion that the manufacture and sale of opium by the East India Company, by which a revenue is acquired and expended for the purpose of Government, is not in contravention of the Act of the 3 & 4 W. IV. c. 85, which statute (on the contrary) must be taken to have intentionally permitted and sanctioned the continuance of such manufacture and sale for this purpose.

2nd. We are also of opinion that the legality of the manufacture and sale of opium by the East India Company is not *directly* affected by the Supplemental Treaty entered into by her Majesty with the Emperor of China in October, 1843. Opium is not mentioned in that treaty, and we are of opinion that the East India Company may manufacture and sell opium (the revenue of which is applied for the purposes of Government) without infringing the treaty.

The true question appears to be, whether the particular manner in which the East India Company's opium is manufactured is open to objection; it appearing by the "Supplemental Memorandum" that the opium in which the Company deals in the province of Bengal is prepared by the East India Company, and before its sale to the dealers specifically for the Chinese contraband trade, by being made up in balls and packed in chests according to Chinese weights. It is true that this practice is in conformity with a course of trade established (as we understand) long before any treaty with China, and even before the importation of opium was prohibited by Chinese law; still we think now that opium is made contraband by the law of China, and that its importation into China is made by Chinese law a capital crime, the continuance of the Company's practice of manufacturing and selling this opium in a form specially adapted to the Chinese contraband trade, though not an actual and direct infringement of the treaty, is yet at variance with its spirit and intention, and with the conduct due to the Chinese Government by that of Great Britain as a friendly power, bound by a treaty which implies that all smuggling into China will be discountenanced by Great Britain; and we think that if the practice in question were to be made the subject of expostulation by the Chinese Government, the British Government would be under an obligation to alter or modify the mode adopted by the East India Company of manufacturing opium, and to abstain from so manufacturing or preparing it as to involve a peculiar adaptation of the article to the Chinese contraband trade as distinguished from other trades, and to adhere to this modification so long as opium is absolutely prohibited in China.

(Signed)   J. D. HARDING.
RICHARD BETHELL.
HENRY S. KEATING.
LOFTUS WIGRAM.

Doctors' Commons, August 5, 1857.

CORRESPONDENCE RELATING TO THE EARL OF ELGIN'S MISSION.

No. 1.

The Earl of Clarendon to the Earl of Elgin.

" Foreign Office, April 20, 1857.

"It will be for your Excellency, when discussing commercial arrangements with any Chinese plenipotentiaries, to ascertain whether the Government of China would revoke its prohibition of the opium trade, which the high officers of the Chinese Government never practically enforce. Whether the legalization of the trade would tend to augment that trade may be doubtful, as it seems now to be carried on to the full extent of the demand in China, with the sanction and connivance of the local authorities. But there would be obvious advantages in placing the trade upon a legal footing by the imposition of a duty, instead of its being carried on in the present irregular manner."

Inclosure in No. 213.

Report on the Revision of Tariff, &c.

. . . " China still retains her objection to the use of a drug on moral grounds; but the present generation of smokers, at all events, must and will have opium. To deter the uninitiated from becoming smokers, China would propose a very high duty; but as opposition was naturally to be expected from us in that case, it should be made as moderate as possible. He urged, however, that inasmuch as when the treaty was signed, opium was not an article within its cognizance, we should not seek to regulate the duty now to be imposed upon it by the five per cent. *ad valorem* principle. . . . They were informed that, according to the data before Lord Elgin, a duty of from fifteen to twenty taels a chest would be a fair rate on the *ad valorem* principle. This, they repeated, could not apply to opium, which must be treated in every way *per se* . . . At length, after naming, apparently more in joke than in earnest, first sixty taels, and then forty taels, a chest, they proposed thirty taels. The British deputies pointed out the fact that twenty-four taels was the duty now levied *sub rosâ* by the authorities at Shanghai, and they were therefore justified in assuming that the Chinese Government would not have fixed upon that sum had the trade been calculated to bear a higher. After much discussion, chiefly upon the probable increase of smuggling in the event of the imposition of too high a duty —a contingency of which the Chinese deputies expressed themselves in no apprehension—it was agreed to put down thirty taels per chest on the duty to be levied."

APPENDIX E.

OPIUM IN BRITISH BURMA.

*Extracts from a Return published by the Government of India:
"Explanation of Causes of Increase or Decrease of amounts
on a Comparison of Revenues and Charges of the Provinces
of British Burma." Calcutta, 1873.*

1856-57. *Pegu.*—"There is no poppy cultivation in Pegu.
The import of opium by private individuals is strictly forbidden. The only opium that comes into the province is
what is supplied, by orders of the Revenue Board, Bengal,
to the Deputy Commissioner of districts, on their indenting
for it. It is retailed by the licensed opium farmers in the
large towns of the province. The use of this deleterious
drug, *strictly prohibited in the Burman time,* has been considerably on the increase of late."

1857-58. *Pegu.*—"In general it may be stated that
spirituous and other liquors are consumed by the European
and Indian inhabitants, and opium by the Chinese and
Burmese. Undoubtedly the consumption of both descriptions of stimulants is increasing. As a practical question
for Pegu, the consumption of spirits and opium could only
be effectually checked by a liquor and drug law applicable
to all inhabitants alike, and as such a law is not likely to be
passed, it only remains, by the imposition of a high rate of
duty, to endeavour to diminish the quantity accessible to the
mass of the population to an amount consistent with the
enjoyment of health and the due exercise of the mental
faculties."

1870-1871.—" Opium-eating is *not a Burman habit; it is a new vice:* and though unfortunately spreading fast, through the evil influence of petty Chinese traders and pedlars, it has not as yet taken such a hold upon the people that any great hardship is involved by such a limit being placed on the number of places to vend, as shall prevent the temptation of opium-eating being thrown in the way of idle young men in large towns and villages by too great facility of supply.

" Accordingly, at the outset, on the annexation of Pegu, the sale of opium in that province was restricted to the principal towns which contain Chinese and other foreigners who consume opium. . . . . Of Arakan the Chief Commissioner (Colonel Phayre) wrote in 1865 : 'Last year a majority of the respectable native Arakanese petitioned me. asserting that their own children and most of the young men of the country had become drunkards, and had acquired within a few years a craving for spirits and opium. . . . In the town of Akyab, which contains twenty thousand inhabitants, there were over ninety shops for the sale of intoxicating liquors and drugs of all sorts. To put an end to this the sale of opium was restricted in 1863-64 to four towns; viz. Akyab, old Arakan, Kyouk Phyoo, and Sandoway. In 1864-65 two farms only were allowed, namely, one in the town of Akyab, and another on the Arakan side of the Chittagong border, in what is known as the Noof district;' sale in the latter being permitted in order to restrain the importation of opium from Chittagong into the Arakan district. In 1868-69, however, the two farms in Kyouk Phyoo (Ramree district) and Sandoway *were re-established.*

    *   *   *   *   *   *   *

" The restriction of the sale of opium to particular towns still continues, with a caution that 'the error should be avoided of limiting sources of supply to such an extent as to make smuggling a remunerative occupation.' . . . . 'A clause has been inserted in the form, binding them to account satisfactorily to the Deputy Commissioner, should the quantity of opium taken fall considerably short of what might be expected from the experience of past years to be the average sale.' At the same time, 'district officers should use their utmost endeavours to prevent the spread of the consumption of this narcotic, as no purely fiscal considerations should be allowed to interfere with the arrangements which may be thought best for the interests of the people committed to their charge.' . . . . Owing, however, to the farmer's supply of Government opium at Rs. 20 a seer, being limited to a quantity less than he could sell, he was able to exact a high price from consumers, which encouraged the importation of opium from Chittagong. To stop this, it was ordered in July, 1870, that the *farmer should be supplied with whatever quantity he might require,* and in 1871-72 the price charged to him was raised from Rs. 20 to Rs. 23 for a seer, on the Chittagong prices."

APPENDIX F.

PROGRESS OF POPPY CULTIVATION IN CHINA.

" IT is now placed quite beyond doubt that the cultivation of opium in China has been very greatly extended of late years, and is at present carried on in the western provinces on a very large scale. The only financial consolation has been the belief that the appetite of the Chinese for the drug was also extending so rapidly as to absorb both the native and the Indian drug; but there was recently a heavy fall in the price of the latter, and weighty opinions, both official and non-official, suggest that the fall is caused by the indigenous cultivation, and that this fall is not only permanent, but warns us of the day, shortly approaching, when the imported opium will no longer be able to bear a heavy duty in competition with the native article, and our Indian revenue from this source will be lost. There have been repeated alarms on this subject, which have blown over; but the present alarm seems more serious and better supported than those which have gone before, and it must at least be felt that our opium revenue is precarious in the future."

(The *Quarterly Review*, vol. 130, Jan., 1871; Article on " The Revenues of India.")

" The principal opium-producing provinces are Kan-Suh, Yun-Nan, Si-Chwan, and Kwei-Chow. In the months of April and May these provinces are white with the poppy flowers. The native article is very cheap in the provinces in which it is grown, and the consumption is very general among the labouring classes. Whilst the foreign article in some parts of Si-Chwan is worth its weight in silver, the price of the native is only tenpence per Chinese ounce. A penny is sufficient to provide an ordinary smoker with enough for a day's consumption. There every one seems to indulge himself more or less in the pipe. The men and the women, the old and the young, seemed to me to be all playing with the insidious poison, and my impression was that it only required a few years more for opium-smoking to become as common as tobacco-smoking in Si-Chwan. I am within the mark when I say that seven out of every ten of the men, and three out of every ten of the women, of Si-Chwan are confirmed opium-smokers. . . . The two other great opium-producing provinces present an aspect similar to that of Si-Chwan."

(Rev. G. John, in the *Nonconformist*, 7th Dec., 1870.)

Letter from Mr. N. Nusserwanjee to the Junior Secretary, Board of Revenue.

"19th January, 1869.

"Having just returned from China, I beg to submit the following information, which I had collected during my stay in that place. It is impossible to give an accurate account of the produce of opium in China; different persons mention different quantities, but I am led to suppose, after inquiry, that not less than 40,000 pounds were produced last year, at a cost of 206 to 250 taels per pecul, and the sales were effected at Canton at about 350 dols. per pecul.

"The produce in former years was considerably less, owing to the restriction on cultivation, and the cost then was about 450 taels per pecul, including charges of transit; but that restriction having been removed by the Chinese Government, the produce is fast increasing, and the drug itself is becoming better in quality and stronger in consistence, the immediate effect of which has led to depress the China market; and the demand of the consumers of both Bengal and Malwa opium is gradually decreasing and their prices falling off. The Chinese, by mixing their drug with the Bengal or Malwa opium, have commenced to imbibe a taste for their own opium.

" Some time ago the Bengal Government, in order to defeat competition, sold 64,000 chests in one year for exportation to China and the Straits, and the prices fell down so much as to frighten the native cultivators, who discontinued cultivating opium for some time through fear of suffering loss.

" Under these circumstances, I beg to submit whether it will not be desirable, both for the interests of Government and the merchants and cultivators of India, to send in future such increased quantities of opium to China, and at such low prices as to prevent indigenous cultivation and competition."

(Papers relating to the Opium Question; Calcutta, 1870, page 218.)

Memorial of Yew Peh-Ch'wan.

"The memorial by the Censor, Yew-Peh-Ch'wan, is published *in extenso* in the *Gazette*. In its preamble it asserts (according to the fundamental maxim) that the 'people are the foundation of the State, and food the heaven (or *summum bonum*) of the people,' and that no greater obstacle to the production of food exists than the cultivation of the poppy. Having spread into other provinces from Kan-suh, the original seat of its growth, the plant is now found occupying land to the extent of upwards of 10,000 mow (or about 1700 acres) in each district (Hien). According to the calculation that has been made, three mow (say half an acre) of rich land will produce sufficient grain for one man's support;

and applying this calculation to a single province, where more than one million mow of land are thus withdrawn from productive cultivation, hundreds of thousands of persons are found to be deprived in this way of the means of subsistence.

" The names of sundry districts are appended : in the provinces of Kiang-su, Ho-nan, and Shan-tung, where, according to the memorialists' information, the cultivation is carried on upon a very large scale, almost equalling that of the cereals themselves. The very children have a rhyming proverb on the subject, which may be translated as follows :—

> 'Everywhere the flower blows,
> Sleep, or waking, still it grows ;
> Reap the profit while 'tis there—
> For the future who shall care.'

" In their greed of gain the inferior classes lose all sight of injurious consequences ; but unless radical measures be instituted to cut off the evil at its source, and pluck it up by the roots, the people's food and livelihood cannot be duly fostered.

"Reiterating the statement that the poppy is usurping lands imperatively required for the production of food, to such an extent that people have actually committed suicide under pressure of starvation, with money in their hands ready to buy food where none was to be had, owing to this cause, the Censor continues with the remark that, as has been observed, the evil caused by opium-smoking is worse than the destruction caused by floods or the ravages of wild beasts ; yet of this the cultivation of the poppy is the very fountain and origin. On these grounds he beseeches the Empress Regent and the Emperor to proclaim stringent prohibition of the growth of the poppy."

(Papers relating to the Opium Question ; Calcutta, 1870, page 232.)

" Sales of Malwa compare favourably, as regards quantity, with the previous year, but average selling prices were at a slightly further decline. The chief feature to remark upon is a falling off in the consumption of Patna, a reason for which is gathered from native sources to be owing to China-grown drug having been in more plentiful supply, roughly estimated at about 1700 peculs against 1000 peculs in the year 1872, as last spring was much milder that 1872, and consequently more favourable for the cultivation of the poppy. The cost is said to be about from 300 to 310 dols. per pecul, but only very small quantities are taken at one time, and probably thereby a le-kim tax is saved. The quality of the drug is, however, rather too thin ; it is found necessary, in order to meet the native taste, to mix fully one-half of Indian growth to furnish sufficient pungency. Persian appears to have been driven out of the field as far as this port is concerned."

(China Consular Reports, 1873 ; Consul Sinclair at Foochow.)

"The amount of native-grown opium is now so considerable, and it competes so seriously with the imported article, that any report on the subject would be manifestly defective that did not take this competition into consideration. Yet the difficulty of procuring any definite or reliable statistics as regards the native industry and its results render it impossible to do more than draw general inferences from such information as may be derivable either from partial observation or common report. These inferences would lead to the conclusion that the native cultivation of the drug is being developed at a rapid rate, and this is confirmed by the fact that the consumption has of late largely increased, whereas it is well known that the import of the Indian drug has been stationary, or nearly so, for several years past. The usual edicts deprecating the cultivation of such a pernicious drug at the expense of cereals and other crops, and prohibiting its culture under heavy penalties, have continued to appear from time to time, and influential Chinese functionaries have not failed, as heretofore, to urge the Crown to take steps towards rescuing the country from the too certain ruin which must be the consequence. But all to no purpose; the drug is so highly prized as an alterative, and the desire for it as a sedative is so general amongst all classes, whilst the local executive are everywhere so easily bribed into connivance, that the cultivation is persisted in, and it will, no doubt, continue to extend until effects are produced which must eventually exercise a vital influence upon the interests of the country at large. The result as regards the rival import from India cannot be doubted. The supply, as I have remarked, has for some time past been limited to about an equal rate year by year; and as it is a maxim in commercial economy that a trade which does not increase must, of necessity, tend towards the opposite direction, it follows that the only too probable event we have to look forward to is a gradual decline and extinction of our share in the trade, whenever the Chinese shall have learnt how to grow and prepare their produce so as to bring it on a par with the Indian staple.

" This is a question which merits serious consideration in connexion with Indian finance. The subject has, I believe and very properly, attracted more than usual attention of late on the part of the Indian Government, and, as you are aware, I have recently ventured to suggest the expediency of at once appointing a commission of inquiry, composed partly of officers conversant with the cultivation in India, and partly of gentlemen in the consular service familiar with the people and language of China, and who might be delegated to make researches throughout the Chinese provinces with a view to establishing the actual truth as regards the extent of cultivation, and its probable effects relatively to the Indian product. I still hope that such a commission may eventually be instituted, and I believe it might further be useful, not only in eliciting valuable information as to the extent to which the drug is consumed in various parts of the country, and its influences upon the people at large, but in establishing a mass of facts with regard to the inland fiscal system, as to the working of which we at present possess but a very vague idea. . . . *Intelligent Chinese ascribe the stagnation of foreign trade to the alarming progress which opium cultivation is making throughout the country. The easy production of the drug, and the remunerative returns it gives, they declare tend to engross the attention of agriculturists, and to sap nearly every other industry. I look upon this suggestion as important, and I cannot but think that it indicates, at any rate, one source of the blight which seems to be affecting branches of the trade with China.*"

(Ibid.; Consul Medhurst, Shanghai.)

"The import of opium, after deducting 190 piculs re-exported, was about 2861 piculs, against 2994 piculs in 1873, showing a falling off of 133 piculs. The decrease is explained by the increased consumption of native opium. The amount reported for taxation at the native Le-kim Tax Office was as follows:—

	1873.	1874.
	lbs.	lbs.
Crude Opium . . .	84,632	169,337
Prepared ditto . . .	996	702
Total	85,628	170,039

The quantity upon which tax was collected in 1874 was therefore *double the amount* taxed in 1873. There is also no doubt that the smuggling of a commodity so easily concealed continued to be carried on extensively. The crop of native opium in Yunnan and Szechuan was large, and the demand continues to keep pace with the supply. Native opium seems, in fact, to be in rather more favour in this part of

China than formerly. It is known to be generally used by the inhabitants of the localities where it is grown, and elsewhere by those who cannot afford to buy the foreign drug. *But it is also stated that many well-to-do Chinese, who had been in the habit of smoking foreign opium, have given it up in whole or in part in favour of the native article, the use of which is believed to be less hurtful to the constitution, and attended with less physical inconvenience. For instance, the confirmed smoker of Indian opium generally passes sleepless nights, whereas smokers of native opium do not suffer to the same extent in this respect.* The Szechuan product contains much less pure opium than is contained in Malwa, the "touch" of the former being, according to the report of an expert, forty-four, of the latter seventy-five. *It is not therefore surprising that, as remarked by travellers, boatmen and other labourers in Szechuan should be able to smoke native opium without being unfitted for work."*

(China Consular Reports, 1874; Hankow, Consul Hughes.)

"There are signs that at no distant date an equalization of the two will occur, and this event must be marked either by the stoppage of the import of Indian opium, or by such a reduction in its cost as will enable it to compete on more equal terms with its Chinese rival. In Manchuria it seems likely that native opium will in a short time take its place as a regular export. As yet the increased production has not had that effect, on either the amount or the price of Indian opium, taken at Newchwang, which might have been anticipated. This is to be attributed to the superior quality of the foreign drug, or possibly to the fact that it still guides the taste of the native consumer. It is probable that much of the drug imported at Newchwang is made use of to strengthen and correct the flavour of the native drug. In such a case it may occur that an export of the native drug may for years to come be coincident with a considerable import of the foreign article. It is very likely owing to this cause that the import of Indian opium at Tien-tsin, as compared with Newchwang, has been continually decreasing; the Manchurian drug, flavoured with Indian opium, being able to compete successfully with the latter in the state of purity. . . . .

"Although nominally the laws of China forbid the cultivation of opium, and although from time to time edicts are issued repeating this prohibition, yet there are signs that the cultivation of opium is likely to be formally legalized. At present, though formally forbidden, it is actually encouraged by the high tariff placed on the foreign drug. At Shanghai, Hankow, and Tien-tsin, again, notwithstanding the formal prohibition of the growth of native opium, le-kin taxes are regularly levied on it, and these taxes are fifty per cent. lower than those charged on foreign opium, so that the native growth is actually protected against the competition of its foreign rival.

"Nor is there wanting amongst influential Chinese a strong party who, acknowledging that opium is deleterious, yet qualify this idea by the assertion that experience has proved it necessary, and who urge on the Government the advisability of making a source of revenue out of what it has proved its inability to entirely restrain. Allied more or less with this party is another, who, taking a mistaken view of political economy, would exclude all imports as tending to draw away wealth from the country. Why should foreigners, they plead, derive all this profit from opium? If we raise the le-kin taxes, and throw obstacles in the way of internal carriage, so that the import of the foreign drug may become unprofitable, the growth of the native will be encouraged, and the wealth which now goes to enrich the foreigner and foreign trade generally will remain amongst our own people."

(Ibid.; Shanghai, Consul Medhurst.)

APPENDIX G.

STATISTICAL.

I.

AMOUNT OF OPIUM IMPORTED INTO CHINA.[1]

	1871.		1872.	
	lbs.	£	lbs.	£
Malwa . .	4,684,393	5,384,770	4,847,584	5,132,669
Patna . .	2,050,328	2,188,314	2,128,931	2,093,519
Benares .	1,011,864	1,035,713	982,072	951,434
Other kinds	170,772	169,656	117,439	118,379
Gross Total	7,917,357	8,778,453	8,076,026	8,296,002
Re-exports	75,741	82,861	36,780	34,621
Net Total .	7,841,616	8,695,592	8,039,246	8,261,381

[1] From Commercial Reports from H. M. Consuls in China, 1872. Part II. page 222.

II.

TOTAL QUANTITY OF OPIUM IMPORTED INTO CHINA DURING THE
YEARS 1864-72.   Compiled from published Returns of the
Chinese Imperial Maritime Customs.

Description.			Quantity.		Value.
			Peculs.[2]	Catties.	Haikwan Taels.[3]
Malwa	India	.	295,730	97	127,164,317
Patna		.	141,662	52	56,665,008
Benares		.	75,374	24	30,149,696
Persian .	.	.	9,204	23	3,773,734
Turkey .	.	.	235	95	89,661
Total	.	.	522,205	291	217,842,416

[2] The Pecul = 100 catties = 133⅓ lbs. avoirdupois.

[3] The Haikwan Tael = 6s. 8d.

N.B.—Out of a total of more than half a million peculs' weight imported in
nine years, Persia and Turkey together only sent 9440 peculs; i. e. not one-
fiftieth of the whole.

III

Summary of the ordinary Income and Expenditure of the British-Indian Empire, broadly and approximately stated in millions sterling and quarter millions by the *Quarterly Review*, vol. 130, p. 104.

REVENUES.	Millions sterling.	EXPENDITURE.	Millions sterling.
Tributes . . .	$\frac{3}{4}$	Charges of Collection	3
Land Revenue . .	21	Treaty Allowances .	$2\frac{1}{4}$
Salt	6	Interest of Debt .	6
Excise on Spirits and		Guaranteed Railways	$1\frac{3}{4}$
Drugs . . .	$2\frac{1}{4}$	Cost of Army . .	18
Customs . . .	$2\frac{3}{4}$	Marine . . .	$\frac{1}{2}$
Stamps . . .	$\frac{3}{4}$	Police . . .	$2\frac{1}{2}$
Opium . . .	$6\frac{1}{2}$	Civil Administration	3
		Justice . . .	$\frac{1}{2}$
Total . . .	40	Education . .	$\frac{3}{4}$
		Telegraph . .	$\frac{1}{2}$
		Superannuation, &c.	$1\frac{1}{4}$
		Public Works . .	3
		Total . . .	43
		Deficit . . .	3

IV.

NUMBER of chests of Bengal and Malwa Opium exported to China and places beyond British India. Finance and Revenue Accounts, No. 65.

Official Year.	From Bengal.			From Bombay to China.	Total Export.
	To China.	Singapore, Penang, &c.	Total.		
	Chests.	Chests.	Chests.	Chests.	Chests.
1834-35	9,480	1,570	11,050	6,812	17,862
1835-36	13,021	1,786	14,807	—	—
1836-37	10,493	2,241	12,734	20,882½	33,616½
1837-38	16,112	3,195	19,307	10,372½	29,679½
1838-39	14,499	3,722	18,221	17,353	35,574
1839-40	3,755	14,755	18,510	—	—
1840-41	5,817	11,593	17,410	12,022½	29,432½
1841-42	10,752	8,987	19,739	14,473	34,212
1842-43	11,867	4,651	16,518	19,369	35,887
1843-44	13,067	4,792	17,859	16,944	34,803
1844-45	14,709	4,083	18,792	18,150½	36,942½
1845-46	16,265	4,288	20,553	17,770	38,323
1846-47	20,668	4,322	24,990	17,389½	42,379½
1847-48	19,434	4,443	23,877	19,391	43,268
1848-49	27,870	4,417	32,287	21,392¼	53,679¼
1849-50	30,996	4,097	35,093	16,513	51,606
1850-51	28,892	4,010	32,902	19,138	52,040
1851-52	27,921	4,385	32,306	28,168½	60,474½
1852-53	31,433	4,745	36,178	24,979½	61,157½
1853-54	33,941	6,854	40,795	26,113½	66,908½
1854-55	43,952	7,469	51,421	25,958¼	77,379¼
1855-56	37,851	7,087	44,938	25,576	70,514
1856-57	36,459	5,982	42,441	29,846½	72,287½
1857-58	31,878	6,735	38,613	36,125½	74,738½
1858-59	33,858	827	34,685	40,849	75,534
1859-60	22,329	3,621	25,950	32,534	58,484
1860-61	15,688	3,621	19,309	43,691	63,000
1861-62	21,332	5,240	26,572	38,680	65,252
1862-63	25,846	6,815	32,661	49,485½	82,146½
1863-64	33,815	8,806	42,621	28,210½	70,831½
1864-65	41,719	8,484	50,203	34,213½	84,416½
1865-66	42,697	11,576	54,273	34,166½	88,439½
1866-67	37,279	4,478	41,757	33,081	74,838
1867-68	40,772	7,484	48,256	38,883	87,139
1868-69	37,985	6,281	44,266	30,683	74,949
1869-70	43,054	6,680	49,734	38,694	88,428
1870-71	40,669	8,054	48,723	36,436	85,159
1871-72	41,569	7,886	49,455	39,334½	88,789½
1872-73	34,009	6,476	40,485	42,369	82,854
1873-74	34,820	8,517	43,337	45,301	88,638

V.

NET OPIUM REVENUE, COMPARED WITH THE GROSS REVENUES
OF INDIA, FROM 1834-35.[4]

| | NET OPIUM REVENUE. | | | GROSS REVENUES OF INDIA (less refunds and drawbacks). |
YEARS.	BENGAL.	BOMBAY.	TOTAL.	
	£	£	£	£
1834–35	694,279	144,171	838,450	26,856,647
1835–36	1,320,162	171,845	1,492,007	20,148,125
1836–37	1,334,097	200,871	1,534,968	22,359,967
1837–38	1,436,724	149,721	1,586,445	21,610,557
1838–39	698,799	254,331	953,130	21,632,680
1839–40	326,076	11,701	337,777	20,151,750
1840–41	649,632	224,645	874,277	20,851,351
1841–42	803,867	214,899	1,018,766	21,840,018
1842–43	1,322,343	254,238	1,576,581	22,616,487
1843–44	1,675,948	348,878	2,024,826	23,586,573
1844–45	1,808,345	372,943	2,181,288	23,666,246
1845–46	2,207,726	595,624	2,803,350	24,270,608
1846–47	2,279,339	606,863	2,886,202	26,084,681
1847–48	1,291,529	371,855	1,663,384	24,908,302
1848–49	1,958,256	887,507	2,845,763	25,396,386
1849–50	2,800,797	729,484	3,530,281	27,522,344
1850–51	2,055,827	694,521	2,750,348	27,625,360
1851–52	2,011,163	1,128,083	3,139,246	27,665,145
1852–53	2,601,043	1,116,889	3,717,932	28,429,275
1853–54	2,394,998	964,022	3,359,020	27,916,058
1854–55	2,232,411	1,101,191	3,333,602	28,959,822
1855–56	2,951,612	1,010,365	3,961,977	30,671,958
1856–57	2,700,712	1,159,677	3,860,389	31,415,559
1857–58	4,286,377	1,631,998	5,918,375	31,643,267
1858–59	3,898,114	1,448,277	5,346,391	35,965,018
1859–60	3,636,453	1,533,325	5,169,778	39,602,850
1860–61	3,316,613	2,441,679	5,758,292	42,728,601
1861–62	2,471,347	2,438,458	4,909,805	43,487,934
1862–63	2,959,789	3,239,409	6,199,198	44,801,686
1863–64	3,044,688	1,480,818	4,525,506	44,279,467
1864–65	2,883,542	2,100,882	4,984,424	45,395,384
1865–66	4,499,227	2,124,767	6,623,994	48,514,749
1866–67	3,873,754	1,851,263	5,725,017	41,590,736
1867–68	4,695,357	2,352,708	7,048,065	48,053,178
1868–69	4,927,150	1,804,180	6,731,330	48,531,763
1869–70	3,776,626	2,354,246	6,130,872	50,241,510
1870–71	3,632,325	2,398,709	6,031,034	50,879,058
1871–72	5,305,402	2,351,811	7,657,213	49,603,015
1872–73	4,259,162	2,611,261	6,870,423	49,673,189
1873–74	3,594,763	2,738,836	6,333,599	— —

[4] From the Calcutta Blue Book, Finance and Revenue Accounts, 1875.
Part III. Accounts No. 2 and No. 64.

VI.

EXTENT OF CULTIVATION, total Produce, Quantity of Opium produced, number of chests made for excise, number of chests made for export, Net Revenue per chest of Bengal Opium, and Revenue per chest on Malwa Opium. Finance and Revenue Accounts, No. 69 and No. 71.

Year of Manufacture.	Quantity of Land cultivated with Poppy.		Quantity of Opium produced.	Number of Akbarry Opium[7] chests made.	Number of Provision Opium[8] chests made.	Net Revenue per chest Bengal Opium.	Duty on Malwa Opium.
September to August.	Beegahs.[5]	Acres.	Mds.[6]	Chests.	Chests.	£	£
1848–49	388,044	242,527	62,994	$398\frac{1}{3}$	35,385	71	40
1849–50	373,616	233,510	60,935	$898\frac{1}{3}$	34,419	64	40
1850–51	412,173	257,608	61,053	$1,412\frac{1}{3}$	33,563	83	40
1851–52	460,322	287,701	70,598	867	39,465	69	40
1852–53	546,031	341,269	87,457	$1,043\frac{1}{2}$	48,322	48	40
1853–54	616,257	385,161	96,278	$1,213\frac{2}{3}$	53,321	46	40
1854–55	595,711	372,319	78,796	$1,432\frac{2}{3}$	$44,441\frac{1}{2}$	61	40
1855–56	582,848	364,280	78,895	$1,833\frac{11}{12}$	43,907	83	40
1856–57	543,897	339,936	59,975	$1,604\frac{1}{3}$	32,693	117	40
1857–58	400,733	250,458	54,867	$3,353\frac{1}{12}$	$27,175\frac{1}{2}$	136	40
1858–59	467,646	292,279	41,329	$1,668\frac{1}{2}$	21,367	147	40
1859–60	434,508	271,567	41,230	$2,182\frac{2}{3}$	21,427	155	{ 40 { 50
1860–61	435,337	272,086	58,168	$3,107\frac{1}{3}$	29,398	112	{ 50 { 60
1861–62	621,165	388,228	75,044	$3,019\frac{2}{3}$	39,656	97	{ 60 { 70
1862–63	748,693	467,933	93,583	3,190	49,727	61	{ 70 { 60
1863–64	808,655	505,409	119,517	2,622	64,269	56	60
1864–65	765,185	478,241	86,276	2,384	47,785	72	60
1865–66	637,830	398,644	81,327	4,157	40,901	116	60
1866–67	702,076	438,798	93,136	4,596	48,895	101	60
1867–68	727,247	454,529	83,750	5,277	43,610	96	60
1868–69	694,340	433,962	86,019	4,458	$46,894\frac{3}{5}$	78	60
1869–70	778,331	486,457	99,124	2,579	$54,072\frac{7}{40}$	92	60
1870–71	834,035	521,272	76,739	3,114	$40,981\frac{1}{5}$	$98\frac{1}{3}$	60
1871–72	863,272	539,545	81,431	$3,680\frac{3}{4}$	42,975	$87\frac{1}{2}$	60
1872–73	828,222	517,639	88,104	$4,292\frac{1}{2}$	45,770	99	60
1873–74	830,593	519,121	99,308	—	54,716	—	—

[5] The Opium Beegah = 27,225 square feet, or $\frac{5}{8}$ of an acre.
[6] The maund = $82\frac{2}{7}$ lbs.
[7] Akbarry Opium is opium for consumption in India.
[8] Provision Opium is opium provided for the Export trade.

VII. OPIUM STATISTICS.

TABLE OF AVERAGES IN GROUPS OF FIVE YEARS.

Compiled from the Finance and Revenue Returns. Part III., Accounts No. 64 and No. 65.

Years.	Net Revenue.			Bengal Chests sold.	Malwa Chests paid duty.	Total number of Chests.	Export.				
	Bengal.	Bombay.	Total.				From Bengal.			From Bombay to China.	Total Export.
							To China.	To Singapore &c.	Total.		
1834-39	1,096,812	184,188	1,281,000	15,437	14,467	29,904	12,721	2,503	15,244	—	—
1839-44	955,573	210,872	1,166,445	17,663	14,301	31,964	9,052	8,956	18,007	—	—
1844-49	1,909,039	566,958	2,475,997	23,941	16,342	40,283	19,789	4,311	24,100	—	—
1849-54	2,372,766	926,600	3,299,366	35,427	23,241	58,668	30,637	4,818	35,455	22,982[9]	58,437
1854-59	3,213,845	1,270,302	4,484,147	42,532	31,452	73,984	36,800	5,620	42,420	31,671	74,091
1859-64	3,085,778	2,226,738	5,312,516	29,226	38,597	67,823	23,802	5,621	29,423	38,520	67,943
1864-69	4,175,806	2,046,760	6,222,566	48,882	33,881	82,763	40,090	7,661	47,751	34,205	81,956
1869-74	4,113,656	2,490,974	6,604,628	45,966	41,457	87,423	38,824	7,523	46,347	40,427	86,774

[9] Previous to 1845-46 the Record of the Export from Bombay is incomplete, and therefore the average could not be calculated.

Printed in Great Britain
by Amazon